BICYCLING THE
pacific coast

*A Complete
Route Guide,
Canada to Mexico*

FOURTH EDITION

BICYCLING THE
pacific coast

*A Complete
Route Guide,
Canada to Mexico*

FOURTH EDITION

VICKY SPRING AND
TOM KIRKENDALL

THE MOUNTAINEERS BOOKS

THE MOUNTAINEERS BOOKS
is the nonprofit publishing arm of The Mountaineers Club, an organization founded in 1906 and dedicated to the exploration, preservation, and enjoyment of outdoor and wilderness areas.

1001 SW Klickitat Way, Suite 201, Seattle, WA 98134

©2005 by Tom Kirkendall and Vicky Spring

First edition, 1984; second edition, 1990; third edition, 1998; fourth edition 2005

Published simultaneously in Great Britain by Cordee, 3a DeMontfort Street, Leicester, England, LE1 7HD

Manufactured in the United States of America

Editor: Christine Clifton-Thornton
Cover Design: Kristy Thompson
Layout: Marge Mueller, Gray Mouse Graphics
Cartographer: Tom Kirkendall

All photographs by the authors unless otherwise noted.

Cover photograph: *Watching the sunset from Lime Kiln Point State Park*
Frontispiece: *A field of hairy checkermallow on Cascade Head overlooks the mouth of the Salmon River.*

Library of Congress Cataloging-in-Publication Data
Kirkendall, Tom.
  Bicycling the Pacific Coast : a complete route guide Canada to Mexico / Tom Kirkendall and Vicky Spring.— 4th ed.
      p. cm.
  Includes bibliographical references and index.
  ISBN 0-89886-954-4 (pbk.)
1. Bicycle touring—Pacific Coast (North America)—Guidebooks. 2. Pacific Coast (North America)—Guidebooks. I. Spring, Vicky, 1953- II. Title.
  GV1046.P17K57 2004
  917.904'34—dc22

                              2004027548

CONTENTS

Table of Essentials 8
Preface 15
Introduction 17

BRITISH COLUMBIA 23
Vancouver to Roberts Creek Provincial Park 26
Roberts Creek Provincial Park to Saltery Bay Provincial Park 34
Saltery Bay Provincial Park to Rathtrevor Beach Provincial Park 38
Rathtrevor Beach Provincial Park to McDonald Provincial Park 43
McDonald Provincial Park to Victoria 50

WASHINGTON 55
Inland Route
The San Juan Islands 61
Anacortes Ferry Dock to Old Fort Townsend State Park 67
Old Fort Townsend State Park to Potlatch State Park 72
Potlatch State Park to Twin Harbors State Park 77
Peninsula Route
Port Angeles to Fairholm Campground 82
Fairholm Campground to Kalaloch Campground 88
Kalaloch Campground to Quinault Lake 93
Quinault Lake to Twin Harbors State Park 96
Combined Route
Twin Harbors State Park to Bay Center 101
Bay Center to the Oregon Border 105

OREGON 109
Washington Border to Nehalem Bay State Park 114
Nehalem Bay State Park to Cape Lookout State Park 120
Cape Lookout State Park to Beverly Beach State Park 124
Beverly Beach State Park to Jessie M. Honeyman Memorial
    State Park 128
Jessie M. Honeyman Memorial State Park to Sunset Bay
    State Park 135
Sunset Bay State Park to Humbug Mountain State Park 140
Humbug Mountain State Park to the California Border 144

CALIFORNIA 149
Oregon Border to Elk Prairie Campground 154
Elk Prairie Campground to Eureka KOA 160

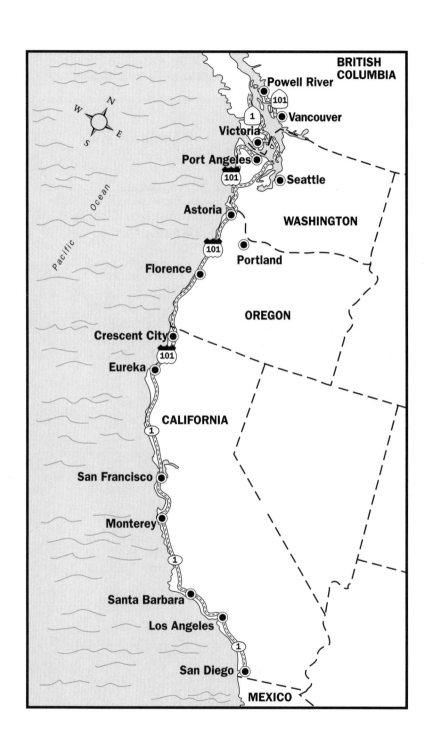

Eureka KOA to Marine Garden Club Grove   164
Marine Garden Club Grove to Standish–Hickey State Park
      Recreation Area   169
Standish–Hickey State Park Recreation Area to MacKerricher Beach
      State Park   173
MacKerricher Beach State Park to Manchester State Beach   177
Manchester State Beach to Bodega Dunes State Beach   181
Bodega Dunes State Beach to Samuel P. Taylor State Park   187
Samuel P. Taylor State Park to Half Moon Bay State Beach   191
Half Moon Bay State Beach to New Brighton State Beach   201
New Brighton State Beach to Vets Memorial Park   206
Vets Memorial Park to Kirk Creek Campground   213
Kirk Creek Campground to San Simeon State Beach   217
San Simeon State Beach to Oceano Campground   220
Oceano Campground to Gaviota State Park   225
Gaviota State Park to Carpinteria State Beach   230
Carpinteria State Beach to Leo Carrillo State Beach   236
Leo Carrillo State Beach to Colonial Inn Hostel   241
Colonial Inn Hostel to San Elijo State Beach   246
San Elijo State Beach to the Mexican Border   255

Useful Phone Numbers and Websites   264
Recommended Reading   265
Index   266

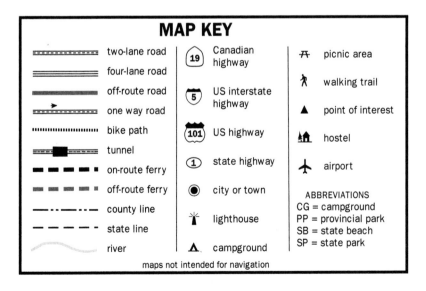

MAP KEY

two-lane road	
four-lane road	
off-route road	
one way road	
bike path	
tunnel	
on-route ferry	
off-route ferry	
county line	
state line	
river	

(19) Canadian highway

(5) US interstate highway

(101) US highway

(1) state highway

⊙ city or town

🗼 lighthouse

▲ campground

⛩ picnic area

🚶 walking trail

▲ point of interest

🏠 hostel

✈ airport

ABBREVIATIONS
CG = campground
PP = provincial park
SB = state beach
SP = state park

maps not intended for navigation

TABLE OF ESSENTIALS

The table on the following pages is designed to let you view all the basic information for each day's ride at a quick glance. The Table of Essentials will help you see what amenities and activities are available along the ride. When considered with the Distance and Difficulty entries, you can quickly calculate how long it will take you to complete the ride and determine the amount of time you will want to spend enjoying the scenery and attractions along the way; or, the table may help you decide if you need to pick up a good book and spend an afternoon relaxing and reading on the beach.

The table is not designed to take the place of the Mileage Log. You will still need to refer to the Mileage Log section of each day's ride for riding directions and distances.

How to Use the Table

Pick the correct table—British Columbia, Washington, Oregon, or California—depending on which state or province you are in. The days are listed in order and by the name of the starting and ending point, as found in the table of contents.

Distance: The miles listed follow the basic routes outlined in the Mileage Log. Any side trips or excursions will add extra miles to the total.

Difficulty: Each day's journey has been rated as either *easy* (E), *moderate* (M), or *difficult* (D).

E In order to receive an *easy* rating the roads must be in fairly good condition with adequate shoulders for most of the distance. Most *easy* rides are less than 60 miles in length. The terrain tends to be rider friendly without too many long hills. Traffic on *easy* rides must be either light or generally rider friendly.

M *Moderate* rides are in that grab-bag category that covers everything that isn't obviously *easy* or truly *difficult*. On *moderate* rides you may encounter long hills, sections where the road is uncomfortably busy, and/or places where the shoulder is missing.

D When a day's ride is rated as *difficult*, there generally are areas that are unpleasant to ride; San Francisco and Los Angeles both received this rating in recognition of the narrow, busy roads that you must ride in order to make it through these municipalities. *Difficult* rides may require constant reference to the directions as the route weaves and wanders through a maze of city streets. Dangerous sections of roads, such as found on sections of Highway 101 in Northern California, where four lanes of traffic are funneled into two lanes with no shoulder, are also reasons for classifying a day's ride as *difficult*.

Bike Shop: Bike shops are available in every large town along the coast. Unfortunately, you can be days away from these major bike shops when your hub suddenly decides to pop or your sealed pedal suddenly unseals itself. The list here is designed to give you an idea of where to start looking for a bike shop. It has been our experience, through several editions of this book, that bike shops come and go frequently in smaller towns. The bike shops that do survive tend to do so by multitasking and may not offer all the services of a large city shop. Your best bet for bike shops is always the big cities and college towns.

Beach Access: This category lets you know if you can plan on an hour or so of beach recreation time during the day's ride.

Hiking Trails: Does your seat hurt? Are your legs screaming for a chance to stretch some different muscles? This column lets you know if you can plan some time for an alternative activity during your day.

Youth Hostel: When you are ready to move indoors, a youth hostel can often offer an inexpensive night's lodging where other guests will not question your choice of attire. Most hostels are booked throughout the summer and it is hard to get a bed without an advance reservation. However, during spring and fall you will have a better chance of finding an empty bed. Please note that hostels also have a tendency to come and go. If you start your trip planning to stay in hostels, secure reservations ahead of time and verify that the listed facilities are still in operation.

Points of Interest: The listed points are the highlights of the day's ride. Days without highlights are great riding days as you can ride without interruption and have plenty of time for relaxing, eating, and laundry at the end of the day.

Ride	Distance	Diffi-culty	Bike Shop	Beach Access	Hiking Trails	Youth Hostel	Points of Interest
BRITISH COLUMBIA							
Vancouver to Roberts Creek Provincial Park	41.5 miles/66.4 kms	M	yes	yes	yes	yes	Stanley Park, Lighthouse Park, ferry ride
Roberts Creek Provincial Park to Saltery Bay Provincial Park	41.7 miles/66.7 kms	E	no	yes	yes	no	Skookumchuck Narrows, ferry ride
Saltery Bay Provincial Park to Rathtrevor Beach Provincial Park	74.2 miles/118.7 kms	M	yes	yes	yes	no	ferry ride
Rathtrevor Beach Provincial Park to McDonald Provincial Park	64.7 miles/103.5 kms	M	no	no	no	yes	two ferry rides, Salt Spring Island
McDonald Provincial Park to Victoria	20.4 miles/32.6 kms	E	yes	no	no	yes	Butchart Gardens, downtown Victoria
WASHINGTON *Inland Route*							
The San Juan Islands	57.9 miles	M	no	yes	yes	yes	Lime Kiln Point State Park, San Juan Island National Historic Park, Moran State Park
Anacortes Ferry Dock to Old Fort Townsend State Park	41.1 miles	E	yes	yes	yes	yes	Washington Park, Deception Pass State Park, Fort Casey State Park, Fort Worden State Park, ferry ride
Old Fort Townsend State Park to Potlatch State Park	64.3 miles	M	no	no	no	no	none
Potlatch State Park to Twin Harbors State Park	74.6 miles	M	yes	no	no	yes	none

Ride	Distance	Diffi-culty	Bike Shop	Beach Access	Hiking Trails	Youth Hostel	Points of Interest
WASHINGTON *Peninsula Route*							
Port Angeles to Fairholm Campground	28.8 miles	M	yes	no	yes	no	Marymere Falls
Fairholm Campground to Kalaloch Campground	61.2 miles	M	yes	yes	yes	yes	Ruby Beach
Kalaloch Campground to Quinault Lake	33.6 miles	M	no	no	yes	no	Quinault Rain Forest
Quinault Lake to Twin Harbors State Park	55.6 miles	M	no	yes	no	no	passenger ferry ride
WASHINGTON *Combined Route*							
Twin Harbors State Park to Bay Center	52.8 miles	E	no	no	no	no	none
Bay Center to the Oregon Border	47.4 miles	M	no	yes	yes	yes	Cape Disappointment State Park
OREGON							
Washington Border to Nehalem Bay State Park	43.9 miles	M	yes	yes	no	yes	Fort Clatsop National Memorial, Fort Stevens State Park, Cannon Beach, Seaside
Nehalem Bay State Park to Cape Lookout State Park	48.2 miles	M	no	yes	yes	no	Cape Meares State Park, Cape Lookout State Park
Cape Lookout State Park to Beverly Beach State Park	57.5 miles	M	no	yes	yes	no	Cape Kiwanda State Park, Devils Punchbowl State Park
Beverly Beach State Park to Jessie M. Honeyman Memorial State Park	60.3 miles	M	no	yes	yes	no	Yaquina Head Lighthouse, Cape Perpetua, Strawberry Point, Devils Elbow State Park, sand dunes
Jessie M. Honeyman Memorial State Park to Sunset Bay State Park	54.9 miles	M	no	yes	yes	no	Oregon Dunes National Recreation Area, Shore Acres State Park, Cape Arago State Park

Ride	Distance	Diffi-culty	Bike Shop	Beach Access	Hiking Trails	Youth Hostel	Points of Interest
Sunset Bay State Park to Humbug Mountain State Park	57 miles	M	no	yes	yes	yes	beaches at Bandon
Humbug Mountain State Park to the California Border	56.2 miles	M	no	yes	yes	no	Boardman State Park, Harris Beach State Park
CALIFORNIA							
Oregon Border to Elk Prairie Campground	61.8 miles	D	no	yes	yes	yes	Redwood National Park, Elk Prairie
Elk Prairie Campground to Eureka KOA	46.3 miles	D	yes	yes	yes	no	Trinidad Memorial Lighthouse
Eureka KOA to Marine Garden Club Grove	51.2 miles	E	yes	no	yes	no	redwoods along Avenue of the Giants
Marine Garden Club Grove to Standish–Hickey State Park Recreation Area	48 miles	D	no	no	yes	no	redwoods along Avenue of the Giants and at Richardson Grove State Park
Standish–Hickey State Park Recreation Area to MacKerricher Beach State Park	39.4 miles	M	no	yes	no	no	trail along beach at MacKerricher Beach State Park
MacKerricher Beach State Park to Manchester State Beach	42.1 miles	M	no	yes	yes	no	coastal scenery is outstanding
Manchester State Beach to Bodega Dunes State Beach	65.4 miles	M	no	yes	yes	no	Point Arena Lighthouse, Salt Water State Park, Fort Ross State Historical Park
Bodega Dunes State Beach to Samuel P. Taylor State Park	40.6 miles	E	no	yes	yes	yes	Point Reyes National Seashore
Samuel P. Taylor State Park to Half Moon Bay State Beach	58.1 miles	D	yes	yes	yes	yes	Marin Headlands, Golden Gate Bridge
Half Moon Bay State Beach to New Brighton State Beach	56.5 miles	E	yes	yes	no	yes	Año Nuevo State Reserve

Ride	Distance	Diffi-culty	Bike Shop	Beach Access	Hiking Trails	Youth Hostel	Points of Interest
New Brighton State Beach to Vets. Memorial Park	40.8 miles	E	yes	yes	no	no	Monterey tour
Vets Memorial Park to Kirk Creek Campground	60.2 miles	D	no	yes	yes	no	Point Lobos State Reserve, Pfeiffer-Big Sur State Park, waterfall at Julia Pfeiffer Burns State Park
Kirk Creek Campground to San Simeon State Beach	40 miles	M	no	yes	yes	no	Hearst Castle
San Simeon State Beach to Oceano Campground	52.6 miles	E	yes	yes	yes	no	sand dunes at Pismo Beach
Oceano Campground to Gaviota State Park	61.6 miles	M	no	yes	yes	no	Gaviota State Beach Hot Springs
Gaviota State Park to Carpinteria State Beach	44.4 miles	E	yes	yes	no	no	Santa Barbara tour
Carpinteria State Beach to Leo Carrillo State Park	47.8 miles	M	yes	yes	yes	no	Channel Islands Visitor Center, Point Mugu State Park
Leo Carrillo State Beach to Colonial Inn Hostel	72.0 miles	D	yes	yes	no	yes	Venice Beach scene, surfers at Huntington Beach
Colonial Inn Hostel to San Elijo State Beach	65.4 miles	D	yes	yes	no	no	Mission San Juan Capistrano, surfers at Trestles Beach
San Elijo State Beach to the Mexican Border	45.3 miles	M	yes	yes	yes	yes	Torrey Pines State Reserve, Scripps Institute Aquarium, Mexican border!

Point Arena Lighthouse is a short but very scenic 2.3-mile side trip off Highway 1 between Manchester State Beach and Bodega Dunes State Park in California.

PREFACE

Why North to South?

If, in 1981, Tom had decided to ride the Pacific Coast south from Canada to Mexico, he would have had a great time, and this book would never have been written. However, in 1981 Tom decided to ride from Mexico to Canada, and the results are as follows.

I rode with him from Mexico to Santa Barbara, ending the short trip with a sunburn and a great enthusiasm for bicycle touring. As he continued to pedal on, I drove north heading to a summer job, certain that I was missing a great ride.

As a West Coast native, I am proud of our beautiful coast and expected Tom to be thrilled by the scenery as well as by the challenge of the ride. I was terribly envious. But something happened as Tom rode on by himself. North of Santa Barbara, he encountered stiff headwinds that blew the fun right out of his adventure. Scenery and the thrill of exploring became secondary to his daily battle with the wind. The wind created an invisible, never-ending hill that had to be constantly climbed. The wind beat dirt into his face, produced an annoying whistling sound through his helmet, and attempted to push him back to Mexico. By San Francisco, riding had become a chore. In Oregon, 80-mile-per-hour winds blew him to a stop while going down a steep hill. In Washington, he had 3 hours of peace when a very wet storm blew through from the south, giving him a much-appreciated tailwind.

When describing that trip, Tom will pull out his trip journal. The beginning of the journal is full of his thoughts and impressions; in the second half he wrote only of the wind. His journal describes how he got up early in the morning to avoid the winds that blew the strongest in the afternoon. The journal describes the miles covered each day, the food he ate, and the interesting people he met along the way, but nowhere in the second half of that book is there any mention of beautiful vista points, magnificent redwood forests, sea otters, sea lions, lighthouses, sand dunes, and fascinating old forts. Nowhere is there any mention of the word *fun*.

The following summer, Tom and I rode back down the coast to prove it *can* be fun. It was an incredible trip. Oh yes, the wind was still blowing, but this time, it was pushing us south. Near the Sea Lion Caves in Oregon, I had to apply my brakes to stop at a viewpoint on a steep uphill grade. The miles flew by, and we had plenty of extra time and energy to stop and explore the forests and beaches. We were surprised

This scenic overlook is a great place to stop and enjoy the beautiful views of the Monterey coast between Vets Memorial Park and Kirk Creek Campground.

to note that the highway department expects cyclists to travel from north to south. We frequently had a good shoulder on the southbound side of the road while northbound cyclists had to dodge trucks and cars on a shoulderless roadway.

To help other bicyclists avoid the disappointment of northbound travel, we spent the following year organizing this guide from Canada to Mexico. We may be biased, but we believe that the magnificent and varied scenery, the temperate climate, and the numerous public facilities designed especially for cyclists make the Pacific Coast the best long-distance tour in the country. When you plan your first tour down the coast, take advantage of the tail winds, head south, and leave yourself plenty of time to explore and enjoy the coast.

Vicky Spring
Seattle, 2004

INTRODUCTION

This book is a guide to the Pacific Coast Bicycle Route (also known as the Coast Route) from Vancouver, British Columbia, south along some of the world's most scenic coastline to palm-lined beaches at the Mexican border. More than a route, this is an adventure where incredible scenery is topped off with visits to national parks, a national recreation area, several national historical monuments, innumerable state parks, museums, forts, and lighthouses. Along the route are friendly towns with bakeries and art galleries, huge bustling metropolises with fascinating museums and excellent restaurants, beautiful forests, lonely sea coasts, and wind-sculptured sand dunes. Included in the adventure are sea otters, sea lions, sea gulls, pelicans, elk, raccoons, chipmunks, deer, and an amazing cross section of people.

It is difficult to draw a generalized description of the Pacific Coast. Nearly all types of road conditions, terrain, and weather may be encountered. A few broad generalities, open to exception, can be drawn as follows: Wind blows from the north in good weather and from the south in bad; the chance of bad weather decreases as you travel south; and the number of facilities for cyclists (and the number of cyclists) increases to the south.

The Pacific Coast Bicycle Route is 1987.3 miles long, excluding side trips. Following the day-by-day descriptions, the entire route may be cycled in 42 days. Some cyclists will ride it in less time. Others will want more time to explore areas of special interest, take side trips, and enjoy leisurely rest days.

For the purpose of simplicity, the book is divided into four chapters: British Columbia, Washington, Oregon, and California. However, the text and maps are arranged so that users may pick out the portions that interest them.

No formalized bicycle route exists for the coast of British Columbia or Washington. However, Oregon and California both established coastal bike routes for the American Bicentennial in 1976, and unless safer or more scenic routes were found, the Pacific Coast Bicycle Route follows these established routes. Oregon has made a commendable commitment to cycling, and the Bicentennial Route is well signed. Due to economic and liability considerations, the state of California no longer maintains the Bicentennial Route and when signs are stolen or otherwise removed, they are not replaced. The state of Washington is still trying to determine if anyone in the state beyond the age of sixteen rides a bike (we are big on studies up north). And, naturally, British Columbia was never part of the Bicentennial Route, even though cycling is well supported in the province.

This book was designed for the cyclists on a budget who plan to stay in campgrounds and cook their own food. However, credit card cyclists will find it easy to adapt the information to suit their own needs, as restaurants and motels are plentiful on the coast. The coast is a popular destination on summer weekends and holidays. Attempt to arrange your itinerary through British Columbia and Washington to avoid the vacation campground congestion.

Pedaling Through the Pages

At the start of each of the four chapters is a discussion of the weather, camping, road conditions, and any problems or conditions unique to that state or province. The chapters are then divided into day rides, starting and ending at campgrounds. The day rides average 52 miles but vary from 28.9 miles to 74 miles, depending on the availability of campsites and number of points of interest along the ride. If the days suggested are too short, cycle farther. If they are too long, shorten them. Most important, have fun in your own special way.

Each day's ride includes a discussion of highlights, road conditions, and possible problems, and suggests alternative camping areas (if any); a map; and a mileage log listing road directions, side trips, and points of interest.

When traveling on a major highway, mileages are accompanied by a milepost number (mp). Mileposts are small signs along the road with a number that indicates the miles from a county or state line. (Mileposts are used by the highway maintenance crews to accurately locate problems. They are not always spaced correctly and some are missing.) For the scope of this book, mileposts serve as another tool to aid in routefinding. They cannot be relied on in place of a cycle computer. In Washington and Oregon, mileposts do not list tenths or hundredths. We have added tenths to the mileage logs to help riders determine whether the point listed is before or after the milepost. In California, mileposts note mileages to the hundredth place. No mileposts were noted in British Columbia; instead we have given distances in both miles and kilometers to help riders correlate information with street signs.

Maps

Additional up-to-date maps and information are always handy. We suggest you obtain city maps of all the major cities you will be visiting (if following the entire route, that means Vancouver, Victoria, San Francisco, Los Angeles, and San Diego). Trace the bike route on these maps to give you a better idea of where you are going before you head into the city. Automobile clubs such as AAA are good sources for city street maps. The Internet and major chain stores, such as REI and Performance, can be helpful in locating other maps and publications.

Hiker-biker Sites

A hiker-biker site is a special area in a campground set aside for people traveling alone or in small groups using nonmotorized forms of transportation. Maximum stay is 2 nights unless otherwise noted. These camps vary in size and fee charged. Some may lack certain conveniences, such as nearby water or restrooms. Space is available on a first-come basis.

The hiker-biker system of campsites is well organized in Washington, Oregon, and California. In these three states, there is virtually no need to worry about full campgrounds or finding a place to stay on busy summer weekends. The fee is moderate, and space is available for a large number of cyclists. Hiker-biker sites may be found in state parks, some forest service campgrounds, and a few county parks.

Hiker-biker sites are a great help to cyclists. When using these campsites, *please* remember they are a privilege and not a right. The fee is modest, so pay it. The campground officials are not raking in a profit from hiker-biker sites, so help them out by keeping the sites clean. Hiker-biker areas may be eliminated if there is too much upkeep involved. Most important, let the campground officials know how much you appreciate having sites like these available to cyclists.

If you are traveling in a group of four or more, a regular campsite will always be less expensive than a hiker-biker site. If you are traveling with a support vehicle, you are required to use a regular campsite. For state park reservations in Washington, call (888) 226-7688. For Oregon state park reservations, call (800) 452-5687. In California, advance reservations can be made by calling (800) 444-7275; for TDD the number is (800) 274-7275. For advance reservations for tours at Año Nuevo or Hearst Castles, call (800) 444-4445.

In southern California, the hiker-biker sites have become favored hangouts for transients. In response to this serious problem, the official hiker-biker sites have been closed in some campgrounds. No cyclists will be turned away; however, you may be moved from one site to another until the official site for the day is chosen.

Yurts

In Oregon, all the state park campgrounds along the coast have yurts for rent. These are very basic structures with room to sleep four or five people, electricity, skylight, a waterproof roof, and a wooden floor. Cooking must be done outdoors. Several parks have added deluxe yurts, which sleep up to seven people and have TV, VCR, refrigerator, microwave, and bathroom with shower, as well as a covered deck with barbecue for cooking.

The reasonably priced yurts have proven to be a popular alternative to tenting along Oregon's often-damp coast. Occasionally you may be able to rent a yurt when you arrive at a park, but, generally, they are rented out months in advance. For more information, call (800) 551-6949 or visit the Oregon State Parks website at *www.oregonstateparks.org.* In 2003, Oregon State Parks was using Reservations Northwest for all its bookings. Their phone number is (800) 452-5687.

Hostels

Twenty-five hostels are located on or near the Coast Route. Hostels are considerably more expensive than a campsite but a lot cheaper (for one person) than a motel. If you run into a streak of miserably wet weather, you may be glad to spend a dry night indoors. For the most current information about hostel locations and charges, check out American Youth Hostels at *www.111traveldirectory.com* or Hosteling International at *www.hihostels.com/opendiscounts.sma.*

Getting Ready to Tour

Before starting a long bicycle tour, it is important to get your body and bicycle into the best shape possible. Numerous excellent books thoroughly cover the subject of how to tour, so we will not pursue it here. These books are available at bookstores and most bicycle shops.

Riding Safely

The first time you ride your bike fully loaded with tour bags is a shock, even to the most seasoned rider. When loaded with an extra twenty to thirty pounds of gear, a lightweight bike behaves like a lopsided tortoise on level ground, and what it does on the uphills defies description. Of course, on the downhill, it takes off like a locomotive. Start off slowly, and take an hour or so to readjust your balance to the extra weight. Pulling a lightweight trailer is an excellent alternative to touring bags. The trailers add drag on the uphill and momentum on the downhill but do not interfere with the bike's balance as much as bags.

On the road, a cyclist's first line of defense is to be as visible as possible to motorists. A bright-colored helmet, brilliantly colored clothing and/or bright fluorescent vests or fanny triangles, and eye-catching touring bags will greatly increase the chances of being seen from a distance, giving motorists a chance to slow down or move to another lane.

Along the Pacific Coast, a cyclist has the same rights and obligations as the driver of a motor vehicle, which means riding single file except to pass, having one hand on the handlebars at all times, obeying stop signs and traffic signals before turning or stopping, and moving as far off the road as possible for rest or repairs.

Large trucks are intimidating to many cyclists, with good reason. An 80,000-pound truck cannot stop quickly or swerve as sharply as a small car if it comes unexpectedly upon a cyclist in the middle of the road. As a large truck passes, its slipstream pulls the relatively lightweight bicycle in toward the center of the road. Lightweight riders, particularly kids, may have trouble with slipstream drag especially from the low-slung chip trucks along the Oregon Coast. When one of these behemoths goes by, parents may want to have the kids actually stop and put a foot on the ground until the slipstream drag passes by.

The following suggestions were made by a logging truck driver: Do not ride in the center of the lane; ride as far to the right as possible, preferably on or to the right of the white line. When traveling in a group, do not string out in a long line down the road; break into groups of two or three, and keep at least a quarter of a mile between groups to allow trucks time to swing out to pass riders and then get back into their lane. When a driver tries to pass a long group, he may be forced to swing in close if he meets oncoming traffic.

Cyclists should be especially cautious in popular tourist areas. Many people are unfamiliar and uncomfortable with the large mobile home they are driving. They are less likely to move over when passing and much more likely than a commercial truck driver to panic in an emergency.

The Necessities

Three necessities are universal to all touring cyclists: food, restrooms, and water. Travel tends to degenerate into a constant search for one or all of these three basics. Public restrooms and water are easily found at numerous parks along the coast. However, in some areas, you are faced with long stretches without any kind of facility at all. Do not plague the small stores and gas stations by begging for water or attempting to leave some. When necessity forces the use of private facilities, try to incorporate this stop with acquisition of the first necessity—food. Do your best to leave a good impression or the next group may be faced with a NO CYCLISTS sign.

Leaving Valuables Behind

The Pacific Coast is a popular area for vacations and a prime location for thieves. It takes only a second for a thief to grab a touring bag—or your entire bike—and throw it into the back of a truck. There is no perfect answer to this problem. Some cyclists never leave gear unattended, always leaving one person with the bikes while the others explore. Others leave their bikes, then worry about them the entire time they are away. Take reasonable precautions: Always take your valuables—money, credit cards, camera—when you leave your bike; always lock your bike when you are away; and get to know your neighbors in camp and watch out for each other. Stashing gear when heading off the main route on a side trip is common, though potentially risky. When stashing gear, make sure no one sees the hiding place, then check to make sure the gear is not visible from the road.

The First Principle of Bicycle Touring
The first and foremost principle of bicycle touring is to have fun. If the days suggested in this book are too long, shorten them. If they are too short, ride farther, take more side trips, or go for a hike. Take rest days when you feel like it. Just be sure to have FUN.

A Note About Safety
Safety is an important concern in all outdoor activities. No guide-book can alert you to every hazard or anticipate the limitations of every reader. Therefore, the descriptions of the roads, trails, routes, or other features in this book are not representations that a particular place or excursion will be safe for your party. When you follow any routes described in this book, you assume responsibility for your own safety. Under normal conditions, such excursions require the usual attention to traffic, road conditions, weather, terrain, the capabilities of your party, the quality of your gear, and other factors. Keeping informed on current conditions and exercising common sense are the keys to a safe, enjoyable tour.

—*The Mountaineers Books*

Opposite: *Point Atkinson Lighthouse, located at the entrance to Burrard Inlet on the ride from Vancouver to Roberts Creek Provincial Park, is reached by a short side trip and a quick stroll off the main route.*

BRITISH COLUMBIA

The 246.9 miles of cycling that make up the British Columbia portion of the Pacific Coast Bicycle Route are unique: The Pacific Ocean is never seen, a minimum of 4 hours and 20 minutes will be spent on the six different ferries that are necessary to the basic route, and for 115.1 miles you will cycle north rather than south.

The British Columbia ride starts in Vancouver and heads north up the beautiful Sunshine Coast to Powell River, a small town near the northern end of Highway 101, which is the true beginning of the Pacific Coast Bicycle Route.

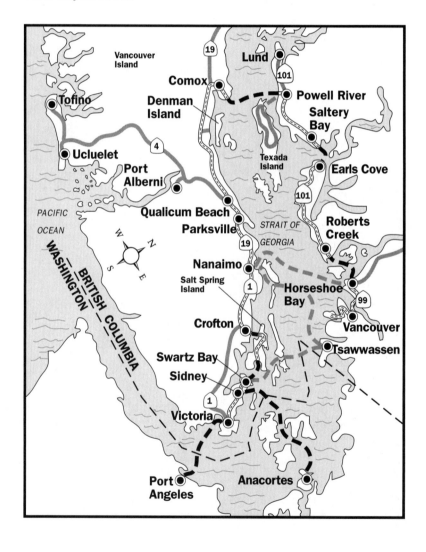

From Powell River, the route heads west across the Strait of Georgia to Vancouver Island before heading south through miles of scenic country and several lovely cities rich with Canadian history. The route ends in Victoria, where you can celebrate with an authentic English tea at the Empress Hotel.

Hopping from peninsula to islands, the route is connected by the British Columbia ferry system. The ferries are reliable and comfortable, and some are downright luxurious. On clear days, the ferry rides seem like expensive cruises to exotic places, where ice-covered peaks form beautiful backdrops as the boats wind through narrow passages between forested islands. Cyclists who become hooked on the British Columbia ferries may find several extra excuses to ride them on side trips to islands off the main route.

Despite being the northernmost section of the Pacific Coast ride, temperatures are mild, averaging 64 degrees F in the summer, and rainfall is just less than 40 inches a year. Riding is best from May through September, when rainfall is at a minimum and daylight hours at a maximum. Wind generally is not a problem, as most of the route is protected by dense forest.

When packing for a ride in British Columbia, plan for wet, cool weather, and then be pleasantly surprised if it's sunny. Fenders and raingear are recommended equipment. Carry a tent or a very good tarp as well as a small stove for hot food and drinks at the end of each day.

Road conditions for bicycling in British Columbia are good. Traffic is moderate except on weekends or during vacations. On Vancouver Island, some sections of the highway have been upgraded to include an adequate shoulder; however, travel on unimproved sections is hazardous due to the steady flow of oversize tourist vehicles and trucks. The most dangerous parts of the ride are on Vancouver Island where the route joins Highway 19 for a portion of the ride. Highway 19 is four lanes with stoplights in some areas and freeway-style on and off ramps in other areas. When encountering an off ramp, the safest choice is to exit and return on the entrance ramp. If you choose to stay on the main highway instead, be extremely cautious at the ramps and wait for a break in the traffic before crossing.

Distances in the trip logs are given first in miles and then in kilometers. No kilometer posts are noted. North of Vancouver, these posts are few and far between. On Vancouver Island, they are located every 5 kilometers, all facing north and nearly invisible to southbound travelers.

The main difficulty for cyclists in British Columbia is finding a campsite. While provincial parks are numerous, only one has a hiker-biker site, called a biker's field. Two others have areas reserved for walk-in camping, which frequently fill up. At the remainder of the campgrounds, sites are available on a first-come basis only. Start your days early in order to get into camp in time to claim a site for the night. Try to schedule trips to avoid weekends during the busy vacation months of July and August.

The city of Vancouver is the center of West Coast Canadian commerce and is readily accessible by air, train, or bus.

United States residents entering Canada should carry some identification establishing their citizenship. This means a birth certificate or passport (it does not need to be current), in addition to a current driver's license. Carry sufficient money—$50 per person per day, or a major credit card, is required.

At the end of the British Columbia portion of the route, you will be faced with three options. To continue south, cyclists may take a Washington State ferry from Sidney, British Columbia, through the San Juan Islands to Anacortes following Washington's Inland Route, or a ferry from Victoria to Port Angeles, Washington, if the Peninsula Route is preferred. Other options are a bus or, in the summer, a ferry to Seattle.

Cyclists wishing to cycle only British Columbia may return to Vancouver by ferry from Swartz Bay to Tsawwassen. (If returning by way of Tsawwassen, check with the Tunnel Office at (604) 277-2115 to be sure the shuttle bus is running at the George Massey Tunnel on Highway 99.) Shuttle service is provided daily from June through August, and on weekends in September and the last *two* weeks of May. The bus picks up cyclists at the highway patrol building at the north end of the bridge and the Town and Country Motel at the south end. If the shuttle is not running, be prepared for a 7.5-mi/12-km detour across the Fraser River via the Alex Fraser Bridge.

Vancouver to Roberts Creek Provincial Park
(41.5 Miles/66.4 Kilometers)

Vancouver is a beautiful city, with numerous parks, vistas, and city views. Bike paths crisscross the city. Cyclists in Vancouver—and there are a lot of them—ride well out in the center of the lane and seem oblivious to traffic. As a one-time visitor, you probably will not have time to achieve that kind of confidence in the drivers. You will also be faced with routefinding on streets that wind over and around rolling hills, requiring careful attention to book and map. If you get off route, ask a local cyclist.

Several city parks provide opportunities along the way to stop, rest frazzled nerves, and take in the outstanding views. The largest is Stanley Park, located on a point at the edge of English Bay. It has a children's zoo, an aquarium, totem poles, hiking trails, and a bike route on the water's edge. With a perfect view over sparkling water to the city's sky-line and towering snow-capped mountains beyond, the park is popular with local residents and visitors alike.

The route described through Vancouver is neither the shortest nor straightest. In order to avoid the more congested streets, the route follows

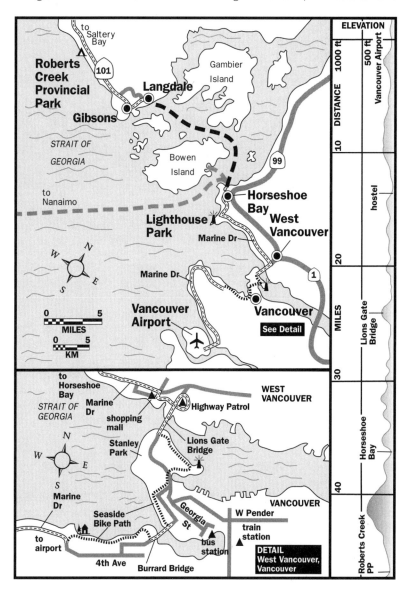

Totem poles are just one of the attractions in Vancouver's Stanley Park. Other points of interest include views of the city, a marina, a lighthouse, a children's zoo, hiking trails, and a bike path along the breakwater.

the coastline, passing through miles of parkland around the University of British Columbia and the popular beaches of English Bay, where the route joins bike paths that take you off the city streets while traversing the downtown area all the way through Stanley Park.

From Stanley Park, the route crosses the Lions Gate Bridge to West Vancouver, the last major city before Victoria, at the end of the British Columbia ride.

North from West Vancouver, a narrow two-lane road leads to Horseshoe Bay, where a luxurious ferry is taken to Langdale and the start of the Sunshine Coast. Roads here vary from narrow with little shoulder to updated with a moderate shoulder. The terrain of the Sunshine Coast is rolling. This is a popular resort area and heavy traffic can be expected on weekends and holidays. After a ferry docks, there is a rush of traffic. If you pull over to the side and wait for a few minutes, the roads will rapidly clear out.

As Vancouver is the starting point of the Pacific Coast Bicycle Route, most cyclists will arrive by bus, train, or air. Since the airport is the farthest point south, the trip description and mileage start from there. For those arriving by ground transportation, the trip is 17 miles/27.4 kilometers shorter. If you arrive late, the youth hostel at Jericho Beach Park (phone (604) 224-3208/(888) 203-4303) is a convenient place to spend the night. The hostel is located on the route from the airport. Those arriving by bus or train may find it by following the route in reverse from downtown Vancouver.

Via Station and Bus Depot
Head right (north) on Station Rd. Take the first left onto National Ave. At the end of 1 block, turn right on Main St. At 0.6 mile/0.9 kilometer from the start, go left on E. Pender and follow it for 0.5 mile/0.8 kilometer before turning left on Cambie St. Follow Cambie St. to its end, then go straight across Pacific Blvd. to find a bike path on the opposite side. Head right (west) for 1 block to Davie St. Go left and descend to the Seaside Bike Path. Head right, passing under the Granville Bridge and then Burrard Bridge to join the route from the airport. Continue on the Seaside Bike Path to Stanley Park.

Mileage Log

0.0 mi/0.0 km From the main terminal at Vancouver International Airport, follow the flow of traffic along the road (Grant MacConache Way) out of the terminal area. Go straight along the broad shoulder of the road, following signs to Vancouver and the Arthur Lang Bridge. Use caution at all intersections, and use extreme caution crossing the freeway-style exit of the road to Highway 99 and Seattle. Wait for a break in the traffic flow before continuing straight, following signs to Vancouver and the Arthur Lang Bridge.

1.9 mi/3.0 km Cross Arthur Lang Bridge on the comfortable security of a 3-ft/1-m shoulder.

2.2 mi/3.5 km At the north end of the bridge, take the Granville St. exit.

2.7 mi/4.3 km Take the first left off Granville St. and follow the bike route signs to SW Marine Dr. This is a difficult crossing and the city bike route planners suggest using the pedestrian crossing. Once across, make an immediate right on SW Marine Dr.

3.0 mi/4.8 km Junction; turn left on W. 70th St., which becomes SW Marine Dr. again. Pass a couple of small city parks as SW Marine Dr. winds its way through expensive residential neighborhoods on a narrow, bumpy road with moderate to heavy traffic.

5.0 mi/8.0 km Junction with W. 49th St. Continue straight ahead.

6.1 mi/9.7 km Major junction with 41st St. As you enter the University Endowment Lands, the road broadens to a four-lane highway with wide shoulders.

7.6 mi/12.2 km Pass a historical site on the left (west) side of SW Marine Dr., where an information board explains the exploration of the Fraser River, once mistaken for the Columbia River.

8.7 mi/14.0 km The road divides. Stay left. The SW Marine Dr. bikeway ends. Continue on around the university on NW Marine Dr., which soon narrows.

9.0 mi/14.4 km Junction; stay on the left side of the university buildings.

9.8 mi/15.6 km Beach access trail, popular with students.

10.0 mi/16.0 km Entrance to the Museum of Anthropology is passed on the left. If you have time for only one stop in Vancouver, consider this beautiful museum, which houses one of the world's finest collections of Canada's First Peoples art, including totem poles, feast dishes, and canoes.

10.2 mi/16.3 km Junction; go left, following NW Marine Dr. as it descends steeply, passing views over English Bay to the Coast Range.

11.1 mi/17.7 km Pacific Spirit Regional Park access is passed on the left. A popular trail descends to the beach. At this point NW Marine Dr. leaves the University Endowment Lands.

11.5 mi/18.4 km Seaside Bike Path begins on the left and parallels English Bay along the Spanish Banks. You can choose between the perils of a big-city bike path or the Bypass Route, which stays on the narrow and often rough-surfaced NW Marine Dr.

11.9 mi/19.0 km Jericho Beach Park and hostel. The hostel is located in a white, three-storied building on the left. Sailboards and kayaks are available for rent. Continue on the Seaside Bike Path or NW Marine Dr., which heads away from the shores of the bay.

12.3 mi/19.7 km Road riders take a left turn on W. 4th Ave., a four-lane road, and follow it for the next 0.4 mi/0.6 km. Traffic volume increases.

12.7 mi/20.3 km Turn left on Wallace St. and descend a few feet before heading right on W. 3rd Ave. Riders who have remained on the Seaside Bike Path also do a quick right here and head down W. 3rd Ave.

13.9 mi/22.2 km Go left on Stephens Rd.

14.1 mi/22.5 km Following the signed City Bike Route, go right on York for 1 block, then go right to cross Cronwell.

14.2 mi/22.7 km Still following the signs for the Seaside Bike Route, ride Pt. Grey Rd. along the coast.

14.6 mi/23.3 km The bike path leaves the road for the next 0.4 mi/0.6 km to the Kitsilano Beach parking area. Bike path riders have the easier routefinding as the path flows seamlessly around English Bay from Kitsilano Park to Hadden Park to Vanier Park.

15.0 mi/24.0 km Road riders still avoiding the bike path should ride through the Kitsilano Beach parking area and head out on Arbutus St.

15.1 mi/24.1 km Turn right on McNicoll Ave.

15.2 mi/24.2 km Go left on Maple.

15.3 mi/24.3 km Take a left on Ogden Ave.

15.4 mi/24.4 km Vanier Park; location of the Vancouver Museum, Maritime Museum, and Planetarium. Ride uphill on Chestnut.

15.7 mi/25.1 km Go left and ride on the shoulder across Burrard Bridge over a marina-filled inlet.

15.8 mi/25.2 km Following the signs, go left and descend on a bike path back to the Seaside Bike Path. Take a right turn at the bikeway intersection and, joining the route from the Via Station and Bus Depot, head to the right along the scenic shoreline.

16.8 mi/26.8 km The Seaside Bike Path enters Stanley Park.

17.1 mi/27.3 km Bike path intersection; go left on a bike path signed to Georgia St.

17.3 mi/27.6 km Stay right and head around a marshy lake.

17.5 mi/28.0 km The path divides; stay left and continue around the lake.

17.7 mi/28.3 km Ride under Georgia St. to a signed intersection for cyclists. If you are in a hurry, the speediest option is to follow Georgia St. to the Lions Gate Bridge. This route description takes the more meandering, scenic approach by following the Seawall Trail along the northeast side of Stanley Park. Scenic Dr. is often less congested than the bike path. Follow Scenic Dr. past the yacht club with views of the bay, city, and mountains. Ride past totem poles, Brockton Point Lighthouse, and a metal sculpture of a girl in a wet suit sitting on a rock; restrooms and water.

19.5 mi/31.2 km Scenic Dr. leaves the bike path and climbs through the forest.

20.9 mi/33.4 km Take a left turn off Scenic Dr. and ride toward Highway 99.

21.0 mi/33.6 km Turn right just before reaching Highway 99 and ride along the bike path/sidewalk as it passes under Scenic Dr. and then over Burrard Inlet on the Lions Gate Bridge.

22.2 mi/35.5 km Ride past the extremely steep Pedestrian Underpass turnoff, and continue on to the end of the bridge.

22.3 mi/35.6 km Ride past a highway building on your right at the end of the bridge and go right following an access road that descends to an intersection. Go right and ride along the lower side of the building and out a gate.

22.5 mi/36.0 km Go right and ride under the bridge, then head right again, on a road that passes an RV park before crossing the Capilano River.

22.6 mi/36.1 km At the base of a shopping mall, turn left and ride around the back side of the indoor complex.

22.8 mi/36.4 km Go left and descend off the road on an unmarked, dirt-surfaced path. This is a tricky turn as parked cars can obscure the start of the path.

22.9 mi/36.6 km Ride under the railroad trestle, then take an immediate right on a wide gravel path paralleling the railroad tracks.

23.0 mi/36.8 km Go straight onto a paved road and continue to parallel the railroad.

23.6 mi/37.7 km Go right on the park access road, which turns into 13th St. and crosses the railroad tracks.

23.7 mi/37.9 km As soon as you cross the tracks, take the first right on Bellevue Ave., a narrow and sometimes crowded street that heads north.

25.2 mi/40.2 km At 25th St., go left. Cross the railroad tracks, then take an immediate right on Bellevue and continue north.

26.7 mi/42.7 km Turn right on 29th Ave. and ride uphill.

26.8 mi/42.8 km Head left (north) on Marine Dr., which is narrow, winding, and shoulderless, and would be completely obnoxious if it weren't for the occasional views. Marine Dr. is a popular training route for local cyclists.

30.2 mi/48.2 km Pass the turnoff to Lighthouse Park on the left. If time allows, ride the 0.4 mi/0.6 km down to the park, then hike the 0.5 mi/0.8 km trail to West Beach for a memorable view of Point Atkinson and the lighthouse. Other park trails lead to viewpoints of Vancouver and to small meadows. Water and outhouses can be found near the lighthouse.

32.0 mi/51.1 km Ride past the congested Eagle Harbor Marina.

33.5 mi/53.5 km A T intersection; turn left and descend to Horseshoe Bay.

33.8 mi/54.0 km Make a right turn on Nelson Rd. and continue to descend.

══════ Brockton Point Lighthouse ══════

Located along the Stanley Park Seawall, overlooking Burrard Inlet, this small lighthouse looks more like a decoration than an important shipping beacon. Most of the time the inlet seems peaceful, with shipping moving in an organized pattern to and from the docks along the inlet. But when Brockton Point Lighthouse was built in 1902, the inlet truly was a busy place, and collisions were common. (There may be over 100 wrecks at the bottom of the inlet.)

Brockton Point Lighthouse had only one keeper. He held the position for twenty-five years and is attributed with saving sixteen people from drowning. He had a house near the lighthouse and kept a beautiful garden. After he retired, his house was torn down and the gardens dug up, and the area was turned into the parking lot we enjoy today.

Located in Stanley Park, the Brockton Lighthouse has been a guiding light on busy Burrard Inlet since 1902.

33.9 mi/54.1 km Go right on Chatham Rd.

34.0 mi/54.3 km Take a well-signed left on Royal and proceed to the ferry dock. Tickets to Langdale are purchased at the Foot Passenger window.

34.2 mi/54.6 km Following the traffic, ride off the dock at Langdale and head up to an intersection and traffic light.

34.4 mi/54.9 km At the light, head straight up the steep hill on Highway 101.

35.9 mi/57.4 km At the top of the hill, go left, heading toward Gibsons on Highway 101.

36.2 mi/57.9 km Intersection; turn right, still following Highway 101 toward Gibsons.

37.4 mi/59.8 km Intersection; go right and ride through the busy town of Gibsons. There are no shoulders here, so ride aggressively out in your lane. A large market is located at the north end of town.

39.9 mi/63.8 km Cliff Gilkner Park; outhouses, picnic tables, and a short hiking trail to a waterfall. Beyond the park is a short section of bike path.

41.2 mi/65.9 km Roberts Creek Provincial Park picnic area; restrooms, water, and beach access. The park is located 0.5 mi/0.8 km off the highway, on the left.

41.5 mi/66.4 km Roberts Creek Provincial Park (Sechelt Campground) on the left (west) side of Highway 101. This campground has large, level, graveled campsites, outhouses, and running water. It does not have beach access, showers, or a walk-in campground. If looking for these features, or if the campground is full, continue on another 7.7 mi/12.3 km to Porpoise Bay Provincial Park.

Roberts Creek Provincial Park to Saltery Bay Provincial Park
(41.7 Miles/66.7 Kilometers)

The Sunshine Coast is justifiably renowned for its beautiful scenery. The rocky inlets, secluded coves, and sheltered beaches are a photographer's dream. Unfortunately, most of this loveliness is hidden from the average cyclist. The majority of the coastal area is privately owned and the coves, inlets, and beaches are accessed only by boat, leaving little reason to linger while heading up the coast.

Narrow, winding roads and a series of long, steep hills provide challenging riding north of Roberts Creek Provincial Park. The scenery varies from enjoyable on the forest-lined road to good at the very occasional viewpoints over Malaspina Strait, where you may catch tantalizing glimpses of little rocky islands and harbors.

The route heads up the Sechelt Peninsula on Highway 101 through lush forest to Earls Cove and the ferry to Saltery Bay. Check your schedule before starting out in the morning, and plan your day's activities around the ferry departure time. The ferry ride is a relaxing 50-minute cruise with views of the Coast Range and forested islands. Once off the ferry, it's only a short, 0.9-mi/1.4-km ride to the campground. End your day by watching the sunset from the benches on the rocky shore of Saltery Bay.

One of the highlights of the Sechelt Peninsula is the Skookumchuck Narrows, where the tidal force of three inlets reaches phenomenal proportions. While it is best to visit at high or low tide, boats working their way through the narrows offer an exciting spectacle at any time of the day. The narrows are reached by a 3.4-mi/5.6-km side trip toward Egmont, followed by a 2.5-mi/4-km forest walk to viewpoints overlooking the narrows. Plan to spend some time watching boats pass in and out of the inlet.

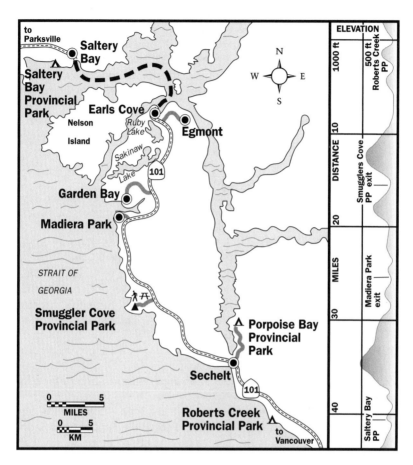

In spring and fall, traffic on this section of the route is light and drivers generally are very courteous, except when they're rushing to catch a ferry. In the summer, however, oversize RVs crowd the highway, and cyclists must ride defensively.

There are only two places to stock up on supplies—Sechelt and Madiera Park. Grocery supplies are not available near Saltery Bay Provincial Park.

Mileage Log

0.0 mi/0.0 km From Roberts Creek Provincial Park, follow Highway 101 north through heavy timber.

1.7 mi/2.7 km Wilson Creek, a private campground.

2.4 mi/3.8 km Brookman Park, a small park with picnic tables.

2.5 mi/4.0 km A short section of highway right along the water's edge at Davis Bay, with unobstructed views over the Strait of Georgia.

5.3 mi/8.5 km Sechelt, a tourist-oriented town with grocery stores, tourist facilities, and a small city park. The town sits on a narrow sand bar, which is all that connects the mainland with the Sechelt Peninsula, to the north. *Side Trip:* Take Wharf St. from the center of town to Porpoise Bay, on the beautiful southern end of Sechelt Inlet. To further explore the bay, follow Porpoise Rd. northeast 2.1 mi/3.3 km to Porpoise Bay Provincial Park; special bicycle camping area, water, showers, beach access, and short hikes.

Continuing north, Highway 101 spends more time climbing than descending as it rolls on through heavy forest.

7.3 mi/11.6 km Turnoff to Sargeant Bay Provincial Park. Located several miles off the highway, this park offers beach access, outhouses, hiking, mountain biking, and backcountry campsites.

13.0 mi/20.8 km Pass a small lake on the east side of Highway 101, a good spot for a breather. The road begins a long descent.

17.8 mi/28.4 km *Side Trip* to Smuggler Cove Provincial Park: This scenic park is reached by a 2.1-mi/3.3-km descent to the parking area. This is followed by a 0.7-mi/1.1-km walk through the forest to reach a small cove on the rocky coast. Campsites are located along the cove; outhouse but no water.

19.5 mi/31.2 km Intriguing views of rocky coves, islands, and summer homes accessible only by boat.

25.2 mi/40.3 km A handy information sign notes location of the grocery store in the town ahead.

27.4 mi/43.8 km A large supermarket lies 0.1 mi/0.2 km to the left (west) off Highway 101, in Madiera Park at the Pender Cove Shopping Center. This is the last chance to shop before Saltery Bay Provincial Park.

31.0 mi/49.6 km Garden Bay turnoff; a small tourist town on the north side of scenic Pender Harbor, 6 mi/10 km west of Highway 101. Beyond the turnoff are more rolling hills and views of two large lakes. The first is Sakinaw Lake, which lies to the west, below the highway.

37.5 mi/60.0 km Highway 101 passes island-dappled Ruby Lake. The road climbs above the east side of the lake and then begins its final descent toward Earls Cove.

40.3 mi/64.5 km *Side Trip* to Skookumchuck Narrows Provincial Park: Follow Egmont Rd. for 3.5 mi/5.6 km east over several short, steep hills. The trail to Skookumchuck Narrows starts at a small parking area on the right side of the road. Push or ride your bike down the first section of the trail on an abandoned dirt road. Mountain bikes can be ridden to the end of the road; touring bikes should be

The ferry crossing from Earls Cove to Saltery Bay is a scenic 50-minute cruise, with views of Sechelt Inlet, the south end of Prince of Wales Reach, Hotham Sound, and the glacier-covered summits of the Coast Range.

securely locked to a tree. At the Narrows, park facilities are limited to picnic tables and an outhouse.

40.8 mi/65.3 km Earls Cove ferry terminal. A waiting room and small restaurant help pass the time. There is no toll booth; fees were included in the price of the previous ferry ride. The scenery is beautiful, making the 50-minute ride pass quickly. The ferry heads east to avoid the large mass of Nelson Island, providing a glimpse of the northern end of Sechelt Inlet and the southern ends of Prince of Wales Reach and Hotham Sound. Miles of green forest connecting the rocky bays to the snow- and ice-covered Coast Range mountains confirm the feeling of being on the edge of the untamed north. Once across, cycle up a short hill away from the dock, then go left, following Highway 101 as it heads northwest.

41.7 mi/66.7 km Saltery Bay Provincial Park, a forested campground with running water, pit toilets, and easy beach access to Mermaid Cove. If the park is full, continue on to one of the numerous private campgrounds that are located between here and Powell River, or have dinner at the Saltery Bay Picnic Area, located 1.2 mi/1.9 km up the road, then continue on and find a primitive, free camp in the forest 4.5 mi/7.2 km farther on along the Powell Lake Canoe Route access road.

Saltery Bay Provincial Park to Rathtrevor Beach Provincial Park (74.2 Miles/118.7 Kilometers)

Saltery Bay Provincial Park to Rathtrevor Beach Provincial Park is not only the longest section of the British Columbia ride, it is also the most scenic. Despite the long distance, the entire day will not be spent riding as the route includes a 75-minute ferry ride from Powell River, on the mainland, to Comox, on Vancouver Island. Start your day early and pedal hard to be in time for the first ferry departure of the day. The Powell River to Vancouver Island ferry is more like a cruise ship than an auto transport. Enjoy the large sitting and dining rooms, decks for lounging or strolling, and tremendous views. On cold, wet days, it is tempting to pay passage back and forth a few times.

The Comox dock at Little River marks the true starting point for the journey south to Mexico. Roads are good and shoulders adequate in most areas. Expect some commercial traffic at all times and considerable tourist traffic during the summer and on weekends. The terrain consists of low, rolling hills with an occasional spectacular view across the Strait of Georgia to the mainland.

If you would like to spend some extra time in this area, consider one or more of four possible side trips off the suggested route, which could extend this section for one or more days. The first is a 35.6-mi/57-km round trip to Lund, at the northern end of Highway 101. It's 1,856.8 miles from Lund to the south end of the Pacific Coast Bicycle Route at San Ysidro, California. The road to Lund is narrow, with few views.

The second side trip is to the island of Texada, just a short ferry ride from Powell River. Several industries are located on Texada Island: limestone quarries, an iron ore mine, and timber. However, intermixed with all this enterprise is some spectacular scenery and very little tourist traffic. Camping is available on the island at Harwood Park.

Once on Vancouver Island, an extra day may be spent hopping between Denman and Hornby Islands. Denman Island is first, then Hornby Island, which has an extinct volcano rising out of its center. Camping is available at Fillongley Provincial Park, on Denman Island. Hornby Island has two provincial park day-use areas.

The fourth potential side trip starts at Parksville, near the end of the day's ride, and heads west across Vancouver Island 29 mi/47 km to Port Alberni. Here you may put your bicycle on a boat and cruise down Barkley Sound, past the Broken Island Group, to Ucluelet and Pacific Rim National Park. At the park there are long, sandy beaches, trails, a rain forest, fishing villages, and tourist attractions such as rental canoes, boat trips, campgrounds, and grocery stores.

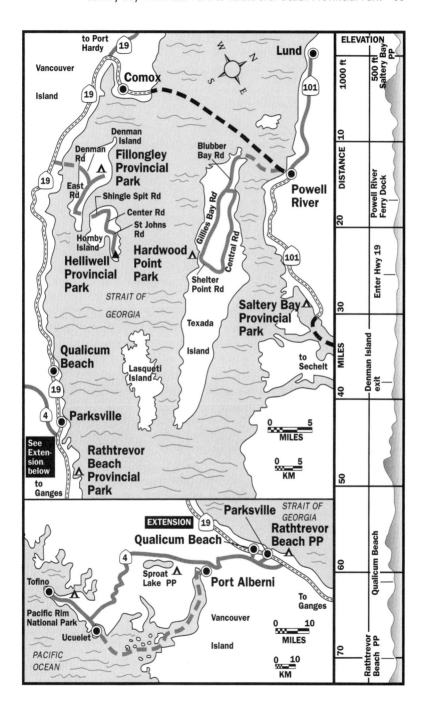

Mileage Log

0.0 mi/0.0 km From Saltery Bay Provincial Park, follow Highway 101, climbing and descending over rolling countryside. Views are few, shoulders are good.

1.2 mi/1.9 km Saltery Bay picnic area; water, restrooms, and limited beach access.

2.9 mi/4.6 km Overgrown viewpoint of Texada Island.

5.7 mi/9.1 km Powell Lake Canoe Route turnoff. It is a rough 3.2 mi/ 5.1 km on a dirt road to primitive campsites on Lois Lake with numerous opportunities to free camp along the way; no campfires.

7.3 mi/11.7 km Lang; small gas station/grocery store and turnoff to Palm Beach (a somewhat invisible park).

7.6 mi/12.2 km Commercial campsite located on the beach.

8.5 mi/13.6 km Long Beach Spawning Channel; picnic tables. Peak spawning time is from late August to October in odd years.

10.0 mi/16.0 km Black Point grocery store.

13.6 mi/21.8 km Myrtle Point; small grocery store and commercial campground.

15.9 mi/25.4 km Road parallels the coast; beach access.

18.3 mi/29.3 km Enter Powell River, a surprisingly large community nestled along the water's edge; commercial campground, grocery stores, and bicycle shops. To the north is the Powell River newspaper plant, the world's largest. A roadside information board relates some of the history of the plant, which may be toured on weekdays.

19.2 mi/30.7 km Turn left on Alexander St., descend 1 block, then go left on Willingdon Ave. to the ferry dock. This turn marks the start of the side trips to Lund and Texada Island. For details, see end of this mileage log.

19.5 mi/31.2 km After the 75-minute crossing, depart from the pleasant luxury of the ferry at Little River and head toward Comox.

19.9 mi/31.8 km Pass a private campground. If the ride proves to be too long, private camp areas can be found all along the route.

21.6 mi/34.5 km A large four-way junction. Continue straight ahead (south) on Anderton Rd.

23.6 mi/37.7 km Comox; bicycle shop and grocery stores.

24.7 mi/39.5 km Road ends at a T intersection located near the edge of the bay. Turn right, toward the business section of town.

25.2 mi/40.3 km Bike lane begins as the road leaves town and descends to low-lying marshlands with views of the snow-capped peaks of Vancouver Island.

26.6 mi/42.5 km Elevated bird observation platform on the left marks the end of the bay.

Mermaid Cove, at Saltery Bay Provincial Park, is a popular destination for kayakers and canoeists.

27.3 mi/43.6 km At the traffic light, go left and ride into downtown Courtenay.

27.5 mi/43.9 km At the second light, go left again, passing several large grocery stores as you ride through town.

28.5 mi/45.6 km The road divides; go straight following the Oceanside Route, Highway 19A. Shoulders are good in this area.

31.6 mi/50.5 km Trent River Bridge; the first of many old-style, narrow bridges where the shoulder disappears on the bridge deck and reappears as soon as you are across. Because the bridges are so narrow, wait for a break in the traffic before venturing across.

36.2 mi/57.9 km Union Bay; small market harbor, bay view, and beach access.

38.8 mi/61.3 km Buckley Bay Rest Area, on the left side of the road, has an excellent view, beach access, and outhouse, but no water.

40.8 mi/65.2 km Convenience store and start of Denman and Hornby Islands side trip. For details, see end of this mileage log.

41.9 mi/67.0 km Fanny Bay; restaurant and small grocery store.

47.2 mi/75.5 km Rosewell Provincial Park; located on the left, 0.1 mi/ 0.2 km off of Highway 19A on Berray Rd. The forested park has an outhouse, picnic tables, a creek, and trails. Continuing south, the shoulders narrow and remain minimal for the next 10 mi/16 km.

53.0 mi/84.8 km Georgia Park; small grocery store.

63.6 mi/101.7 km Cedar Grove; a private campground with a water slide and nearby store.

64.2 mi/102.7 km Qualicum Beach; grocery stores and nice grassy park along the edge of the bay.

65.0 mi/104.0 km Public restrooms.

65.4 mi/104.6 km Turnoff to Qualicum Beach city center and first turnoff to Port Alberni.

68.4 mi/109.4 km Lasqueti Island ferry turnoff. The ferry runs a couple times a day on most days during the summer season. The ferry does not take cars, so bicycles are a popular mode of transportation along the dirt roads of the island. There is one commercial campground on the island.

70.3 mi/112.5 km Parksville. Stock up on food supplies for the night. Road widens from two to four lanes and the shoulder disappears.

71.8 mi/114.9 km Second turnoff to Port Alberni and Pacific Rim National Park. See end of this mileage log for details.

73.2 mi/117.1 km Cross Englishman River, then climb a short hill.

73.6 mi/117.7 km At the top of the hill, turn left to Rathtrevor Beach Provincial Park. Once across, go left again, then take the first right and descend into the park.

74.2 mi/118.7 km Rathtrevor Beach Provincial Park; camping, walk-in campsites, restrooms, water, showers, hiking trails, and beach access. The walk-in sites are located in an open field next to the entrance booth.

Lund Side Trip

Cyclists continuing north to Lund, at the end of Highway 101, should stay on the main road through Powell River. There are few views along the 14-mi/23-km ride. Several private campgrounds are passed en route, and groceries may be purchased at Powell River and Lund.

Texada Island Side Trip

From the same dock as the Comox ferry, catch the small ferry from Powell River to Blubber Bay, an old whaling port on Texada Island. Ride to Shelter Point Regional Park, located 17 mi/27 km from the ferry dock.

When you return to Blubber Bay, purchase a ferry ticket to Comox, on Vancouver Island, with a stopover at Powell River—this is cheaper than two separate tickets.

Denman and Hornby Islands Side Trip

Take the ferry across Buckley Bay to Denman Island. Head directly across the island from the ferry landing. Follow Denman Rd. 3 mi/5 km to Swan Rd., then turn left and ride 1 mi/1.6 km to Fillongley Provincial Park; camping, water, restrooms, nature walks, and beach access. Set up camp here before continuing on.

From the provincial park turnoff, continue on Dennman Rd., which becomes East Rd., riding along the shores of Lambert Channel for 3.4 mi/5.5 km to the Hornby Island ferry. Hornby Island has several resorts but no camping. Mountain bike riding is a year-round activity on the island, and if you are riding a fat-tire bike, you may want to take the opportunity to try out some of the island's single- and double-track routes. Talk to the locals to find out which routes would be appropriate for your bike. To ride to the scenic Helliwell Park on the east end of the island, follow Shingle Spit Rd. for 2.2 mi/3.5 km. Turn left on Central Rd. and ride 4.1 mi/6.5 km, then go right on St. Johns Rd. for the final 2.2 mi/ 3.5 km to the park.

Pacific Rim National Park Side Trip

From Parksville, take Highway 4 west 29 mi/47 km to Port Alberni. The road is hilly and twisting, passing lakes, Little Qualicum Falls Provincial Park, and Cathedral Grove Provincial Park, where trees are 300 to 800 years old. The road crosses 1,230-foot/375-meter Port Alberni Summit at 25 mi/40 km, then descends to town. Stop at the visitor information center at the east end of town to pick up maps and information on campgrounds, roads, and the sailing schedule for the *Lady Rose.* Facilities in Port Alberni include several commercial campgrounds, supermarkets, motels, and restaurants.

From Port Alberni, take the beautiful and scenic boat ride on the *Lady Rose* to Ucluelet. The alternative is to ride 60 mi/90 km to the coast on Highway 4, which is steep, narrow, and busy, but very scenic. Evenings are the best time to ride, when the logging trucks are off the road. The *Lady Rose* leaves Port Alberni at 8:00 A.M. on alternating days and carries only 100 people. Be sure to sign up early and specify that you will be taking your bicycle with you. If riding, stock up on supplies at Port Alberni.

Once you reach Ucluelet, ride north to find camping, hiking trails, the rain forest, and long, sandy beaches.

Rathtrevor Beach Provincial Park to McDonald Provincial Park (64.7 Miles/103.5 Kilometers)

Spanning great changes in scenery and climate, the ride from Rathtrevor Beach Provincial Park to McDonald Provincial Park brings you out of the raw north to the warmth of the southern Gulf Islands. From the summits of the Coast Range gleaming across the island-studded Strait of Georgia, to ships and boats cruising this inland passage to and from Alaska, the scenery is outstanding.

In this section, the route follows Highway 19 and Highway 19A south along the east coast of Vancouver Island. The roads are extremely busy. In Nanaimo, the route takes a relaxing break from the noisy highway and follows a city bike path for several miles before returning to the wide shoulders of the main highway. To end the day, the route leaves the hustle and bustle of the four-lane highway and jogs east on rural roads to catch the ferry to Salt Spring Island, one of the Gulf Islands, followed by a second scenic ferry ride to Sidney.

Salt Spring Island is a fun steppingstone on your journey south. The island, the largest and most populated of the Gulf Islands, is also a popular resort and vacation center. It has several provincial parks, trails for hiking, art galleries galore, and beaches for relaxing.

The bike route heads directly to Fulford Harbor where you board the second ferry of the day, to Swartz Bay. From the massive ferry terminal on the northern end of the Saanich Peninsula, it is a short ride to McDonald Provincial Park.

The main point of interest in this section is the town of Nanaimo. At the hub of this thoroughly modern area is the old town, with beautiful rock buildings and immaculate parks. Stop at the tourist center and pick up a tour map outlining various points of interest, from rose gardens to totem poles and petroglyphs. Spend time at the small but well-designed museum, and explore a coal mine and coal miner's cottage, an important part of Nanaimo's heritage.

In the center of Nanaimo's harbor lies Newcastle Island, a provincial park. The island is a perfect picnic spot, and the ferries run frequently throughout the day during the summer months. Enjoy an hour on the island, hike its many trails, or spend the night at the campground.

Nanaimo

The prosperous yacht harbor, lovely parks, floral gardens, well-laid-out bike paths, and cultured museum all seem at odds with Nanaimo's rough-and-tumble coal mining past. The area's original residents were members of five bands of the Coast Salish, and the city's name was derived from the native word *Sneneymexw,* which meant either "The Whole" or "The Meeting Place."

In 1852, the Hudson's Bay Company established an outpost here and the coal mining began. At one point there were ten working mines extending out under Newcastle Island into the Strait of Georgia. In 1853, The Bastion was built to protect the miners against attacks by natives who wanted their homes back. Nanaimo's colorful history can be explored in depth with a stop at the Nanaimo Museum.

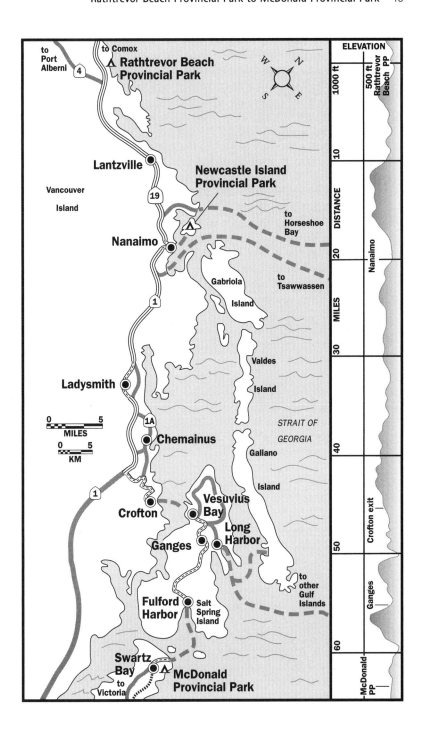

Mileage Log

0.0 mi/0.0 km From Rathtrevor Beach Provincial Park, enjoy a final view of the Sunshine Coast across the Strait of Georgia, then cycle west on the park access road back to Highway 19A.

0.7 mi/1.2 km Intersection; go left, cycling past several resorts.

1.3 mi/2.0 km Go right on Resort Way and head back to Highway 19A.

1.4 mi/2.1 km Using caution and a lot of patience, wait for a break in traffic and cross over to the southbound side of Highway 19A, which has four lanes with wide shoulders.

2.5 mi/4.0 km Highway 19A merges with Highway 19. Continue south on the comfortable shoulders of this busy freeway.

8.0 mi/12.8 km Nanoose Bay Rest Area; picnic tables but no water. This inlet is beautiful when the tide is in and an enticing clam-digging area when the tide is out. Across the inlet from the highway is a naval station, where large ships of war are frequently moored. Beyond the bay the road turns inland, passing several privately operated campgrounds.

10.3 mi/16.4 km Pass the first of several exits to Lantzville, a small commercial area with most of its facilities located off the main highway. Beyond Lantzville, forests are replaced by farms, which in turn are replaced by shopping centers, gas stations, and ware-houses.

12.4 mi/19.8 km Enter Nanaimo; all facilities, including bike shops and supermarkets.

13.1 mi/21.0 km Leave Highway 19 at the Highway 19A exit and ride past a seemingly endless parade of shopping centers, malls, and strip malls. Highway 19A is a four-laner with a shoulder that varies from poor to nonexistent at the beginning and improves as you go.

14.9 mi/23.8 km Turn right at Mostar Rd., then take an immediate left onto the E & N Bike Path. The path is sketchy at first, part path and part sidewalk. Ride past the Wholesale Club Store (that was what it was in 2003) to find the path on the left, just before the railroad tracks. (*Special Note:* The tracks are crossed several times by the bike path in the next couple of miles. Use caution when crossing. Despite their abandoned look, the tracks are traversed by the VIA commuter train several times each day.)

18.2 mi/29.1 km Unless you are planning to return to Horseshoe Bay, ignore the bikeway turnoff and underpass on the left.

19.6 mi/31.3 km After riding over the train tracks, the E & N Bike Path empties out onto Holly Ave., a quiet residential street. Continue south on the road or bikeway/sidewalk.

19.8 mi/31.6 km Turn left on Rosehill St., following the City Center bike

Nanaimo is a popular destination for boaters, and the marinas are over-flowing with pleasure craft throughout the summer.

route signs. Descend for 1 block, then go right on Caledonia Ave.

20.0 mi/32.0 km Stay left as the bike route leaves the road and heads across a wide pedestrian bridge. Once across, go right and ride across a parking area to a road. Go left and descend on Prideaux St.

20.3 mi/32.4 km Ride around a parking area, then follow the bike path through an underpass, crossing to the east side of Highway 19A to reach an intersection with the Harbor Path. Take the first right and ride across a large parking area to Comox Rd.

20.4 mi/32.5 km Go left on Comox Rd. and head east into the heart of the old town. *Side Trip* to Newcastle Island Provincial Park: Ride approximately 500 ft/150 m on Comox Rd., take a left, and descend to the ferry terminal at Maffeo Sutton Park, located directly behind the arena. The island park has campsites, fast food, swimming, play fields, and enough artifacts to keep a history buff happy for several days.

20.6 mi/32.9 km Comox Rd. bends to the right and turns into Front St. Pass to the right of The Bastion, an old Hudson's Bay Company fort-turned-museum, open in the summer.

21.0 mi/33.6 km *Side Trip* to the Nanaimo Museum: The building sits atop a small knoll with access up a short, steep road. The view from the top is excellent.

21.2 mi/33.0 km Pass Gabriola Island ferry dock. There are 20 mi/32 km of pleasant touring on the island. No camping.

21.4 mi/34.2 km The road divides; stay to the left, following the waterfront as Front St. turns into Esplanade.

21.5 mi/34.3 km Turn right on Crace St., then take an immediate left on Haliburton, following the green city bike route signs.

23.5 mi/37.6 km Just before reaching the main highway, turn left. You are still on Haliburton.

24.0 mi/38.4 km Return to the busy highway using the traffic signal and continue south on the Trans-Canada Highway 1. The road is a busy four-laner with a wide shoulder.

25.2 mi/40.3 km Following the bike route signs, ride up the freeway-style exit to Duke Bay Rd. Once up top, a bike path will return you to Highway 1.

29.6 mi/47.3 km Pass a rest area located on the left side of the highway; no water.

30.3 mi/48.4 km Ride over a broad, level plane, passing the Nanaimo Airport.

34.3 mi/54.8 km Ladysmith; commercial district and grocery stores are located off Trans-Canada Highway 1.

36.5 mi/58.4 km The Chemainus turnoff is the start of an *Alternate Route* to Crofton. Highway 1A through Chemainus offers a scenic escape from the Trans-Canada Highway 1. The road is narrow and recommended only on weekends, when the lumber mills are closed.

42.5 mi/68.0 km Pass Henery Rd. and the turnoff to the Thetis Island ferry dock at Chemainus. (Thetis Island is mainly a residential area without parks or public beach access.)

45.3 mi/72.4 km Leave the Trans-Canada Highway 1 at Mount Sticker Rd. and go east toward Crofton and the Salt Spring Island ferry. The best way to make this turn is to go right on Mount Sticker Rd. and, using the light at the intersection, make the crossing of the busy highway. The Mount Sticker Rd. is narrow with little shoulder.

45.7 mi/73.1 km Intersection; go left on a narrow road through a residential area.

46.7 mi/74.7 km Road ends. Turn right, joining Highway 1A from Chemainus, and follow the narrow road over several very short, steep hills to Crofton.

48.0 mi/76.8 km A large lumber mill marks the entrance to Crofton. In town, you will find a supermarket and, on a clear day, a grand view of Mount Baker over Salt Spring Island.

49.0 mi/78.4 km Intersection; go left and head straight downhill to the ferry dock.

49.4 mi/79.0 km Crofton ferry terminal. After a 20-minute ride, the ferry docks on Salt Spring Island at Vesuvius Bay. Let the ferry traffic go by, then head right, following Vesuvius Rd. Riding on the island is fun, and many cyclists relax their strict road disciplines on the quiet country roads. Unfortunately, though traffic on the island is sparse, cars travel at high speeds. Remember to ride defensively while enjoying the scenery.

51.7 mi/82.7 km Intersection; turn right (south) on Lower Ganges Rd. and follow it for a roller-coaster ride through island farmlands.

54.2 mi/86.7 km Ganges; a small, crowded tourist town with a grocery store, bakery, picturesque harbor, and small picnic area. Ride through town to a T intersection facing the picnic area. Turn right. *Side Trip* to Mouat Provincial Park: Ride 300 ft/0.1 km to the base of a steep hill, then turn right on an unmarked road full of potholes. The park is located at the end of Seaview Rd.; limited campsites, Frisbee golf course, and trails.

57.5 mi/92.0 km Pass the turnoff to Mount Maxwell Provincial Park. It is a 5.6 mi/9 km climb to a viewpoint at the summit; picnic tables and outhouses.

61.8 mi/98.8 km Stop sign; turn left toward Fulford Harbor, past a small park on the right.

62.8 mi/100.4 km Fulford Harbor; descend to the ferry dock and the main part of town; grocery store and small restaurant. The crossing from Salt Spring Island to Swartz Bay, on the Saanich Peninsula of Vancouver Island, takes 20 minutes, much too brief to fully appreciate the view that stretches across the Gulf Islands to Mount Baker in Washington State. *Side Trip* to Ruckle Provincial Park: For those wishing to stay awhile on Salt Spring Island, Ruckle Provincial Park offers the best camping on the island. From the turnoff to Fulford Harbor, go left on Beaver Point Rd. 5.9 mi/9.5 km to the park entrance. There are seventy walk-in campsites, 5 mi/8 km of trails, access to the shore, and a lot of island history to explore at this scenic park.

When you disembark at Swartz Bay, follow the well-signed bike route along the shoulder of Highway 1.

64.1 mi/102.5 km Following the bike route and signs to McDonald Provincial Park, exit Highway 1. At the top of the exit ramp, go left.

64.3 mi/102.8 km At the base of a hill, go right, still following the signed bike route.

64.6 mi/103.3 km Entrance to McDonald Provincial Park. Turn right into the park and ride up the steep hill.

64.7 mi/103.5 km The walk-in campsites are located across the road from the park warden's house. The park has outhouses, running water, and split wood for campfires.

McDonald Provincial Park to Victoria (20.4 Miles/32.6 Kilometers)

The final leg of the British Columbia section of the Pacific Coast Bicycle Route has three possible endings. Cyclists heading back to Vancouver take the ferry from Swartz Bay to Tsawwassen. If planning to head south on the Inland Route through Washington, ride to Sidney and take the San Juan Islands ferry east to tour the islands before heading on to Anacortes. The Coho ferry to Port Angeles is the proper choice if the objective is the Peninsula Route through Washington. It departs from the heart of downtown Victoria. (The San Juan Island and Coho ferries have limited daily departures; check with a tourist information center for an up-to-date schedule.)

No matter what route off Vancouver Island is chosen, plan to spend at least half a day touring Victoria. The city, often accused of being more English than England, is easy to explore by bicycle. Major attractions are within a few blocks of each other, and there are well-signed bike routes heading out in every direction. Popular attractions include the Maritime Museum and Royal BC Museum (hours can be spent here), Thunderbird Park, Empress Hotel, Parliament buildings, and Beacon Hill Park, with beautiful gardens and an excellent view south. Stop at any tourist information office for a city map.

Just north of Victoria is the spectacular Butchart Gardens, open year round. The 35-acre gardens display almost every variety and color of flower known to man in such exotic settings as the Sunken Garden, English Rose Garden, Japanese Garden, and Italian Garden.

McDonald Provincial Park is the best campground near Victoria, and there is an excellent hostel located on 516 Yates St. in the downtown area. Call ahead for reservations: (604) 385-4511.

The route from McDonald Provincial Park to Victoria is entirely on the extensive and brilliantly designed regional trail system. The trails are not entirely paved; expect some dirt and mud on rainy days. However, the hardened surface is easy to ride even for traditional touring bicycles with 27-inch or 700-c wheels. The trails follow old railroad grades and for the most part are level. The easy riding means that even riders taking the late afternoon ferry to Friday Harbor on San Juan Island should be able to tour Victoria and still be back in time to go through customs before boarding the ferry at Sidney.

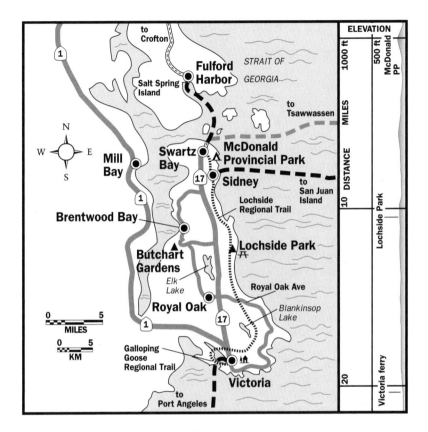

Mileage Log

0.0 mi/0.0 km Leaving McDonald Provincial Park, go right and head south on McDonald Park Rd. The next driveway passed leads to Blue Heron Day-use Park, located along the southern boundary of the provincial park. The day-use park has sports fields, restrooms, picnic tables, and running water.

0.8 mi/1.2 km Intersection; continue straight ahead. Highway 17 is now in sight, on the right.

0.9 mi/1.4 km Go straight ahead to find a bike path paralleling Highway 17. (This bike route is part of the Lochside Regional Trail and is well signed.)

1.9 mi/3.0 km A large intersection marks the entrance to Sidney, a tourist-oriented town with flower-lined streets, numerous coffee shops, restaurants, bakeries, grocery stores, bike shops, art galleries, a museum, picturesque marinas, and several small, immaculately maintained parks. The bike path continues straight at the intersections, skirting around the downtown area.

2.2 mi/3.5 km At the yellow posts, take a left turn off the wide bike path. Ride the narrow path for 15 ft/5 m to a city street. Make a short jog to the right, then continue straight east toward the harbor.

2.5 mi/4.0 km At the visitor information building, pick up a map of the regional bike trails as well as a tourist map of downtown Victoria. If you are heading directly to the twice-a-day ferry to Anacortes (once a day from mid-September to mid-May), go straight 0.2 mi/ 0.3 km to the gated waiting area. For Victoria, go right at the visitor information building and ride south on Lockside Dr.

2.7 mi/4.3 km Tulista Park on the left; great place for views of the island-studded Sidney Harbor.

4.3 mi/6.8 km The road narrows and the bike lane disappears. No problem; traffic is not overwhelming in this area.

4.4 mi/7.0 km CY Thompson Park; outhouses, a trail, beach access, and views of the Gulf and San Juan Islands.

5.2 mi/8.3 km Enter the Municipality of Central Saanich.

6.5 mi/10.4 km Turn right on Mt. Newton X Rd. and head west for 1 block.

6.6 mi/10.5 km Cross Mt. Newton X Rd. Ride the sidewalk past a gas station to find a hardened-surface bike path on the left. Go left, paralleling Highway 17 south.

7.4 mi/11.8 km Pass Saanich Historical Artifacts Society's Heritage Museum, which features outdoor displays of an historic train and farming implements.

7.7 mi/12.3 km The Lochside Trail returns to pavement at the museum's entrance. Continue straight ahead on country roads through neatly tilled farm fields.

8.2 mi/13.1 km Intersection; go straight.

9.0 mi/14.4 km Cross another paved road; continue straight.

9.3 mi/14.8 km Pavement ends; continue on a hardened dirt surface.

9.6 mi/15.3 km Ride on a brief section of pavement before heading out over more hardened-surface road.

11.1 mi/17.7 km Return to pavement at Lochside Park; restrooms, water, play fields, and picnic tables.

11.2 mi/17.9 km Cross to the left side of the park access road just before it bends, and ride the paved bike path, which climbs up into a residential area.

11.3 mi/18.0 km The bike path crosses a busy intersection and resumes with a short, steep climb from the southwest corner.

11.4 mi/18.2 km The bike path ends; cross the road and head slightly left before taking the first right, on Lochside Dr.

12.4 mi/19.8 km Ride past Doris Page Park; forested trails.

13.0 mi/20.8 km Go right on a hardened dirt path and cross above McMinn Park; water, restrooms, trails, play area, picnic tables.

13.1 mi/20.9 km Return to Lochside Dr. and continue straight through an upscale residential district.

13.5 mi/21.6 km Cross a major street at the traffic light and continue straight, descending back into an area of farms and marshy lakes.

14.9 mi/23.8 km Blankinsop Lake; a wooden trestle takes you across this marshy area, replete with ducks. Look for grebes and woodducks, along with mallards and Canada geese.

15.5 mi/24.8 km Return to pavement at the edge of a busy urban area.

The Parliament buildings are a stately reminder that Victoria is the capital of British Columbia. Bagpipers are often seen strolling the streets and grounds, adding a touch of old England to the New World.

15.7 mi/25.1 km Intersection; head right on Cedar Hill X Rd. to the next intersection.

15.8 mi/25.2 km Turn left on Bordan St. and cruise downhill to the next intersection.

15.9 mi/25.4 km Go straight across McKenzie Ave. Once across, go left and ride up on the sidewalk to find the paved Lochside Regional Trail heading off at a diagonal.

17.2 mi/27.5 km After passing through a tunnel, the trail reaches a major pedestrian intersection, which marks the end of the Lochside Regional Trail. Go left, heading toward downtown Victoria on the Galloping Goose Regional Trail. Climb over Switch Bridge, then head through an industrial park.

18.7 mi/29.9 km After crossing the Inner Harbor on the wood-slatted Selkirk Trestle, reach an intersection. Stay left, paralleling the Inner Harbor waterway.

19.2 mi/30.7 km The bike path ends; head left and ride the roadway until it bends. Go left on the bike path and climb a short hill.

19.5 mi/31.2 km Go left and ride the Johnson St. Railway Bridge across the Inner Harbor waterway.

19.7 mi/31.5 km Enter downtown Victoria. You are now on the wrong side of a crazy intersection. The safest way to cross is to ride straight up to Store St. and then, when the traffic is agreeable, head right, directly across the intersection, to ride Wharf St. south to the main tourist center. The Victoria Hostel is located here, at the intersection of Wharf and Yates.

20.3 mi/32.4 km At the central Inner Harbor tourist area is a visitor information center with maps and suggestions about what to see and do, from museum hopping to whale watching excursions. Get something to eat at one of the local cafes or just sit and enjoy the ambiance.

20.4 mi/32.6 km As soon as Wharf St. merges with Government St., the road reaches a major intersection. The Royal BC Museum is across Bellevue St.; the Parliament buildings are to the right. To reach the Coho ferry to Port Angeles, go right on Bellevue for 1 block.

Opposite: *A small waterfall tumbles down the hillside along the road on the south side of Quinault Lake.*

The coastal region of Washington prides itself on its lush vegetation, lakes, rivers, rugged coastline, glacier-capped mountains, and rich, green forests. If you think that all the verdant growth and abundant water are indicators of a very moist climate, you are correct. The generous and frequent rainfall discourages some cyclists, but the hardy don raincoats and find much to enjoy. Of course, everyone hopes

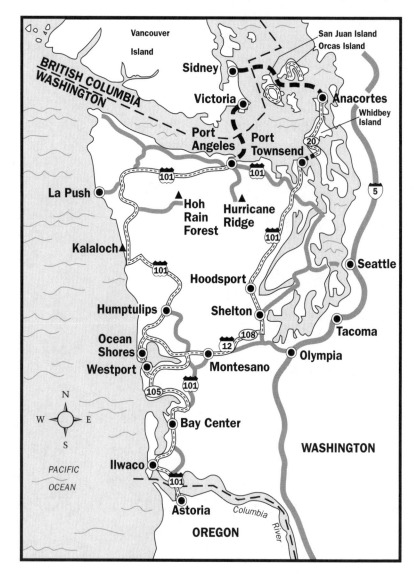

to catch one or more of the sixty days a year when it is perfectly clear, the sky is a sparkly blue, and the great snow- and ice-covered peaks of the Cascade and Olympic Ranges gleam brightly over the open waterways and forested foothills.

Two different routes through the northern portion of the state are catalogued in this section. We have named them the Peninsula Route and the Inland Route. The Peninsula Route heads south from Victoria to Port Angeles on the Coho ferry, then follows US 101 south around the west side of the Olympic Peninsula, totaling 344.5 miles to the Oregon border. The Inland Route travels down Puget Sound, island-hopping from the San Juan Islands to Fidalgo and Whidbey Islands. The route then crosses to the west side of the Sound and follows Hood Canal to Shelton before turning west to join the Peninsula Route at Westport, for a total of 329.9 miles to the Oregon border.

The two routes are designed for riders with different goals. Riders taking the Peninsula Route should not be planning a quick dash through the state. To fully enjoy the Olympic Peninsula, it's necessary to take long side trips off US 101 and pedal up steep roads to alpine meadows; descend long, shoulderless roads to beachcomb the rugged coast; and follow forest roads inland to wander through the moss-hung rain forests. Weather plays an important role on the Olympic Peninsula, and riders should be prepared for heavy fogs and rain (over 140 inches of rain fall each year in the Hoh River Valley). The roads around the Olympic Peninsula are narrow and see considerable logging truck traffic. Grocery stores, restaurants, and motels are few and far between, making this route best for more experienced cyclists who are prepared to camp and carry their food supplies for long distances.

If you are not interested in long side trips and miles of forest, or prefer your route to be dotted with bakeries and ice cream shops, then the Inland Route is the way to go. Points of interest are easily accessible from the main route. Riding conditions are generally good, and the climate, protected by a coastal range of mountains, is drier. In addition to numerous state parks, old forts, and Victorian towns, riders can expect to enjoy beautiful scenery and classic Northwest views. The route starts with a ferry ride to one of the best-known cycling areas in the country, the San Juan Islands, then heads south along the edge of the scenic Hood Canal. Moderately rolling terrain and good roads make this route enjoyable for all cyclists.

Eleven state parks in Washington have primitive campsites for cyclists. These sites are small, with trail access to the water and restrooms. Cyclists are charged per tent (or tarp) rather than per person. These sites do not require reservations. National forest and national park campgrounds are filled on a first-come basis, and finding a campsite may be

The San Juan Islands are a well-known destination for touring cyclists, and you can expect to have a lot of two-wheeled company on the ferry rides between the islands.

difficult on weekends and holidays. To ensure a site in these national forest or national park campgrounds, it's best to make camp by early afternoon.

National park campgrounds are open year-round. Most forest service camps close from September through May. Most state parks are open year round, with limited services in the winter. Future budget cuts may result in the closure of some parks during the winter months.

If planning to travel during the winter months, check ahead to be certain the parks are open.

Due to the moist climate, fenders and raingear are recommended. Take a tent or heavy-duty tarp and a stove, so you can cook at least one hot meal each day when it's raining. However, it's a documented fact that if you load up on raingear and warm clothing, and forget your sunglasses, you will have excellent weather the entire time you are in the state.

The climate is mild. Temperatures average in the low 60s during June, July, and August. Winds blow from the south when the weather is bad and from the north when it's good. Rainfall averages 45 inches a year on the Inland Route and up to 144 inches a year on portions of the Peninsula Route.

Mileposts in Washington decrease from north to south, and only whole numbers are indicated. Tenths have been added to the mileage logs to increase accuracy. For cyclists heading north to south, if the milepost number reads 25.7 in the mileage log, the point indicated will be passed 0.7 mile before milepost 25 (or 0.3 mile after milepost 26).

Finding an easily accessible point to start the Washington tour is difficult. Ideally, the tour should start from the Canadian border at Victoria; however, it's less expensive to fly to either Vancouver or Seattle and ride (very easy) or take ground transport to Victoria. Air, train, and bus service to Vancouver is excellent. From the Vancouver Airport, it is a relatively straightforward ride to Tsawwassen, where you pick up the ferry to Swartz Bay. Air, train, and bus service to Seattle is also excellent. Seattle has the added advantage of direct ferry service to Victoria. Port Angeles, the starting point for the Peninsula Route, is an easy two-day ride from Seattle. It also can be reached by Greyhound bus from Seattle or by ferry from Victoria.

If ending your trip at the southern end of the state, it is best to cross the Columbia River to Astoria, Oregon, then ride inland on Highway 30 to Portland or box the bikes and take a Greyhound bus to Seattle or Portland. A bicycle shop is a possible source of bike boxes for bus travel. See the introduction to Oregon for bike routes to the bus depot, train station, and airport in Portland.

Seattle-Tacoma (Sea-Tac) International Airport

Cyclists choosing to start from the Sea-Tac International Airport (located at the south end of Seattle) are faced with a maze of freeways. You may find a bus or taxi to carry your gear to your chosen ferry dock or downtown accommodations. If riding from the airport, you may avoid the downtown congestion by heading to the Fauntleroy ferry. Pick up bikes and gear at baggage claim, pack up, then head out along the sidewalk or the road, following the flow of traffic. At the end of the terminal

A ferry loads at Orcas Island. The island has a direct ferry link to both Friday Harbor, on San Juan Island, and Anacortes, on the mainland.

buildings, the road passes a bus loading and parking area. Ride to the end of the bus area to find a city bike route sign that leads you to a sidewalk. Follow the sidewalk 0.1 mile to International Blvd. (Highway 99). Cross the road and head left (north), either on the road with the traffic or on the wide sidewalk. At 0.8 mile, turn left on S. 170th St. and ride under a freeway. Turn right on Air Cargo Rd. at 1.1 miles and ride north through a complicated intersection. At 2.3 miles, cross S. 154th St. and go straight on 24th Ave. S. Make a left turn on S. 136th St. at 3.5 miles and ride west for 1.8 miles. At 5.3 miles, turn right on 4th Ave. SW. (*Note:* Do not turn on 4th Ave. S., which is passed right after you cross over Highway 509.) After 1.9 miles, go left on SW 108th St. and head west. When SW 108th St. ends, jog right on 12th Ave. SW, then take the first left on SW 107th St., which will turn into SW 106th St. At 9.8 miles, SW 106th ends. Go right on Marine View Dr. SW for 0.8 mile. At SW Wildwood, turn left and descend to reach the small Fauntleroy ferry dock, 11 miles from the airport. Be sure to catch a ferry going all the way across Puget Sound to Southworth.

Once on the west side of Puget Sound, follow Highway 160 west. After 3.7 miles, pass the turnoff to Manchester State Park. (This small state park has limited camping 2.5 miles north. Call the state parks reservation line at (888) 226-7688 before leaving home to ensure that a site will be waiting for you.) Highway 160 merges with Highway 16. Shortly after, at 11.7 miles from Southworth, head west on Highway 3 for 7.4 miles to Belfair (there is a state park just 3 miles off the route). Continue east on Highway 106 for 19 more miles to join the Inland Route just south of the town of Potlatch. If cycling up to Port Angeles, head north on Highway 3 to the Hood Canal Bridge, then west on Highway 104 to US 101; the shoulder is excellent the entire way.

For cyclists heading to the center of Seattle to catch the train to Vancouver, the ferry to Bremerton or Winslow, or simply to spend some time in the downtown area, continue straight on 24th Ave. S. until it ends, 4.8 miles from the airport. Go right (east) on S. 116th Way and descend 0.5 mile. Make a left turn onto (unsigned) Pacific Highway S. After 0.7 mile, reach a confusing intersection. Go right and, after a few cranks of the pedal, go right again on Airport Way, which loops through a narrow canyon and then heads north along Boeing Field. At 6.7 miles from Sea-Tac Airport, pass an entrance to the Museum of Flight (one of Seattle's finest museums). When riding through Mill Town at 10.1 miles, stay right and cross the overpass above the train tracks. Turn left on Royal Brougham at 12.9 miles and head west. To reach the train station, turn right at 13.5 miles on Occidental, then, 0.4 mile beyond, turn right again on S. King St. Go straight to the train depot. For the Bremerton, Bainbridge, or Victoria ferries, follow Royal Brougham to its end, then go right on Alaska Way S. (also called Highway 519) and follow the signs.

Inland Route: The San Juan Islands (57.9 Miles)

The Inland Route through Washington heads east from Sidney, British Columbia, by ferry through the San Juan Islands to Anacortes. During the summer there are two departures each day. One is a nonstop cruise to Anacortes; the other makes a single stop at San Juan Island. While touring the islands is not essential to the southward journey, it is an opportunity you should not pass up.

The San Juan Islands are a cyclist's paradise. Even their size is perfect—too small to be toured enjoyably by car, and too large to be easily explored on foot. The islands that have ferry service are the ideal size for a day-long tour including plenty of time to explore the viewpoints, parks, and historic monuments.

Of the many islands that make up the San Juans, only four have state ferry service—San Juan, Orcas, Shaw, and Lopez. These four islands offer invigorating riding and excellent camping opportunities (limited

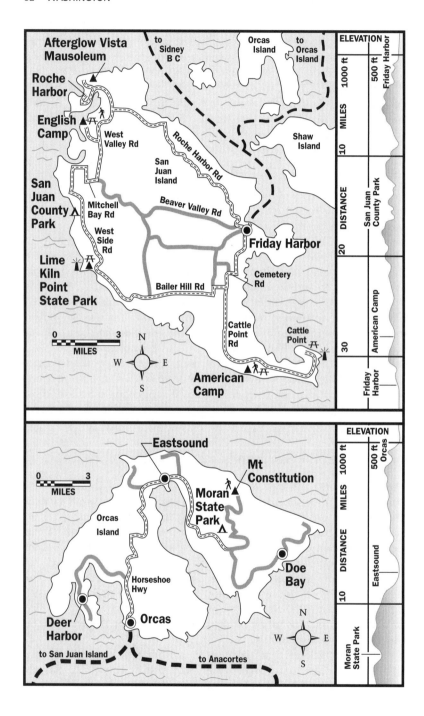

Afterglow Vista Mausoleum

Roche Harbor

to Sidney B C

Orcas Island

to Orcas Island

English Camp

West Valley Rd

Roche Harbor Rd

San Juan Island

Shaw Island

San Juan County Park

Mitchell Bay Rd

Beaver Valley Rd

West Side Rd

Friday Harbor

Lime Kiln Point State Park

Bailer Hill Rd

Cemetery Rd

0   3
MILES

N
W   E
S

Cattle Point Rd

Cattle Point

American Camp

ELEVATION

1000 ft   500 ft   Friday Harbor

MILES   10

DISTANCE   20   San Juan County Park

30   American Camp

Friday Harbor

Eastsound

Mt Constitution

Moran State Park

0   3
MILES

Orcas Island

Doe Bay

Horseshoe Hwy

Deer Harbor

Orcas

to San Juan Island   to Anacortes

N
W   E
S

ELEVATION

1000 ft   500 ft   Orcas

MILES

DISTANCE   Eastsound

10

Moran State Park

on Shaw). Shaw and Lopez offer pleasant roads with low traffic volume but are very limited in the way of scenic or historical highlights and will not be mentioned further here. San Juan and Orcas offer numerous points of interest and should not be missed by southbound cyclists, even those with tight schedules.

San Juan Island is the site of the farcical Pig War between the Americans and the English. The war, allegedly over a pig, actually disputed the boundary between Canada and the United States. It lasted from 1859 to 1871, with only one shot fired, and only one casualty: the pig. The sites of the two camps are on opposite sides of the island—and are "musts" on the tour itinerary. Roche Harbor is of scenic and historical interest. Hotel de Haro has housed two American presidents and is now the center of a yachtsmen's paradise. Near the harbor is the Afterglow Vista Mausoleum, the bizarre and strangely beautiful tomb of the McMillin family, who made a fortune mining lime in the area. In the center of the mausoleum is a marble dining table with chairs arranged as they had been during the family's life.

San Juan Island has several private campgrounds and a county park with a hiker-biker site near the water with an excellent view. (This is a very popular park; call ahead for reservations at (360) 378-1842 between the hours of 12:00 P.M. and 4:00 P.M. PST, March through August, or go to the park website at *www.co.san-juan.wa.us.*) Late arrivals will also appreciate the easy access to commercial Lakedale Campground, which almost always has room for a couple more bikes, located 4.5 miles from the ferry dock on Roche Harbor Rd.

Orcas Island's chief attraction is Moran State Park, which covers more than 4,900 acres. The park has two large lakes, numerous hiking trails, campgrounds, and outstanding viewpoints over Puget Sound from the summit of Mount Constitution. If time allows, explore the miles of back

San Juan Islands

There are more than 170 beautiful islands that make up the San Juans. Many of the islands were named in rather a casual fashion. In 1790, two Spanish explorers spotted the islands from a high point near the current site of the town of Victoria. On Spanish ships at the time, sailors were expected to pray to a different saint every day. That day the saint was San Juan—hence the name of the islands. Other island names, such as Orcas and Lopez, are also attributed to the Spanish. An merican captain tried to rename the islands, but except for Shaw Island (named for Captain John D. Shaw, who fought the Barbary Coast pirates in 1815), the Spanish names stuck.

roads off the main island tour that lead to beautiful secluded coves and small resorts, including the Doe Bay Village Resort Hostel (call (360) 376-2291 for reservations, or check their website for more information at *www.doebay.com*). Sea kayaks may be rented if you wish to continue your explorations on the water.

The San Juan and Orcas Island tours are best spread out over 2 days. Spend the first night at San Juan County Park and the second at Moran State Park. The ride back across Orcas Island fits nicely into the next section heading south from Anacortes to Old Fort Townsend State Park.

Island travel is popular, and spring and fall are the recommended times to avoid crowds. When you need to stop and consult the book or a map, please pull your bike completely off the road to avoid blocking traffic, or use the specially marked cyclist pullouts.

Mileage Log

San Juan Island

0.0 Leave the ferry at Friday Harbor and head uphill; tourist shops, whale museum, grocery stores, bakery, and bike shop.

0.2 At Second St., turn right, heading up and out of town.

0.4 Turn right on Tucker St., which dips down past small resorts and a delightful view over Friday Harbor to Mount Baker.

Historic Hotel de Haro is located at Roche Harbor, a popular destination for pleasure boaters on San Juan Island.

0.7 Intersection. The right fork leads to the University of Washington's marine research laboratories, open to the public Wednesdays and Saturdays from 2:00 P.M. to 4:00 P.M. during the summer. Take the left fork and continue around the island on Roche Harbor Rd.

4.5 Pass Sportsman Lake, popular with bird watchers and fishermen.

7.0 Roche Harbor–English Camp junction. Bear right to Roche Harbor if making the full island tour. (If you are running late, go left toward the campground and come back another day.)

8.2 Roche Harbor. Pass the entrance gate and take a left. Coast down the steep road to the harbor and hotel.

8.6 After checking out the area, return to the entrance gate and head north for 0.2 mile to the mausoleum trail.

8.8 Afterglow Mausoleum Trail, a short 0.25-mile walk. Imagine the area as it was when the mausoleum was built, with a sweeping view west over Haro Strait.

9.8 Return to the Roche Harbor–English Camp junction and head south to English Camp on West Valley Rd. The terrain is rolling (hills moderate to steep); the road is narrow and shaded.

11.5 English Camp National Historic Park. Ride down the access road to the parking area, then walk the trail down to the camp area. Tour the restored buildings on the pretty little harbor, then hike one of the park trails. A visitor center offers a movie, information, a small museum, and restrooms, but no running water. Open during the summer only.

13.3 Intersection. Turn right on Mitchell Bay Rd. toward Snug Harbor. (West Valley Rd. continues back across the island to Friday Harbor.)

14.6 Curve left on West Side Rd.

16.4 San Juan County Park; hiker-biker site, restrooms, but no showers. The closest grocery stores are located in Friday Harbor. The park has a lovely western exposure for watching the sun set over Vancouver Island and the Olympic Mountains. This is a popular whale-watching area.

19.7 Turnoff to Lime Kiln Lighthouse and the remains of a limekiln. This is a very popular whale-watching site. The offshore water is deep and the pods cruise in close to shore.

21.7 West Side Rd. bends east and becomes Bailer Hill Rd. as it heads inland across green farmland.

24.8 Turn right on Little Rd.

25.2 Intersection. Go right again on Cattle Point Rd. and follow it to windswept American Camp.

28.0 American Camp National Historic Park; information center, restrooms, and drinking water. A nature trail winds around the campsite to an excellent viewpoint over Cattle Point. The park has the

Lime Kiln Point State Park is a well-known whale-watching area located near San Juan Island County Park.

best beach access on the island.

From American Camp, cycle back north along Cattle Point Rd. for 3.2 miles, passing the Little Rd. turnoff.

31.2 Turn right at Cemetery Rd. and head downhill.

31.8 Bear left as Cemetery Rd. joins Argyle Rd.

31.9 Return to Friday Harbor, completing the San Juan Island tour.

Orcas Island

0.0 The ferry docks at the little town of Orcas; small grocery store and several restaurants. Following the Horseshoe Highway, the tour starts by climbing the first of numerous steep hills while heading across the center of the island. The road is narrow; watch for cars.

4.5 Bicyclist rest stop; no facilities.

8.3 Eastsound, largest town on Orcas Island; good-size grocery store and a small pioneer museum. The town is scenically situated on the edge of East Sound, a long, narrow passage that nearly cuts the island in two.

8.8 Start of steep climb to Moran State Park.

12.5 Moran State Park entrance. Road descends to Cascade Lake.

13.0 First of three campgrounds along Cascade Lake. Go to the entrance booth for directions to the large hiker-biker area (located beyond the car camping area); hot showers, boat rentals, and numerous hiking trails. From the state park, retrace your route back to the ferry dock. The round trip on Orcas Island, including a trip to the summit of Mount Constitution (see below), is 35.4 miles.

Mount Constitution Side Trip

The chief attraction of Moran State Park is the view from the 2,409-foot summit of Mount Constitution, located just 4.7 miles above 351-foot Cascade Lake. To say the road is steep is definitely an understatement. However, cyclists sweat their way to the summit every day. Be sure to deposit all heavy baggage at the bottom. For those without low gears, try the 4-mile hiking trail.

There are two viewpoints, one at each end of the mile-long summit; visit both to enjoy the sweeping views over hundreds of islands to the Cascade Mountains where Mount Baker is the star, the Coast Range, Vancouver Island, and the Olympics.

Inland Route: Anacortes Ferry Dock to Old Fort Townsend State Park (41.1 Miles)

The short ride from the Anacortes ferry dock to Old Fort Townsend State Park is designed to allow plenty of time in the morning for the long, leisurely ferry trip from Sidney or one of the San Juan Islands to Anacortes and later in the day a second ferry ride from Keystone to Port Townsend. Neither of these ferries runs frequently, so expect to spend an hour or more waiting at the ferry dock.

The ferry dock at Anacortes is located on Fidalgo Island, a large body of land solidly connected to the mainland. From the dock the road heads up, launching the day's ride over a long series of steeply rolling hills. The route to the Keystone/Port Townsend ferry dock travels over Fidalgo Island, across Deception Pass, and on to Whidbey Island.

Do not expect the same island feeling found in the San Juans. Both Fidalgo Island and Whidbey Island are securely linked to the mainland and bustle with activity from several large towns and a naval air base at Oak Harbor.

To avoid the busy main highway on Fidalgo and Whidbey Islands, most of this ride is on the back roads. Scenery varies from forest to beautiful views west over Puget Sound to the Olympics and east to the snow- and ice-capped Cascade Range.

The area between Anacortes and Old Fort Townsend State Park is rich in history. Two of the towns, Coupeville and Port Townsend, were important seaports in the late 1800s and have beautifully maintained Victorian-style buildings. Port Townsend was settled in the 1850s and was a thriving seaport until the mid-1890s, when Seattle became the

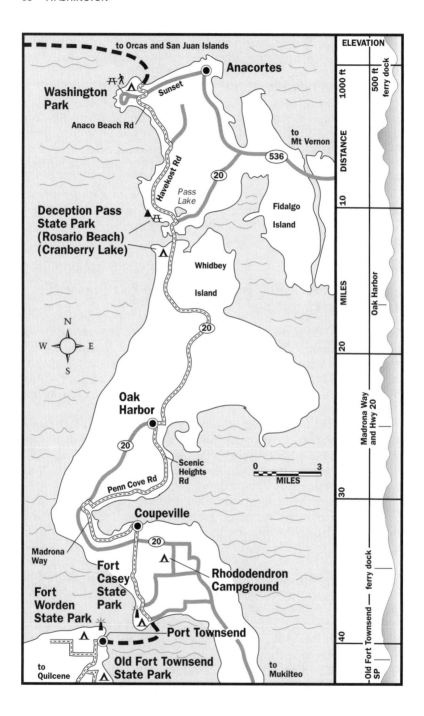

to Orcas and San Juan Islands

Anacortes

Washington
Park

Sunset

Anaco Beach Rd

to
Mt Vernon

536

Havekost Rd

20

Pass
Lake

Fidalgo

Deception Pass
State Park
(Rosario Beach)
(Cranberry Lake)

Island

Whidbey

Island

20

N
W   E
S

Oak
Harbor

20

Scenic
Heights
Rd

Penn Cove Rd

0   3
MILES

30

Coupeville

20

Madrona
Way

Fort
Casey
State
Park

Rhododendron
Campground

Fort
Worden
State Park

Port Townsend

to
Quilcene

Old Fort Townsend
State Park

to
Mukilteo

ELEVATION

1000 ft

500 ft

ferry dock

DISTANCE

10

MILES

Oak Harbor

20

Madrona Way
and Hwy 20

30

Old Fort Townsend — ferry dock

40

Old Fort Townsend
SP

western terminus of the Union Pacific Railroad. Today, the downtown and bluff area is a designated National Historic District with buildings dating back to the 1880s. Stop at the information center and pick up a free guide map to the historic buildings, art galleries, antique shops, and Jefferson County Museum.

Three old forts are passed along the route. Two were designed to protect Puget Sound from enemy invasion, the third to fight native Americans. These massive structures never were tested in battle, which was a good thing, as they tended to become obsolete as soon as they were built. The forts are fun to explore and great places to sit and watch the view. Fort Casey and Fort Worden also have lighthouses overlooking broad waterways.

Four large and scenic parks as well as a couple of smaller parks are passed on this ride, so plan extra time between your ferry rides to enjoy them. Washington Park, near the Anacortes ferry dock, has a not-to-be-missed 2.3-mile loop road around a small headland with viewpoints of the San Juan Islands and Rosario Strait, framed by wind-sculptured trees.

Deception Pass State Park (6.2 miles south of the Anacortes ferry dock) spans Fidalgo and Whidbey Islands and has miles of trails, lakes, beaches, and views, as well as picnic and camping facilities. Stop at Pass Island, a small chunk of rock in the center of the rushing, rolling waters of Deception Pass, and watch boats challenge the dangerous currents.

A small city park in Oak Harbor is a fun place to visit after a stop at the bakery. The city beach has a majestic windmill that looks as though it came straight from the Netherlands.

Fort Casey State Park is located next to the ferry dock at Keystone. While waiting for your ferry, take time to explore the old fort, or check out the lighthouse and museum. If you miss your ferry, stay in the state park campground overlooking the ferry terminal.

If time allows, take a side trip from Fort Casey to Rhododendron Campground, a county park. In May, this forested park is bright with flowering rhododendrons. Free camping is the main attraction the rest of the year. Also within easy riding distance of Fort Casey is a Washington State game farm specializing in pheasants. Visitors are welcome.

You do not have to be a history buff to enjoy the pleasant, almost lazy atmosphere of the islands. The scenery is excellent and the beaches, especially in the Deception Pass area, are fun to explore and teaming with life. Bakeries, espresso stands, and coffee shops abound. For the hungry cyclist on a budget, there are several supermarkets and a lot of fast-food eateries.

The Keystone ferry takes you on a scenic, 35-minute ride across Puget Sound to Port Townsend. Nearby Fort Worden State Park is a great place to spend an hour or two. On a clear day, the sunset over Mount Baker is spectacular. Fort Worden has a partially restored military fort, a working lighthouse, a marine science center, a youth hostel, and miles of beach with views of the Strait of Juan de Fuca, San Juan Islands, and Admiralty Inlet.

The day ends at Old Fort Townsend State Park. This park is open from April 1 to the end of September. Stay at Fort Worden State Park during the off-season.

Mileage Log

0.0 Anacortes ferry dock. Follow the main stream of traffic uphill to the first intersection.

0.5 Intersection. Take a sharp right (west) on Sunset, a quiet, narrow, county road. The left fork heads east 8 miles to Anacortes; tourist facilities, bike shop, and large grocery stores.

0.6 Intersection. Turn left (south) on Anaco Beach Rd. and skim through housing developments, past views, and over a few steep hills. *Side Trip* to Washington Park: Continue straight on Sunset for 0.6 mile past Anaco Beach Rd. to the park; scenic loop, restrooms, running water, picnic area, hiker-biker (primitive) site, and forested trails to viewpoints over the San Juan Islands and Olympics.

3.4 Anaco Beach Rd. ends. Go right on Havekost Rd. Follow this somewhat busy road, staying right at a large unmarked Y intersection.

6.2 *Side Trip* to Rosario Beach picnic area, part of Deception Pass State Park: Follow signs 0.5 mile to the picnic area, restrooms, and running water. There are tide pools to poke into and several trails, including a 0.2-mile loop to wide-flung views from Rosario Head.

6.7 *Side Trip* to Bowman Bay picnic area and campground, another section of Deception Pass State Park: Turn right and follow the road 0.4 mile west to its end at a picnic area and campground. A trail heads south around the bay to Reservation Head, where a short, scenic loop is made around Lighthouse Point. Total hike is 2 miles.

6.8 (mp 43.0) Join Highway 20 at Pass Lake and turn right. The road narrows as it heads south off Fidalgo Island.

7.4 (mp 42.4) Deception Pass Bridge. The bridge is narrow, with a broad sidewalk for pedestrians. In the middle of the bridge lies Pass Island. Walk down the rocks to the water's edge for the best views. The rocks are slippery, so take off cleats before starting. Turnoffs on either end allow you to park your bike and gaze at the spectacle of small boats rushing to challenge the pass's amazingly strong currents.

8.3 Cranberry Lake Campground; wonderful hiker-biker site, showers, restrooms, marshes, cliffy beaches, lake for swimming, trails,

Cyclists take a lunch break on Pass Island, below the Deception Pass Bridge. This is an excellent location to watch small boats battle the currents through the narrow channel.

and views. A small convenience store is located just 0.1 mile south of the campground entrance. Beyond the campground, Highway 20 widens to include broad shoulders. This is a settled area with farms and stores.

16.3 Oak Harbor; numerous supermarkets, a bakery, and a host of fast-food restaurants. Follow Highway 20 straight into town to a large intersection near the waterfront.

17.7 Stay with Highway 20 as it turns right (west) and heads uphill. ***Side Trip:*** To visit a windmill that looks like it came straight from the Netherlands, turn left at the intersection and go 1 block.

18.1 About halfway up the hill, make a left turn off Highway 20 onto Scenic Heights Rd.

19.1 The road divides; stay right on Badla Rd.

20.4 Badla Rd. becomes Morre Beck Ln.

20.7 A right turn takes you back on Scenic Heights Rd., which soon descends into Penn Cove, where the name changes to Penn Cove Rd.

24.4 Go right on Holbrook.

24.5 Turn left onto Highway 20 and ride around the end of Penn Cove on a good shoulder.

25.5 At the west end of the cove, leave Highway 20 by making a left turn onto Madrona Way. Ride around the south side of Penn Cove, past groves of madrona trees.

29.3 Intersection. Go straight and descend on Madrona.

29.4 At Cloveland, turn right and continue descending into the quaint town of Coupeville, with its renovated Victorian harbor and small museum. Explore the waterfront before heading up N. Main St.

29.7 Head steeply up N. Main St. to Highway 20.

30.3 Highway 20. Go straight across the highway, past a large grocery store. The road starts off narrow but soon gains a rideable shoulder.

34.1 Fort Casey State Park; campground, hiker-biker site, showers, trail, fort, lighthouse, and museum all located near the ferry dock. The first park entrance leads to the fort, lighthouse, and museum. It is best to continue on to Keystone and check the schedule for the ferry, then come back and explore.

34.2 Keystone ferry dock. After a 35-minute crossing, the ferry lands in Port Townsend. Go left on Water St. (which is actually Highway 20), passing supermarkets and the information center. The main historic area is located to the right on Water St.

34.8 After crossing Kearney St., Water St. turns into Sims Way, which in turn becomes Highway 20. The shoulder is good except at bridges. The interesting smell is from the nearby paper mill. **Side Trip** to Fort Worden State Park: Turn right on Kearney St. and follow the well-signed route 2.8 miles to the park. The park has a hiker-biker area, a youth hostel, hot showers, hiking trails, a restored fort, a lighthouse, and a marine science center.

38.4 Cross a narrow bridge; no shoulder.

39.3 Turn left and follow signs east on a narrow road to Old Fort Townsend State Park.

41.1 Old Fort Townsend State Park; hiker-biker area, running water, restrooms, historical area, beach access, and hiking and mountain biking trails. Open May through September only.

Inland Route: Old Fort Townsend State Park to Potlatch State Park (64.3 Miles)

Weaving south through the byways of Puget Sound country, the Inland Route heads across a peninsula, dividing the Strait of Juan de Fuca from Puget Sound, then climbs the side of a steep mountain before descending to the shores of Hood Canal. The canal (a spur of Puget Sound and a popular for area for scuba diving, clam digging, sailboarding, boating, shrimping, and fishing) is followed for the final 34 miles of the ride to Potlatch State Park.

Very little of the area's abundant scenery is visible from the road. Occasional glimpses of the Olympic Range highlight the pastoral areas and river valleys. Along Hood Canal, the hillsides rise steeply from water's edge, climbing steadily to the crest of the Olympics Mountains. Vegetation is rich and abundant, growing with such enthusiasm it creates

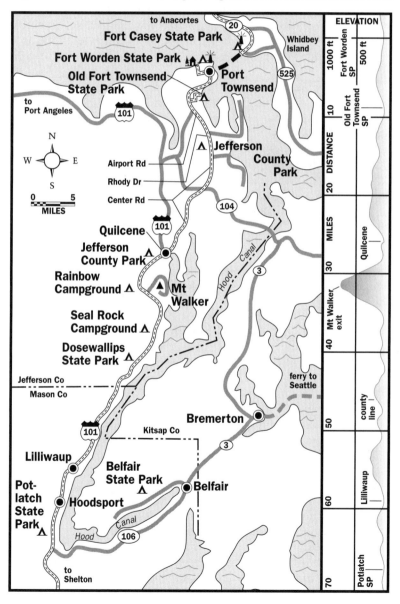

a nearly impenetrable wall and riders catch only an occasional glimpse of sparkling waters through the trees. The most entrancing views occur when the highway dips into coves and the forest is replaced with low scrub at the edge of the mud flats. Birds abound in these tidal zones, and heron and cormorants are common sights.

To really see the area, you must take a 5-mile side trip to the summit of Mount Walker. From the mountain's top you can look down on the bays, islands, and large cities of Puget Sound. Unfortunately, this is a very difficult ride on a steep, gravel road and simply not for all bikes or all riders.

Several Olympic National Park access roads are passed in this section. These accesses are designed for hikers intent on exploring the miles of wilderness found in the park's interior and are basically useless for a touring cyclist. If you wish to include the park in your itinerary, now is the time to turn east toward Port Angeles and the Peninsula Route.

This is a long section; however, the riding is fairly easy. Expect a steady stream of commercial and tourist traffic along US 101. The shoulders vary from comfortable to nonexistent, disappearing just when they would be most appreciated. Hills are common on this ride. If you are not climbing a hill, you are probably descending. Some of the hills are rather steep, but, except for the hill just south of Quilcene, most climbs are short.

Potlatch State Park, at the end of the day's ride, has a pleasant location on the edge of Hood Canal. Pick up groceries 3.7 miles north, at Hoodsport.

Mileage Log

0.0 From Old Fort Townsend State Park, ride back to Highway 20.

2.0 Go left on Highway 20. The shoulder is adequate except at bridges.

2.4 The road divides; stay left (east) on Airport Cutoff Rd. and watch for low-flying aircraft. Highway 20 heads west, toward Port Angeles, Olympic National Park, and the Peninsula Route.

4.8 When Airport Cutoff Rd. ends, bend left on Rhody Dr.

7.1 Pass Chimacum Jefferson County Park; limited camping, water, picnic shelter, pit toilets, and a somewhat abused dragon.

7.7 A four-way intersection with a confusing sign for cyclists. Ignore the sign and take a right turn on Center Rd., heading toward the town of Quilcene on a wide shoulder. The Olympic Mountains form a dramatic backdrop for farmlands, clearcuts, and forest.

13.0 Intersection; continue straight on Center Rd.

14.7 Center Rd. passes under Highway 104.

22.9 (mp 294.5) Center Rd. intersects US 101 and ends at the small town of Quilcene; grocery store, campground, historical museum, and fast-food outlets. Quilcene prides itself on its oysters; the largest oyster hatchery in the world is located southwest of town on Linger Longer Rd. Go left and ride south through town on US 101. (*Note:* The mileage on mileposts in this section of US 101 increases from north to south; shoulder width is narrow.)

23.3 (mp 294.9) Quilcene Jefferson County Park; campsites, picnic area, water, restrooms, and a Best tractor.

23.7 (mp 295.1) Quilcene Ranger Station offers information on campgrounds and upcoming attractions. Open weekdays only.

25.3 (mp 296.7) After crossing a shoulderless bridge, US 101 begins a steep climb over Walker Point, wandering in and out of Olympic National Forest. Shoulder width increases and logging truck drivers are adept at avoiding cyclists.

26.9 (mp 298.4) Falls View Campground; picnic area, water, and trail into Falls Canyon. No hiker-biker site.

28.3 (mp 299.9) Rainbow Campground; another forest service area offering campsites, water, and a hiking trail. No hiker-biker facilities.

28.4 (mp 300.00) Summit of the Walker Point climb. It's a downhill

The Olympic Mountains make a rare appearance along Highway 101 north of Shelton.

glide for the next couple of miles. **Side Trip:** From the highway summit, a gravel road on the left climbs 4 steep miles to the true summit of Mount Walker and two outstanding viewpoints over Hood Canal, to the Cascades, and to the Olympics. (Suitable for mountain bikes only; leave gear at the bottom. You may also reach the viewpoints by walking a 2-mile trail starting 0.2 mile from the highway.)

31.9 (mp 302.4) US 101 winds along the edge of Hood Canal, climbing in and out of small bays. During open seasons, the beach is lined with clam diggers when the tide is out. The sections of the canal marked with buoys are oyster farms. With a little luck, you can spot blue herons. Enjoy the scenery, but remember to keep a sharp lookout for traffic; the shoulder varies from adequate to none.

34.1 (mp 305.4) Seal Rock Campground; a forest service area with campsites, picnicking, running water, and beach access. No hiker-biker facilities.

34.5 (mp 305.9) Brinnon; a small resort town with a general store, restaurant, and motel. Use caution when crossing the narrow, shoulderless bridge over the Dosewallips River at the south end of town.

35.6 (mp 307) Dosewallips State Park has camping on the west side of the highway, and beach access and a picnic area on the east. Amenities include a hiker-biker (primitive) site on the banks of the Dosewallips River, hot showers, running water, access to an oyster shell–covered beach, a beach viewing platform, hiking trails, and excellent mushroom picking in August.

38.9 (mp 310.3) Duckabush River Bridge. No shoulder; use caution when crossing.

43.3 (mp 314.5) Triton Cove State Park; a day-use area with picnic tables, toilets, and boat dock.

43.4 (mp 314.6) Leave Jefferson County and enter Mason County.

47.9 (mp 319) Eldon; a very small community with a restaurant and a mini-mart on the left. Use caution; the shoulder often disappears on the corners, making it difficult for drivers of big trucks to slow down in time when suddenly encountering cyclists. Look back and check for traffic before heading around blind corners.

51.9 (mp 323) After passing an area where the road is etched into steep hillsides, the terrain moderates and the shoulder improves.

55.1 (mp 326.1) Public beach access and roadside parking.

56.2 (mp 327.2) Lilliwaup; small grocery store, motel, and restaurant. The town spreads south of the main commercial area with cottages butting right up to the edge of the highway, leaving little room for a shoulder.

60.5 (mp 331.3) Hoodsport; a resort town with a market, restaurants, bakery, motels, and even wine tasting. An information center for Olympic National Park and Olympic National Forest is located on the right side of the road. Pick up groceries for the night here.

62.7 (mp 333.6) Potlatch. This small town is the center of the Skokomish Indian Reservation; fireworks stands, shellfish, and smoked salmon are the specialties.

63.8 (mp 334.6) Tacoma Power Plant (right) and picnic area (left) overlook The Great Bend of the Hood Canal.

64.3 (mp 335.1) Potlatch State Park has a picnic area and beach access on the east side of the highway, and a campground on the west. Amenities include a hiker-biker (primitive) area, hot showers, beach access, and two trails into the forested uplands west of the camp area. Oyster picking and clam digging are popular in season. Both activities require a license. At times these succulent mollusks carry high levels of a toxic red algae that is that extremely dangerous for humans to ingest. Be aware of "red tide" postings; also do not harvest out of season.

Inland Route: Potlatch State Park to Twin Harbors State Park
(74.6 Miles)

This section of the Inland Route takes you through the southern reaches of Puget Sound country and then turns west to the Pacific Coast. With no specific stops or side trips between Potlatch and Twin Harbors State Parks, you can concentrate solely on riding.

This is a long ride. The terrain is rolling, with several short, steep hills interspersed by long, level sections where, if there isn't an onshore wind, the miles seem to speed away. If you are just starting down the coast and not ready for a long ride, divide the ride in two parts and spend the extra night at Lake Sylvia State Park, near Montesano. This will ensure plenty of time to get that rented surfboard waxed just the way you want it before braving the first wave at Westport. Or, if you are pressed for time, you may take a short cut on Highway 107 from Montesano and head south to rejoin the main route at Raymond.

Scenery along the route varies from cooling towers of a defunct nuclear power project to blue herons fishing in the mud flats of Grays Harbor. At the end of the ride is Twin Harbors State Park, located on a thin peninsula between Grays Harbor, Elk Bay Harbor, and the Pacific Ocean (which is sometimes peaceful and sometimes not, but always interesting).

Twin Harbors State Park is located near the town of Westport, a bustling resort town, and host to an endless stream of visitors during the

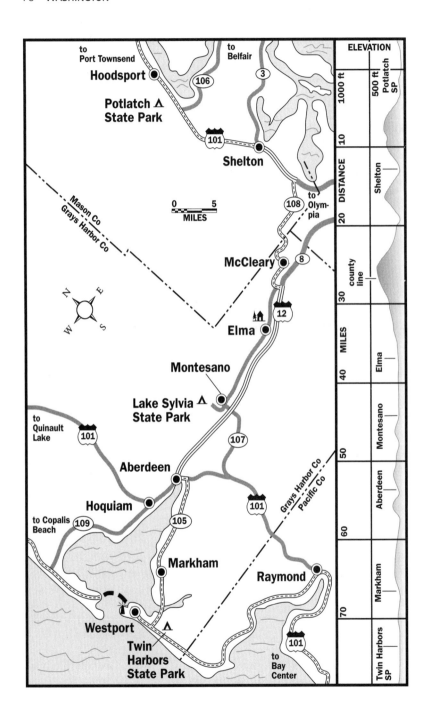

ELEVATION

1000 ft

500 ft Potlatch SP

to
Port Townsend

to
Belfair

Hoodsport ●

106

3

Potlatch △
State Park

101

10

Shelton ●

Shelton

DISTANCE

MILES

0   5
MILES

108

to
Olym-
pia

20

McCleary ●

8

county
line

30

12

Elma ●

MILES

Mason Co
Grays Harbor Co

N
E
W
S

40

Elma

Montesano

Lake Sylvia △
State Park

●

Montesano

to
Quinault
Lake

101

107

50

Aberdeen ●

101

Grays Harbor Co
Pacific Co

Aberdeen

Hoquiam ●

to Copalis
Beach

109

105

60

Markham ●

Raymond ●

Markham

Westport ●

△

70

Twin
Harbors
State Park

to
Bay
Center

101

Twin Harbors
SP

summer. Westport is a great place to spend an hour or a day, strolling the beaches and harbor. Watch kayakers and surfers challenge the waves, and, if you are brave and very warm-blooded, rent a board (and wet suit) and catch a few waves yourself. Check out the long fishing piers, watch the fishing boats, then work your way through the ice cream shops and bakeries. Top off the day with fresh oysters, crab, or salmon purchased from a little roadside stand.

Mileage Log

0.0 (mp 335.1) From Potlatch State Park, head south on US 101, paralleling the mud flats of The Great Bend of Hood Canal. The ride starts off on a 2-foot shoulder, which narrows somewhat as you go south.

2.0 (mp 336.8) Highway 106 branches off to the left, heading east to Bremerton and the Seattle ferries. This area is part of the Skokomish Indian Reservation; grocery store/smoke shops, fruit stands, and firework stands line the road.

4.5 (mp 339.5) Purdy Cutoff, an alternate access to Highway 106 and Bremerton. On the right is a turnoff to the Skokomish Valley Recreation Area. Campground and recreation facilities are a long way west of the highway. US 101 now climbs above the lowlands of Hood Canal and cruises past miles of Christmas tree farms.

10.2 (mp 345.3) First turnoff to Shelton (known as Christmas Town U.S.A. because of the large number of Christmas trees grown in the area). A large shopping center is located left (east) of US 101. Continuing south, US 101 is now a freeway. Use caution when crossing entrances and exits.

18.3 (mp 353.4) Exit US 101 and head west on Highway 108 to McCleary. A medium-size grocery store, the last for 10 miles, is located near the exit. Highway 108 heads past farms, then through forest. The shoulder is narrow, and traffic is moderate. Expect an occasional logging truck.

26.3 (mp 4.3) Leave Mason County and enter Grays Harbor County. The road narrows.

27.5 (mp 3.1) Start shoulder.

28.6 (mp 2.1) Intersection. Still following Highway 108, turn left (south) and enter McCleary.

29.5 (mp 1.2) At the center of town, turn right (west) toward Elma. Ride past several small stores and restaurants, as well as a small city park with running water, restrooms, and a display of old logging equipment.

30.5 (mp 0.2 and mp 6.1) Intersection. Go left, still on Highway 108, for 100 feet to join Highway 8, a freeway. Head west; shoulders are broad, traffic volume is heavy, and the head wind is frequently strong. Cooling towers of the abandoned Satsop nuclear plant are visible to the south.

36.6 (mp 0.0) Highway 8 merges with Highway 12. Continue west on Highway 12.

37.1 Elma; a small town with several grocery stores, a city park (no facilities), a hostel, and fairgrounds (the fair takes place during the second week of August). If tired of the traffic on Highway 12, Elma is a good place to exit. Follow the McCleary–Elma Rd. west,

A portion of the Lake Sylvia loop trail crosses a scenic boardwalk. The lake was created in 1878 when a dam was built for the purpose of creating a log pond for the sawmill.

through town, where it becomes the Elma–Montesano Rd. Beyond Elma, the shoulders are good.

39.8 Satsop; small grocery store to the right (north) of Highway 12.

44.8 Montesano; large grocery store, restaurants, fast food, historic county courthouse, and Lake Sylvia State Park. The state park is located on a forested lake 1 mile above town. To reach the park, ride to the center of town. At the intersection with Highway 107, continue straight for 3 blocks, then take a right on 3rd St. and follow the signs to Lake Sylvia State Park. The park has a hiker-biker area, hot showers, lakeshore campsites, boat rentals, swimming, hiking trails, and some interesting artifacts from the turn of the century logging industry.

47.3 (mp 6.7) Wynoochee River Bridge. Wait for a break in the traffic before crossing this shoulderless bridge.

49.4 (mp 4.6) Central Park; market on the left.

54.5 Enter Aberdeen.

55.5 River Park; picnicking, restrooms, and access to historic waterfront area. The park is reached by making a left turn just before a large shopping center.

56.0 Cross the Wishkah River on a narrow bridge. Follow the US 101 S. signs and prepare for a left turn 2 blocks beyond the bridge.

56.2 (mp 0.0 and mp 88.4) Turn left on US 101 and cross the Chehalis River on a wide bridge. When traffic is heavy, cyclists may prefer to follow the pedestrian route.

57.0 (mp 87.8 and mp 48.8) On the south side of the bridge, go straight on Highway 105 (US 101 turns left here). Two large supermarkets, located on the left side of the highway at the intersection, offer an excellent opportunity to pick up your groceries for the night. Highway 105 (a Washington State Scenic and Recreational Highway) heads west, paralleling the tide flats on the south side of Grays Harbor. The highway is busy and shoulderless in town. Soon after passing a large shopping center, the road narrows from four to two lanes with a comfortable shoulder.

67.6 (mp 38.2) Markham; home of Ocean Spray fruit juices. No tasting room or retail outlet.

72.0 (mp 32.4) Bay City; small town with a grocery store. Shoulder comes and goes in this area.

74.5 (mp 30.0) Westport; a resort town with charter boats, salmon fishing, aquarium, museum, ocean beaches, campground, grocery store, motels, restaurants, ferry to Ocean Shores, tourist shops, bakeries, and kite shops. Grocery stores and restaurants are found 2 miles north, in the center of town. A small market is located at the turnoff. Continue straight ahead on Highway 105 for another

200 feet, then turn left to reach Twin Harbors State Park.

74.6 Twin Harbors State Park; hiker-biker (primitive) area, hot showers, beach access, kitchen shelter, clam-cleaning shed, nature trail through the sand dunes, and hiking trails to the beach.

To continue south, go to the Combined Route: Twin Harbors State Park to Bay Center, *on page 101.*

Peninsula Route: Port Angeles to Fairholm Campground
(28.8 Miles)

The Coho ferry from Victoria takes 90 minutes to cross the Strait of Juan de Fuca and dock in Port Angeles, the starting point of the Washington State portion of the Peninsula Route. During the summer months, the first ferry arrives midmorning, so this day's ride is intentionally short.

In good weather, adventure-minded riders may prefer to linger in Port Angeles and spend the afternoon riding to Hurricane Ridge, one of the state's scenic highlights. The ridge is part of Olympic National Park (a designated World Heritage Site) and the only place a cyclist may sample the alpine aspect of this diverse area. The ride up Hurricane Ridge is long and difficult. Only strong cyclists will find pleasure in the climb, which gains 5,300 feet in just 18 miles; however, everyone who reaches the top will enjoy the view and the screaming descent. If the ride is more than you wish to tackle, consider an alternate, shorter, and easier side trip to the Olympic National Park Visitor Center.

The Elwha River Valley, located 9.8 miles west of Port Angeles, offers a second opportunity to leave the main route and explore more of the national park. This lowland valley has campgrounds, numerous trails (including one to Hurricane Ridge), a large lake, and, if you go far enough, a hot springs.

Heading south of the Elwha River Valley, you will encounter a notorious section of US 101 in the Lake Crescent area. The road around this beautiful lake has minimal shoulders, with blind corners, and, despite the moderate 35-mile-an-hour speed limit, fast-moving auto and truck traffic. If ever there were a place to install flashing lights to let motorists know when cyclists are on the road, this is it. The state, however, has placed signs at each end of the lake, recommending riders take one of the rare public busses around the lake.

The Storm King area, located about halfway around Lake Crescent, is the one easily accessible national park feature along this portion of the route. Along with the obvious attractions of restrooms, picnic tables, and running water, Storm King has several short trails to explore. The 2-mile round-trip walk to Marymere Falls is one of the not-to-be-missed

highlights of the park, and the nearby nature trail is an excellent introduction to the lowland forest community. Maps can be picked up at the
ranger station, open summer only.

The day's ride ends at Fairholm Campground, a relatively small,

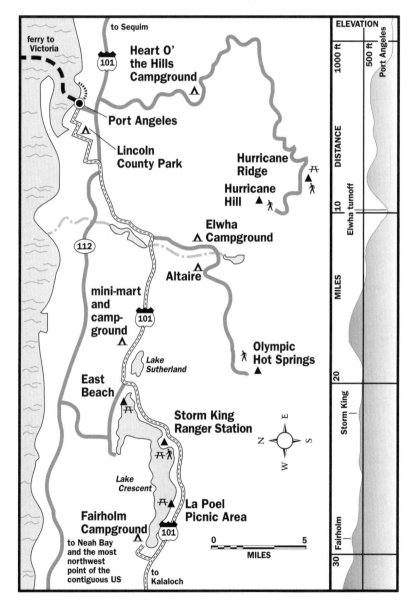

eighty-seven-site facility that fills up almost every night during the summer and always on weekends. Cyclists are encouraged to arrive as early as possible to secure a site. If no site is available, consider filling up your water containers and finding a tent site on national forest land at the top of the next hill.

Mileage Log

0.0 The day starts at the Victoria (Coho) ferry dock. After passing through international customs inspection, everyone (that includes cyclists planning to ride up to Hurricane Ridge) should turn right on Railroad St. and follow it along the waterfront. (As Port Angeles has the last large grocery stores before Fairholm, anyone who needs to stock up on food should take a side trip into town. Follow the signs for US 101 south to the supermarkets at the upper end of town.) **Side Trip:** For a quick look at the Port Angeles area, go left after you exit the ferry and ride a short 0.1 mile east along the waterfront. When the road turns, continue straight ahead to a parking area. Lock up your bike and wander the dock area. The Arthur D. Fiero Marine Science Laboratory is an excellent facility designed

Lake Crescent is almost 9 miles long and about 1 mile wide. It is the largest lake in the Olympic Mountains and the third largest natural lake in Western Washington.

for children (perfect for most touring cyclists) with a large touch tank. When in port, you may take a tour of a Coast Guard vessel (afternoons only) or climb the viewing tower for a look across the Strait of Juan de Fuca.

0.1 Railroad St. bends left and the name changes to N. Oak.

0.2 The road divides; stay to the right and continue along the waterfront on Front St.

0.4 Bear right on Marine Dr. (also called W. 1st St.).

0.6 Intersection; continue straight (trucks go left).

0.7 Turn left on Tumwater St. (this is the first left after the truck route), and gear down for a 0.3-mile climb.

1.5 Tumwater St. turns into W. 5th St.

2.3 Turn left on I St. and head inland.

2.6 I St. ends; go right on W. 16th St., which takes you past the fairgrounds and magically turns into 18th St.

2.9 Take the first left, on L St.

3.2 Go right on W. Lauridsen Blvd. If planning to make the side trip to Hurricane Ridge, or if you just need a convenient place to spend the night, go left 0.2 mile to the Lincoln County Park campground; hiker-biker area, water, restrooms, and a small store across the road. (Open for camping summer only.) This marks the starting point for the side trip to Hurricane Ridge. For details, see the end of this mileage log.

3.3 When the road divides, stay to the right, on Edgewood Dr. This road twists and turns through a rural residential area for 2.7 miles.

6.3 (mp 242.9) Go right on US 101, which is blessed with a comfortable shoulder except at bridges.

6.6 (mp 242.4) Highway 112 branches off to the right; watch for turning traffic.

7.9 (mp 241.1) Pass a viewpoint overlooking the Elwha River Valley. US 101 now descends.

9.8 (mp 239.5) Turnoff to Elwha River Valley and campgrounds on the left (east). *Side Trip:* Cycle up the Elwha River Valley to Olympic National Park on a narrow road, which passes through cool, shady groves of moss-covered maples. The first campground is located 3 miles off US 101; running water and walk-in campsites. Shortly beyond is a ranger station, then a second campground. The road is gated 4 miles before its end at Olympic Hot Springs. Bicycles may continue on up the rough road to a primitive camp area near the hot springs; pick up a backcountry permit at the ranger station if interested.

16.7 (mp 233.0) Gas station with a mini-mart and an adjoining private campground. Tents are welcome. As you climb, Lake Sutherland

It is just a short hike from the Hurricane Ridge Visitor Center to a glorious view of glacier-topped Mount Olympus.

is visible through the trees to the left.

17.8 (mp 231.9) Pass turnoff to East Beach, Piedmont, and Spruce Railroad Trail.

18.4 (mp 231.3) The shoulder narrows as US 101 leaves Olympic National Forest and enters Olympic National Park. The road descends steeply toward Lake Crescent. Tighten your grip—the next 10 miles are nerve-wracking and the road is often rough.

18.5 (mp 231.2) Sign warning cyclists about hazards ahead and a note about the bus service. (Where is the sign for *motorists* to use caution over the next 10 miles?) Viewpoints allow you to make frequent stops to let traffic by, if needed. Watch for grooved pavement on the corners.

21.7 (mp 227.9) Barnes Point-Storm King turnoff. **Side Trip:** Go right 0.1 mile to Storm King Ranger Station; restrooms, water, picnic tables. This busy area is the starting point for several short trails. Highly recommended is the easy 2-mile round-trip hike through stately old trees to beautiful Marymere Falls. The trail starts in front of the ranger station. The Moments in Time Nature Trail leads to a view of the lake and is an easy 1-mile round trip.

26.0 (mp 223.7) La Poel Picnic Area; running water, vault toilets, and limited lake access.

28.5 (mp 221.0) Fairholm Grocery; limited groceries, deli, and boat rentals, open during the summer months only. Shoulder widens as US 101 begins to climb away from the lake.

28.7 (mp 220.8) Fairholm Campground; go right (west) on Camp David Jr. Rd. Ride past the lake access and boat launch.

28.8 Turn right and descend into the campground. The walk-in sites along the lakeshore are scenic and often vacant after the rest of the sites are full. The campground has restrooms, running water, and a boring nature trail. Small boats may be rented at the Fairholm Grocery. There is a designated swimming area at the boat launch. (When this campground is full, you may continue on US 101 to Klahowya, Walhgren, or Tumbling Rapids forest service campgrounds. Or cook your dinner at Fairholm, then ride on and find a free campsite on national forest land.)

Hurricane Ridge Side Trip

Pack plenty of warm clothes, shoes for walking, a lot of food, a couple quarts of water, and a set of bike lights for the tunnel. Food service is available during the middle of the day at Hurricane Ridge.

0.0 Once you have unloaded your bike at the Lincoln County Park campground, retrace your route back to the waterfront. Carry plenty of warm clothing and food for the trip.

2.5 Stay on Marine Dr., which becomes W. 1st St. Once across Lincoln St., W. 1st St. joins US 101; continue east for 0.8 mile.

3.6 Turn right (south) on Race St., following signs to Hurricane Ridge. From this point, it's all uphill to the ridge. Buy groceries before leaving town.

4.6 Olympic National Park headquarters; park and weather information, restrooms, and water.

10.6 Park entrance. If you did not bring your own lights, you will be loaned one for the ride through the tunnel. Just beyond the entrance station is Heart O' the Hills Campground, elevation 1,957 feet. The road above Heart O' the Hills is steep and narrow, with numerous turnouts, all on the left side.

21.5 Hurricane Ridge Visitor Center; restrooms, water, and information. The views from the top are unforgettable, extending over the Strait of Juan de Fuca, Vancouver Island, the Cascades, and Mount Olympus. The roadside meadows burst with colorful wildflowers mid-July through mid-August. For your own safety, make the descent to the campground before dark. If the weather turns bad, head back immediately.

🚲

Peninsula Route: Fairholm Campground to Kalaloch Campground (61.2 Miles)

From the clear blue waters of Lake Crescent, the Peninsula Route heads south to the popular ocean shores of the Kalaloch Beach unit of Olympic National Park. The route follows US 101, heading south through stump-covered clear-cut forests and stump-covered pastures to the town of Forks. Beyond town, the terrain becomes increasingly hilly and the countryside increasingly forested as the road winds its way out to the coast. Shoulders are mostly good in this section, disappearing at bridges. With only an occasional view of the mountains over massive clearcuts to distract you, the miles fly by.

The Kalaloch area beaches are easily accessed from the main highway. Ruby Beach has a couple of large sea stacks and is most like the wilderness beaches of the north sections of the park. Fourth Beach has

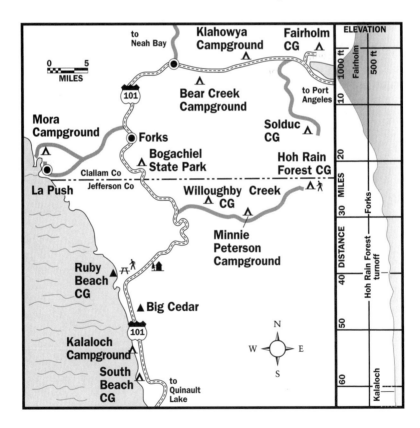

excellent tide pools on the near-shore rocks and is the scene of daily naturalist talks. Kalaloch and South Beaches are great for barefoot strolls through the sand.

The day ends at Kalaloch Campground. The 177 campsites usually fill by noon. Luckily, there is an overflow campground at South Beach just 3 miles to the south. There is no water or garbage pickup service. You may find it convenient to set up camp at South Beach, then ride back to Kalaloch Campground and cook your dinner at the picnic area.

Kalaloch is a full-service area, with excellent accommodations (usually booked months in advance), a small grocery store, a coffee shop, and a restaurant.

This day's ride will take you by three major national park access points. To visit any of these areas requires a full day excursion off the main route. If you have time or the inclination to explore one or more of these areas, your efforts will be rewarded with incredible scenery. Just 1.5 miles south of Fairholm Campground is the Solduc Hot Springs turn-off. The hot springs are located in a beautiful rain forest and reached by a 12-mile ride along the edge of the Solduc River. In the spring and early fall, when the salmon are heading upstream to spawn, their incredible journey can be watched from the overlook at the Salmon Cascades. Solduc Hot Springs have been commercially developed with a beautifully maintained swim area and hot pools for soaking. A substantial admission fee is charged. You may stay at the national park campground (which usually fills by noon) or rent a cabin (expensive) and eat at the restaurant. Other than the hot springs, the area's chief attraction is a beautiful falls that is reached by a 0.9-mile walk through the rain forest.

The incredibly wild and untamed beaches of the Wilderness Coast

======== The Iron Man of the Hoh ========

As you cycle up the Hoh River Valley toward the Olympic National Park boundary and the rain forest, take note of an old farm located about 6 miles up. This is the old Huelsdunk homestead, settled in 1892. Farming was not a sustainable occupation in this country of huge trees, giant stumps, and endless rainfall, so John Huelsdunk supplemented his income and food supply by fur trapping and logging. Occasionally he would hike into Forks over a rugged and muddy trail for supplies. Legend has it that one day a neighbor saw Huelsdunk hiking back to his cabin with an iron kitchen stove on his back. When asked if the stove wasn't uncomfortable to carry, Huelsdunk is said to have replied, "No, but I wish I could find a way to keep those four 50-pound bags of flour inside from shifting around all the time."

Massive old maple trees covered with moss are the principle attraction at road's end in the Hoh Rain Forest.

unit of Olympic National Park is the second of the three accesses passed. Several of the beaches are reached by well-maintained forest trails; however, for the cyclist, Rialto Beach offers the easiest access. Here you may hike past giant drift logs to towering sea stacks and walk through Hole-in-the-Wall. The tide pools are teaming with life, and bald eagles are frequently spotted. Nearby Mora Campground is an excellent place to spend the night (usually fills by early afternoon).***Warning:*** Before hiking on wilderness beaches, check the tide chart posted at the trailhead to avoid becoming stranded for several hours while waiting for the water level to go down.

The third park access takes you up the Hoh River Valley to the Hoh Rain Forest, which lies at the western edge of the Olympic Mountains and receives more rainfall than any other spot in the continental United

States. Although connotations of a rain forest have little to attract cyclists, you should not bypass the Hoh. The rain forest is a world colored in green, from the lush vegetation of the forest floor to the giant trees covered with lacy moss. Plants grow at fantastic rates and trees grow to record heights. Elk, deer, and a multitude of small forest animals thrive in this environment. The large national park campground is an ideal location to spend the night (fills by noon) and a great base for exploring the nearby nature trails. The small, cozy information center is an excellent place to browse for an hour on a wet day.

Mileage Log

0.0 From Fairholm Campground, ride back to US 101.

0.1 (mp 220.8) Go right (south) and start the climb away from Lake Crescent on US 101. The road has three lanes and a decent shoulder for grinding up the hill.

1.6 (mp 219.3) Crest of the hill and start of an easy riding section over gently rolling terrain. *Side Trip* to Solduc Hot Springs: The scenic road up the Solduc River Valley begins on the left. It climbs gradually for 12 miles to the hot springs resort and campground and then continues on another 0.9 mile to end at the Solduc Falls trailhead.

8.9 (mp 213.9) Klahowya Campground; restrooms, running water, and nature trail.

14.7 (mp 205.8) Bear Creek Campground (on the left side of US 101); restrooms, running water, and three short walks along the Solduc River.

16.2 (mp 204.3) Enter Sappho; a small cafe and a good-size bar.

16.6 (mp 203.8) Pass turnoff to Neah Bay.

16.9 (mp 203.5) Tumbling Rapids Rest Area; restrooms but no running water; often closed.

20.1 (mp 200.4) Lake Pleasant Grocery.

24.2 (mp 196.2) Olympic National Park and National Forest Information Station.

27.2 (mp 193.2) *Side Trip* to Mora Campground and Rialto Beach: If planning to explore the Wilderness Beach unit of Olympic National Park, go right (west) toward La Push. Follow this narrow road 7.9 miles to a junction with a small but very complete grocery store on the corner. Go right for a final 3.8 miles to Mora Campground; restrooms and running water. Once you have set up camp, grab your best bike lock and ride on the final 2 miles to the end of the road, at Rialto Beach. Walk the beach north as far as time and tides will allow.

28.3 (mp 192.1) Enter Forks, a logging town with full tourist facilities as well as two large supermarkets and a private campground with hot showers. At the center of town there is an information center, and at the south end of town is the Timber Museum.

33.0 (mp 186) Bogachiel State Park; a campground with running water, restrooms, covered cooking areas, and two hiker-biker (primitive) sites set in a grove of stately trees. This is a popular fishing area.

34.5 (mp 184.5) Leave Clallam County and enter Jefferson County.

40.4 (mp 178.9) *Side Trip* to the Hoh Rain Forest: Turn left (east) off US 101 on Hoh River Rd., heading inland to the rain forest. The road is narrow and winding, a perfect road for riding if there were no cars. Use the turnouts to let traffic pass or to stop for a breather. The road passes through ugly clearcuts, then peaceful forest. Wear bright, visible clothing to help motorists see you. Terrain is rolling and some of the short hills are steep.

40.5 (mp 178.8) Forest display explaining the topography of a clearcut, located on the left side of the road.

41.5 (mp 177.7) Turnoff to Cottonwood Recreation Area, a private campground.

41.8 (mp 177.4) Hoh-Oxbow Campground, a private facility on the right.

42.7 (mp 176.0) Turnoff to Hoh-Clearwood State Forest (campgrounds are miles away from US 101).

43.2 (mp 175.5) Small store and RV park with cabins.

49.3 (mp 169.3) Rain Forest Home Hostel; open all year. Call ahead for reservations: (360) 374-2270.

51.0 (mp 167.6) Hoh Tribal Center turnoff.

51.8 (mp 166.8) Enter Olympic National Park. The road runs through heavy forest with occasional views over the ocean.

53.9 (mp 164.7) Ruby Beach; views over the rugged Pacific Coast, beach access, and vault toilets.

55.2 (mp 163.4) Destruction Island viewpoint. A small turnout with an information board relating the not-so-happy history of the island.

56.0 (mp 162.6) Beach 6; vault toilet, whale-watching area, and beach trail.

56.4 (mp 162.2) Big Cedar; a very old and abused tree located 0.3 mile off US 101 on an easy-to-ride dirt road.

58.3 (mp 160.3) Beach 4; parking lot, restrooms, and path to the beach. This is an excellent place to stop and explore tide pools. Park naturalists are often here at low tide to explain the complexities of intertidal life.

59.1 (mp 159.5) Beach 3; another beach access.

61.2 (mp 157.8) Kalaloch Campground; restrooms, running water, nature trail, and beach access. A small grocery store can be reached by a 0.5-mile trail from the campground.

Peninsula Route: Kalaloch Campground to Quinault Lake
(33.6 miles)

This is a short ride, designed to ensure plenty of time to explore the temperate rain forest environment that makes this area so unique. If you rode right past the roads to the Elwha, Solduc, and Hoh River Valleys, do not miss this opportunity to regenerate your mental and physical energies with a walk through the fertile forests around Quinault Lake. The greens are intensely pervasive. Noise is muted by the vegetation. The feeling of growth and vitality permeates the air. It's a wonderfully healthy break from the dirt and grime of the road.

Leaving the coast, US 101 turns southeast, heading inland through miles of forest and logging clearings. Without views or other points of interest, this is a good section to just cover some miles. Shoulders are just barely adequate and the terrain is gently rolling.

The day's ride ends back in Olympic National Park at a campground at the edge of Quinault Lake. This is a rain forest area, with lush, green forests, fern-filled canyons, and moss-covered trees. At the end of the mileage log is a tour guide to the Quinault area.

Ruby Beach is a virtual playground, with stumps, logs, rocks, sea stacks, tide pools, sand, and even a small, freshwater creek for wading.

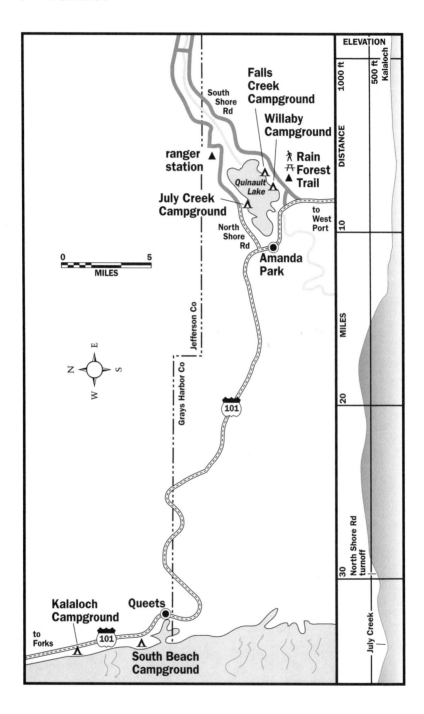

ELEVATION

1000 ft

500 ft Kalaloch

South Shore Rd

Falls Creek Campground

Willaby Campground

DISTANCE

ranger station ▲

🚶 **Rain**
🪑 **Forest**
▲ **Trail**

▲
Quinault Lake ▲
▲

July Creek Campground
▲

to West Port

10

North Shore Rd

● **Amanda Park**

0   5

MILES

Jefferson Co

MILES

E

N ✦ S

W

20

Grays Harbor Co

🛡101

30 North Shore Rd turnoff

July Creek

Kalaloch Campground   **Queets**

to Forks

🛡101

▲

▲

South Beach Campground

Mileage Log

0.0 (mp 157.8) Leaving Kalaloch Campground, head south along the coast on US 101. The road has a good shoulder.

0.5 (mp 157.4) Kalaloch Resort; small store, cabins, coffee shop, and beach access.

0.7 (mp 157.2) Olympic National Park Ranger Station; information, displays, and restrooms.

1.6 (mp 156.1) Beach 2; parking area with a path to a sandy beach.

2.5 (mp 155.2) Beach 1; beach access and restrooms.

3.5 (mp 154.3) South Beach campground and picnic area. The primitive campground is an overflow area for Kalaloch Campground, open midsummer only. Beyond the campground, US 101 leaves the national park and turns inland to bypass a section of the coast owned by the Quinault tribe. The ocean is not seen again until Copalis Beach, 61.4 miles south. Terrain is mostly level. Expect some truck traffic.

6.1 (mp 151.8) Queets; a very small grocery store is located on the left, 0.5 mile off US 101 on an unsigned road.

6.5 (mp 151.4) Leave Jefferson County and enter Grays Harbor County. The terrain remains almost level as the route makes its way inland, passing acres of clearcuts and stumps with occasional views of the Olympic Mountains.

10.0 (mp 148.0) Leave Grays Harbor County and reenter Jefferson County.

13.6 (mp 144.4) Queets Valley turnoff. This very primitive area in Olympic National Park is reached by a 14-mile gravel road. The road-end campground does not have potable water and the main trail up the valley to a beautiful grove of trees begins with a difficult ford of the Queets River.

13.8 (mp 144.2) Leave Jefferson County and reenter Grays Harbor County. The shoulder width varies here from 0.5 to 1.5 feet wide. For scenery you have a vast array of clearcuts in different stages of regrowth and a few decrepit lumber and shake mills.

27.8 (mp 130.2) Enter Olympic National Forest.

29.2 (mp 128.8) Pass a small gas station/store on the left.

29.9 (mp 127.9) Turn left (east) off US 101 onto North Shore Rd. A small grocery is located here. (If this store is closed, another is located 1.7 miles south.) Follow the narrow and shoulderless road into Olympic National Park.

33.6 July Creek Campground; a walk-in-only area with restrooms and running water located on the shores of Quinault Lake. If this campground is full, try one of three forest service campgrounds located on the south shore of the lake.

Exploring Quinault Lake—North Side

0.0 Starting at July Creek Campground, go right and head east along North Shore Rd. The road is narrow, winding, and heavily shaded from both the sun and the rain.

6.5 Quinault River Ranger Station. This is one of the best places to see the rain forest. The ranger station has a small visitor center with displays of the rain forest environment; open summer only. A self-guided nature trail makes a 0.5-mile loop through a glade of stately old maples, fancifully draped in long streamers of moss. Chances of seeing deer are very good; you may even see an elk. Consider walking the loop at least twice.

Although the scenery is good for the remainder of the distance around the lake, pavement ends in another 2.4 miles. If you would like to sample more of the rain forest scene, now is a good time to turn around and ride the pavement to South Shore Rd. (*Note:* If your bike is equipped for rough roads, the entire lake loop is just 27 miles long.)

Exploring Quinault Lake—South Side

0.0 From July Creek Campground head left, back to US 101.

3.7 Go left on US 101 and descend along the west side of the lake.

5.4 Ride through Amanda Park, passing a small grocery store.

5.7 Go left on South Shore Rd.

6.9 Junction; stay left.

7.3 Go right into a large parking lot with running water, restrooms, and picnic tables. This is the Quinault Rain Forest trailhead. You may choose trail combinations that vary in length from a 0.5-mile nature loop through the big trees to a 10-mile ramble past waterfalls and fern grottos.

Be sure and lock the bikes up before heading out.

If you wish to ride farther, 0.3 mile east is the little community of Quinault, which has a small grocery store, a large lodge, and a Forest Service Information Center.

Peninsula Route: Quinault Lake to Twin Harbors State Park
(55.6 Miles)

This ride depends on a small passenger ferry that crosses the narrow mouth of Grays Harbor Bay between Ocean Shores and Westport. Unfortunately, it is a seasonal ferry, running a regular schedule from the fourth week of June through Labor Day only. The ferry runs on weekends from the fourth week of May to the fourth week of June, and from

Labor Day through the third week in September about once every hour and a half between 11:00 A.M. and 6:00 P.M. If you have questions, call ahead: (360) 289-3386.

When the passenger ferry is not running, you must follow US 101 through the congested twin cities of Hoquiam and Aberdeen, then head west on Highway 105, winding around Grays Harbor Bay to Twin Harbors State Park. The off-season route is 10 miles longer than the summer route, uses congested roads, and is monotonous.

No matter which route you follow, the day starts with a good warm-up

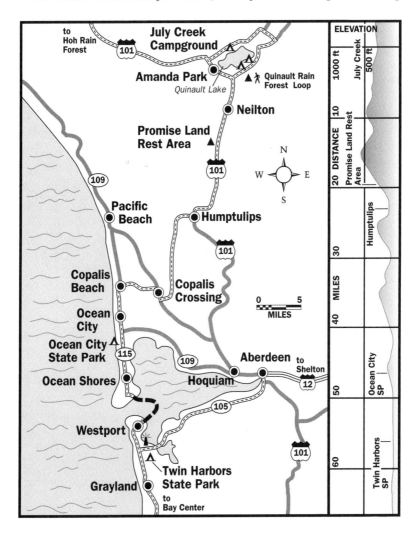

on US 101. The highway passes through alternating clearcuts and small bands of second-growth timber. Expect considerable truck traffic for these first 22.6 miles.

At Humptulips, the summer route leaves US 101 and heads west on country roads to return to the salt-tanged air of the Pacific Ocean at Copalis Beach. Grocery stores, motels, RV campgrounds, restaurants, beach cabins, and tourist shops abound. Some of these long, sandy beaches are open to motor vehicles. Clam digging, kite flying, and sunbathing are popular activities.

Once the route reaches the ocean, it turns south, paralleling the coast. The terrain is level, the roads often shoulderless. After riding through several small towns, reach the tip of a sandy peninsula where the small passenger ferry to Westport is located. The ride continues south from Westport for another 3 miles to Twin Harbors State Park. For Peninsula Route riders, hot showers are the most notable feature of this destina-

Kite flying is a popular activity along the coast. Purchase your kite at Ocean Shores or Westport, and practice flying it as you continue down the coast.

tion (the first showers encountered in Washington—enjoy). Twin Harbors State Park is the junction of the Peninsula and Inland Routes. *The* Combined Route, *found later in this section, continues south; see page 101.*

Mileage Log

0.0 From July Creek Campground, head back to US 101 on North Shore Rd. and make your final adieus to Olympic National Park.

3.7 (mp 128.4) North Shore Rd. ends. Head left and continue your journey south on US 101. The first hills encountered are steep, shoulders adequate.

5.4 (mp 126.9) Amanda Park; grocery store.

5.7 (mp 126.6) Pass South Shore Rd.; access to the Quinault Rain Forest nature loop trails.

6.7 (mp 125.1) Pass second turnoff to Quinault. As you continue up, the road enters the Quinault Natural Area, a deeply shadowed virgin forest.

8.8 (mp 123) Neilton; small grocery store.

14.1 (mp 118.1) Leave Olympic National Forest.

19.8 (mp 112.3) Promise Land Rest Area; large gazebo at the edge of a salmon spawning pond lets you hide from the rain or dodge the sun when open.

22.6 (mp 109.5) Humptulips; small grocery store.

22.7 (mp 109.4) Summer route heads right, following signs to OCEAN BEACHES. Be sure your food supplies are in good order; no towns for 12.6 miles. (See end of this log for off-season route description.)

23.2 Riverview Campground; a private facility with campsites and rental cabins. Beyond the campground, the road is narrow without shoulders.

24.2 After passing a large fish hatchery, the road climbs steeply.

24.8 Top of the hill; check out the view.

34.4 Enter Copalis Crossing; cafe.

34.6 Go right (north) following a sign to BEACHES on Copalis Beach Rd.

35.2 Turn left (west) toward BEACHES, passing a small mini-market on the right.

40.0 (mp 21.3) Intersection. Go straight on Highway 119 into Copalis Beach; grocery store, cafe, motels, and beach access.

40.4 (mp 20.9) Pass the first of many beach access roads. The beach, located 0.4 mile west, may be used as a highway for several miles south to Ocean City when the tide is out. Highway 119 is narrow and congested.

41.0 (mp 20.3) Pass a privately operated campground with beach cabins.

42.9 (mp 18.4) Ocean City; motels, grocery stores, and restaurants.

43.4 (mp 18.0) Beach access.

45.4 (mp 16.0 and mp 0.0) Intersection. Go right on Highway 115 and head to Ocean Shores. The wide shoulder offers a chance to relax.

46.3 (mp 0.9) Ocean City State Park; hiker-biker site, showers, beach access.

47.4 (mp 2) Highway 115 ends. Go left, following signs to PED FERRY. Enter Ocean Shores; grocery stores and tourist amenities.

47.8 Intersection; continue straight ahead. The road turns into a three-laner. The road name will soon change to Pt. Brown Ave.

51.9 Intersection; go right.

52.1 Stop at the Silver King Motel to buy tickets for the 30-minute ferry ride to Westport, then go left into the marina. The ferry docks at Westport, a tourist town on a narrow peninsula, with the Pacific Ocean to the west and Grays Harbor Bay to the east. Near the tip of the peninsula is Westhaven State Park, a day-use area and popular surfing beach. The town is a resort for sport fishermen, with numerous hotels, motels, and restaurants, and a grocery store. Seafood is readily available; try a restaurant or purchase it from a roadside vendor.

52.3 Once off the ferry, go left for 2 blocks, then turn right.

52.5 Take a left on Harbor Blvd. and ride south, passing a large grocery store.

55.5 Turn right on Highway 105.

55.6 Twin Harbors State Park; hiker-bike sites, hot showers, beach access, and dune trail.

Off-season Route

Continue south from Humptulips on US 101 for 20 miles to Hoquiam. Follow US 101 south through the congested downtown area. Shoulders disappear; however, traffic moves slowly through town. When crossing the Hoquiam River, cyclists may use the sidewalk on the left side of the extremely narrow, steel-grate bridge.

Hoquiam flows into Aberdeen, with more supermarkets and tourist facilities. Continue to follow US 101 as it makes a sharp bend to the right (south) and crosses the Chehalis River on a wide bridge. On the south side of the bridge, leave US 101 as it takes a sharp bend to the left at a traffic signal. Go straight on Highway 105 and head west for the next 18.2 miles. (Two large supermarkets are located on the left side of the highway at this intersection.) Highway 105 (a Washington State Scenic and Recreational Highway) skirts the tide flats of Grays Harbor. The highway is narrow, and shoulders vary from good to none.

Enter Westport 42.6 miles from Humptulips. The road skirts the edge of town; grocery stores, restaurants, and the ferry to Ocean Shores are located 2 miles north, at the town center. Turn left to Twin Harbor State Park.

Combined Route: Twin Harbors State Park to Bay Center
(52.8 Miles)

The Peninsula and Inland Routes join at Twin Harbors State Park and unite for the final push south to the Columbia River and the Oregon border.

The southern coastline of Washington is broken by large bays, which force the route to turn inland below Twin Harbors State Park. Cyclists can expect a lot of tree plantations with occasional views of either the ocean or vast mud flats (depending on the tide) as the route heads southeast around massive Willapa Bay to rejoin US 101 at Raymond. If you can drag yourself away from the delightful views of artistic deer and elk grazing along the road in Raymond, you may escape the noise of the

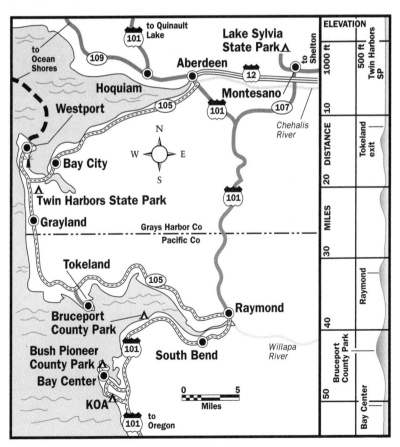

A realistic-looking sheet-iron sculpture is located along the bike path overlooking the Willapa River between Raymond and South Bend.

main highway by following a 2.5-mile bike path west along the Willapa River to South Bend.

Start the day with full water bottles and plenty of extra food; few stores or restrooms are found along the route. With little to break the rhythm of the ride, the miles tend to speed by. Cyclists arriving at Bay Center may understandably be tempted to continue south another 33 miles to Cape Disappointment State Park, near Ilwaco. Not a bad idea, if you use the time gained to explore the historically interesting and very scenic Columbia River mouth.

This is a quiet area. Both Highways 105 and 101 receive only a low volume of traffic, leaving time to hear the surf and listen to the shore-birds. Shoulder width is good except for a short stretch as you enter Raymond and the final section to Bay Center.

The economy in this area is based on the forest industry, so be pre-pared for logging trucks on the highways. Always give these huge trucks as much space as possible, or even get off the road to avoid being trapped in a squeeze play. Most truck drivers are very friendly to cyclists (many ride themselves), but those trucks are big, heavy, and difficult to ma-neuver, and most drivers are paid by the load.

The day ends at Bay Center, a small town in a formerly thriving oyster farming community with two campgrounds. The public facility is Bush Pioneer County Park. This forested park has ten campsites, a picnic area, restrooms, and limited beach access. The park is open during the months of July and August only. The alternative is a commercial KOA campground with all the amenities.

Mileage Log

0.0 (mp 30.1) From Twin Harbors State Park, head south on Highway 105. Shoulders are narrow, and traffic is moderate to light.

2.8 (mp 27.5) Grayland; a small resort town with motels, grocery store, and deli.

3.4 (mp 26.9) Beach access; toilets.

4.6 (mp 25.6) Turnoff to Grayland Beach State Park; water, restrooms, showers, hiker-biker sites, interpretive trails, and beach access. This park is oriented to the needs of campers with recreational vehicles.

4.7 (mp 25.5) Leave Grays Harbor County and enter Pacific County.

6.5 (mp 24) Pass the first of several beach access points. The highway lies inland here, away from the beach. The land between the highway and the beach is private except for the occasional access provided by the state park system.

7.9 (mp 22.3) North Cove; a very small town with a very small market.

9.8 (mp 20.6) Highway 105 parallels ocean along the edge of North Cove.

11.2 (mp 19.3) Enter the Shoalwater Indian Reservation. Groceries, motels, and fireworks may be found near the turnoff to Tokeland, a small community with a fishing dock and a rather plain-looking historic hotel. The highway turns east here, crossing a forested peninsula and then paralleling the shore of Willapa Bay. The bay is very shallow, and the ebbing tide exposes miles of tide flats. To the south lies Leadbetter Point (the northern tip of the North Beach Peninsula), as well as the objective for this day's ride, Bay Center. The route skirts around Willapa Bay for the next 63 miles.

20.4 (mp 10.1) After passing a commercial campground, the highway crosses North River, then Smith Creek. Across the bay, the mills of South Bend and Raymond come into view.

30.3 (mp 0.8) Raymond; a lumber town with art sculpture that will put a smile on your face. You will find just about everything for the touring cyclist here except a good bike shop. There are motels, restaurants, a supermarket, and camping at the county park.

31.5 (mp 0.0 and mp 59.6) Highway 105 ends; turn right on US 101 and cycle across the North Fork Willapa River.

32.0 (mp 59.1) Pass a city park on the left side of the highway; restrooms and running water.

32.5 (mp 58.5) Leave US 101 when it intersects Highway 6 at a stoplight. Go straight across the intersection then turn right and go up on the sidewalk, starting the bike path to South Bend. Continue straight ahead, passing a sculpture of kayakers and cyclists, then cross the Willapa River. *Alternate Route:* Stay on US 101.

32.7 Go left and follow the bike route up a city street.

32.8 Find the bike path and follow it around the south side of the Willapa Market Place shopping center.

33.2 The path ends. Go straight down a well-signed street.

33.4 Return to the bike path. The path parallels US 101 along the Willapa River. (In the early 1900s, there were twenty working lumber mills along this portion of the river.)

35.6 Bike path ends. Go left on Summit St., then right, to return to US 101 just as it enters South Bend, a small, charming town first settled in 1860. Many old buildings remain. Amenities include a city park, public restrooms, a grocery store, tourist facilities, and an RV park that accepts tents.

37.2 (mp 54.0) Pacific County Museum, a small, friendly facility. Public restrooms are located on the north side of the street beyond the information center and parking area. Beyond South Bend, the road is level for several miles. The shoulder starts off comfortably, then gradually narrows.

42.7 (mp 48.6) Bruceport County RV Park; picnic area, eight tent sites, restrooms, running water, and hot showers. Campsites overlook Willapa Bay and are available on a first-come basis.

45.3 (mp 46.4) Historical marker relating the story of Bruceport's origin.

47.5 (mp 44.0) Naipikipi River Bridge.

48.7 (mp 42.6) Palix Creek Bridge. Mileposts become "confused" shortly beyond the bridge.

50.1 (mp 42.4) At Bay Center Dike Rd., turn right (west) and ride toward Bay Center and the campground. Cycle along the water's edge, passing huge piles of oyster shells; no shoulder.

52.5 T junction at Bay Center. The small grocery store and Bush Pioneer County Park are to the right. (The commercial KOA campground is to the left.)

52.8 Bush Pioneer County Park. This is a primitive park with ten campsites, a picnic area, restrooms, and limited beach access. The park is only open during the short summer season from July through August. If you prefer more amenities, try the KOA campground located just south of Bay Center on Bay Center Rd. (The KOA campground has hot showers, laundry, a shelter just for cyclists, a store, and beach access.)

Combined Route: Bay Center to the Oregon Border (47.4 Miles)

The journey through Washington ends at the Columbia River, just a few miles inland from its turbulent terminus at the Pacific Ocean. This scenic area is rich in history. Native Americans lived and fished here for thousands of years before European explorer Captain Robert Gray charted the location of the river mouth in 1792. In 1805, Lewis and Clark ended their long western trek to the Pacific Ocean on the south side of the river near Astoria and wintered a few miles inland from the ocean.

The tricky sandbar at the Columbia River entrance caused many problems for early settlers, and over the years it has been the scene of many shipwrecks. Despite the building of lighthouses, the marking of the

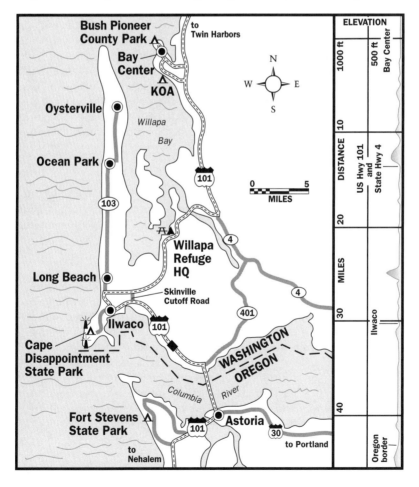

channel, and the taming of the waters by numerous upriver dams, the Columbia River mouth retains many of its navigational challenges. The designing of a very special Columbia River rescue boat gives testimony to the strength and danger of the river.

The ride from Bush Pioneer County Park to Oregon is an easy one, leaving plenty of time for exploring. Along the way you will pass the Willapa National Wildlife Refuge, inhabited by migrating ducks and geese in the spring and fall, and a host of shorebirds year round. Two blinds for viewing and photographing the birds are situated near US 101 at the refuge headquarters. The next point of interest is the Long Beach Peninsula. Its most visible attractions are tourist oriented: "World's Longest Driving Beach," innumerable restaurants, motels, and amusement centers.

At the southern end of the Long Beach Peninsula is Cape Disappointment State Park, formerly known as Fort Canby State Park. The old fort is now the site of an excellent museum commemorating the Lewis and Clark Expedition. Museum exhibits lead visitors on an imaginary journey over the Lewis and Clark Trail. Two lighthouses, North Point and Cape Disappointment, are located within easy walking distance of the park. North Point is the most photographed lighthouse in Washington.

No public campgrounds are located at the state border, so Cape Disappointment State Park is the recommended overnight stop. The small town of Chinook, 5.3 miles from the border, has two commercial campgrounds that accept tents.

Mileage Log

0.0 The day starts at Bay Center, either from Bush Pioneer County Park or the KOA; however, miles start from Bush Pioneer. Ride south on the shoulderless road through Bay Center and continue straight on Bay Center Rd.

0.8 KOA, a commercial campground that is open year round.

Ilwaco

The founder of Ilwaco was a true scoundrel by the name of Elijah White. After making himself notorious in Oregon, he came to the north side of the Columbia River and filed for 640 acres of land under the Homestead Act. He then went east and sold parcels of land in his made-up town to the prospective settlers. Dr. White, as he then styled himself, convinced one investor to build a fancy hotel. The U.S. government eventually became involved, taking over the land claim by White. The hotel, however, was built on legally purchased land and it became the nucleus of the town of Ilwaco.

North Head Lighthouse is located on a cliffy headland at Cape Deception State Park. The lighthouse is open on weekends throughout the summer.

3.8 (mp 41.5) Bay Center Rd. ends; head right (south) on US 101, which has a wide shoulder in this area.

17.0 (mp 29.0) Junction of Highway 4 and US 101. The bicycle route follows US 101 as it turns sharply right (west). The shoulder is narrow to nonexistent. ***Alternate Route:*** Highway 4, in conjunction with Highway 401, may be used as a short cut to Astoria, bypassing 11.1 miles of riding. No camping facilities or points of interest on this route.

19.4 (mp 26.4) Naselle River Bridge marks the return of a shoulder. Beyond, US 101 parallels the shore of Willapa Bay. The road is narrow and winding, with turnouts if you wish to stop and look over the sloughs and scenic mud flats.

22.0 (mp 24.1) The Willapa National Wildlife Refuge headquarters, on the left (east) side of US 101, has information on what to see and where to see it. Check out the bird blinds, but don't expect to see too much in the middle of the day.

25.9 (mp 20.2) Green Head Slough.

30.9 (mp 15.2) Intersection of US 101 and Alternate US 101, called the Skinville Cutoff. The bicycle route continues straight on US 101 to the Long Beach Peninsula, Ilwaco, and Cape Disappointment State Park. The 0.2-mile-long cutoff short cuts 6.1 miles of road, bypassing the Long Beach Peninsula and Cape Disappointment State Park.

33.3 (mp 13.6) Intersection of US 101 and Highway 103 at Seaview; grocery stores and complete tourist facilities. The bicycle route bears left (south), following US 101. Highway 103 heads right, to the town of Long Beach and the northern end of the Long Beach Peninsula.

34.8 (mp 12.1) Enter Ilwaco. The town is located on the Columbia River and has tourist facilities and a grocery store.

35.3 (mp 11.6) *Side Trip* to Cape Disappointment State Park, lighthouses, and Lewis and Clark Trail Museum: Turn right (west) when US 101 makes a sharp turn left (east) in the center of Ilwaco. Go straight until the road branches. Either branch may be followed for the 3-mile ride to the park; hiker-biker (primitive) campsites, hot showers, beach access, lighthouses, museum, and hiking trails.

37.5 (mp 10.4) Intersection of US 101 and Alternate US 101 (the Skinville Cutoff Rd.). Continue straight on US 101 as it parallels the Columbia River through farmland. A commercial KOA campground is located at the intersection.

42.1 (mp 5.6) Chinook, a small town with a grocery store and two commercial campgrounds. Beyond town, pass a county park with campsites for RVs only.

44.3 (mp 3.5) Fort Columbia State Park; picnic tables, trails, running water, restrooms, gun turrets, museum, and rental houses.

44.4 (mp 3.4) Pass through a short, straight tunnel. Before entering, set off the blinking light that warns motorists of your presence.

45.0 (mp 2.8) Lewis and Clark Campsite, a small area set aside to commemorate one of the expedition's overnight stops. (No camping here.)

46.9 (mp 0.9) Intersection of US 101 and Highway 401 at the Astoria Bridge. Follow US 101 south across the bridge. The roadway is narrow, shoulderless, and difficult to ride when the wind is blowing. Take a deep breath and head across at a quick pace. Do not stop until you reach the other side.

47.4 (mp 0.0) The Washington–Oregon border is located on the Astoria Bridge over the center of the Columbia River.

Opposite: *There are dramatic views of Canon Beach and the coast south from Indian Beach, in Ecola State Park. The park is reached by a 2-mile side trip from Canon Beach.*

OREGON

The Oregon Coast Bicycle Route has 378 miles of spectacular ocean views, long beaches, sand dunes, wave-sculptured sea stacks, and rugged headlands. This is a popular tourist area, so finding food and lodging poses few problems. The Oregon Coast section of the Pacific Coast Bicycle Route is well marked, and, for the most part, the road is wide enough to accommodate a comfortable shoulder, making it enjoyable for first-time cycle tourists as well as expert riders.

The Oregon Coast should be savored at a leisurely pace. Save the

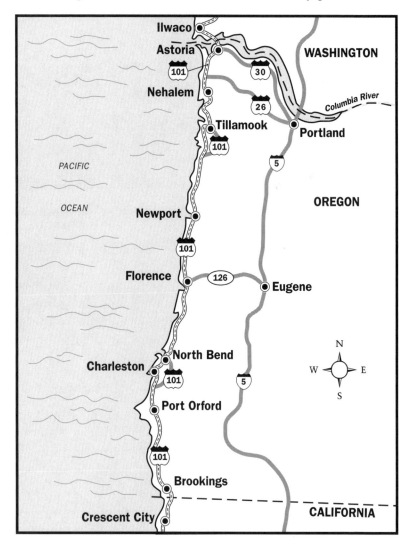

marathon days for a tour across the Great Plains. Slow down, hike, explore, or just sit and watch the sun set.

Cyclists on the Oregon Coast should carry waterproof gear for protection against long, rainy days. Bright, visible clothing and bike lights are essential for surviving the heavy, wet fog that can engulf the coast during the summer months. Fenders are a much-appreciated accessory when it rains, protecting you and your gear from the grime of wet roads. The months of July, August, and September are the driest. Expect heavy rains from October through June. Coastal winds gust up to 60 miles per hour in the summer months (most often from the northwest), and the winds are even stronger in the winter.

The Oregon Highway Department expects the majority of riders to be heading from north to south. Where the road is narrow, the southbound shoulder has been developed at the expense of the shoulder on the northbound side of the road. Most key intersections have been marked with Oregon Coast Bicycle Route signs; unfortunately, these

Touring with young children is especially challenging. Packing the extra gear and pulling the extra weight is the easy part; keeping the kids entertained on the long hauls between frolics on the beach is the hard part. PHOTO: BRENDA JONES

are popular home decorating items, so keep a close eye on the directions and map.

The two tunnels on the Oregon Coast cannot be avoided except by flying. Flashing signs, activated by cyclists before entering, warn motorists that bicycles are in the tunnels. Despite this convenience, tunnels are very hazardous, so be cautious. Strap on a light that will be visible to vehicles approaching from behind, then wait for a lull in traffic before starting out. All these precautions notwithstanding, the tunnels are nerve-wracking, so pedal fast.

The popularity of the Oregon Coast extends beyond the bicycling world. People flock to the coast in the summer, many driving oversized motorhomes—you know the kind: with picture windows, microwaves, showers, televisions, and toilets. Many of these vehicles are rental units, and drivers of these bus-size "camping" machines may lack experience in handling them. Ride defensively and try to anticipate the problems these drivers will have when they pass. Most of all, pray that the next gas shortage will send these "campers" back to hotels.

In Oregon, the milepost signs note miles in whole numbers, starting with 00 at the Washington border and increasing to the south. In the mileage logs, mileposts are noted in tenths for increased accuracy; a milepost number of 25.7 indicates that the point of interest is located 0.7 mile past (south of) milepost 25. On some mileposts the number is preceded by a Z to indicate that the milepost does not follow the normal numeric sequence. In other words, these mileposts are out of order.

State parks provide sixteen hiker-biker camps for cyclists along the coast. The sites are primitive and generally tucked away from regular camping areas. Water, restroom facilities, and showers are available but may be somewhat removed from the campsite. These areas are rarely full, no reservations are required, and the cost is reasonable. However, since the charge is per person, groups of four or more may find the regular campsites a better bargain. Larger groups should always reserve campsites ahead of time. The state parks have recently started building yurts in their campgrounds. All the state park campgrounds on the Oregon Coast have them. These shelters are usually booked throughout the summer. Off-season travelers may find a vacancy during the week. The yurts have mattresses, chairs, and a heater inside. All cooking must be done outdoors. If a regular campsite or yurt is desired, be sure to call ahead for reservations at (800) 452-5687, Monday through Friday, 8:00 A.M. to 5:00 P.M., from 2 days to 9 months in advance.

Between November 1 and mid-April, only eleven state park campgrounds are open. Oswald West, Umpqua Lighthouse, Sunset Bay, William M. Tugman, and Cape Blanco close during the winter.

Many of the state park day-use areas now charge entry fees. If you spent the previous night at a state park campground, your receipt will allow you to use the day-use area of that park. When no one is present to collect the fees, leave the receipt prominently displayed (taped) on your handlebars.

Portland has the closest major airport and train access to the northern Oregon Coast. The only form of public transportation from Portland to Astoria is the bus; bicycles must be boxed for the trip.

If planning to ride from Portland to the coast, Highway 30 (95 miles to Astoria with a good shoulder most of the way) or Highway 26 (80 miles to Cannon Beach with moderate shoulder, some freeway riding, and one tunnel) are recommended.

Neither route offers camping. Highway 30 is easier to reach from the airport, train, or bus station, and has numerous small towns with restaurants and motels along the way. To ride to Highway 30 from the Portland airport, follow the main road from the arrival area and merge right onto NE 82nd, heading east. After 1.2 miles, go right on NE 82nd Way for 1.7 miles. When the road ends, head left on busy Highway 213 (also called 82nd), then take the first right onto NE Alberta St. Follow this road until it ends (it will turn to gravel), then take a left on NE 75th Way and follow it to the first major intersection. Go right on NE Prescott, which soon turns into an official city bike route. After 2.1 miles, jog left on NE 38th, then take the first right back onto Prescott for another 0.2 mile. Turn left at 33rd Ave. and follow it for a short 0.1 mile before going right on Skidmore St. Ride Skidmore for the next 1.1 miles until you reach 17th, where you take a short jog right, then return to Skidmore St. for another 1.7 miles. Go right on Concord Ave. and grind up the pedestrian overpass. Once across, continue straight for 0.2 mile and then take a left on N. Alberta. After 0.2 mile go right on N. Denver Ave. for 0.5

═══════════ Oregon Lighthouse Trivia ═══════════

- The oldest lighthouse on the Oregon Coast is Cape Blanco, built in 1870. It is also the most westerly of the Oregon lighthouses.
- The least-used lighthouse was at Yaquina Bay. It was in service for only three years before being replaced by the Yaquina Head Lighthouse, located just 3 miles to the north.
- There have been three lighthouses at Cape Arago. The sandstone island it sits on continues to erode at a rapid rate, and eventually the current light station will have to be moved.
- The tallest lighthouse tower in Oregon is Yaquina Head Lighthouse, which reaches up a lofty 93 feet. The highest light above sea level is Cape Blanco. The light shines from an elevation of 245 feet, for 21 miles out to sea.

mile, then take a left on N. Ainsworth for 0.6 mile. Turn right on scenic Willamette Blvd. and follow it for 4 miles. Cross the Willamette River at St. Johns Bridge, and head west on Highway 30. (It is best to pick up a Portland map—AAA has them—before you leave home and trace your route through town.)

From the train or bus station (located next to each other in downtown Portland), head up 5th or 6th Ave. to Olisan and turn right. In 0.6 mile, turn right again on NW 18th. After another 0.6 mile, take a left on Raleigh and follow it for 1 mile, then turn right on 28th St. After 0.2 mile, go left on Thurman for 0.2 mile. Turn right on 29th St. for 0.3 mile to a major intersection. Go left here, onto Highway 30 (also called St. Helens Rd.). Traffic is heavy on weekends.

At the southern border of Oregon, riders leaving the Coast Route are once again faced with transport problems. The only public transportation in Brookings is the bus, and the trip to Portland takes 6 hours on the express. Bikes need to be boxed. The alternative is to continue south 21 miles to Crescent City, California, and rent a car or take a commuter flight to larger cities inland (however, these small airlines may refuse to transport your bicycle).

Note: Cyclists have experienced difficulties in obtaining bicycle boxes in Brookings. To avoid hassles, have a friend ship you a bike box by bus.

Washington Border to Nehalem Bay State Park (43.9 Miles)

The northern coast of Oregon is as excellent for bicycle touring as it is for sightseeing. The Oregon Coast Bicycle Route starts high above the Columbia River on the Astoria Bridge and follows US 101 from the state border through farm country, past historical landmarks, to the wild and scenic coast.

US 101 is busy. The shoulder is good for the first 33 miles, then disappears in Oswald West State Park. To add to the challenges, the first of the Oregon Coast tunnels is encountered. Use all precautions for tunnel travel suggested in the introduction to this chapter: Strap on a light, wait for a lull in traffic, activate the warning signals, and pedal like mad.

Although the ride is short, you can easily spend 2 days here checking out all the side trips and exploring the many state parks. The first side trip is into Astoria, where a collection of photographs and memorabilia at the Maritime Museum depicts the colorful marine history of the Oregon Coast, with emphasis on the problems caused by the turbulent entrance to the Columbia River.

The Lewis and Clark Expedition ended its westward journey near Astoria in November 1805. A couple of the expedition members spent the winter boiling sea water for salt at a place that is now called Seaside, while the main body of the expedition took shelter from the damp weather at Fort Clatsop. The second side trip leads to a national memorial at the site of the rebuilt fort.

More recent history is explored on a third side trip to Fort Stevens State Park, where the remains of the *Peter Iredale,* shipwrecked in 1906, lie just offshore. This once-mighty, four-masted British sailing ship is a reminder of the many ships that sank trying to enter the placid-looking

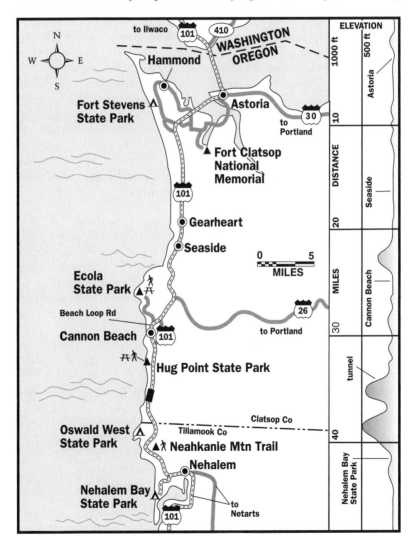

mouth of the Columbia River. The fort can also be explored. The old structure has been abandoned for many years, but at one time it guarded the river entrance and was the only West Coast fort ever shelled.

Farther south, at Hug Point State Park, a short beach walk leads to the remains of the first highway along the Oregon Coast. Most of this early roadway was right on the beach, and drivers had to schedule their travel for low tide. One exception was at Hug Point, where the narrow, single-lane road blasted into the side of a sea cliff can still be seen today.

Not to be forgotten is the tremendous scenery along the way. In Astoria, a side trip to the Astoria Column reveals sweeping views of the Columbia River, Pacific Ocean, Oregon's Coast Range, and parts of Washington. A side trip to Ecola State Park, at Cannon Beach, gives you a chance to enjoy a view of Tillamook Head Lighthouse (currently a mausoleum) and a broad vista over Cannon Beach. Farther south, the highway climbs over a large shoulder of Neahkahnie Mountain, with breathtaking views south over Nehalem Bay and beyond. Leave the bicycles and hike 2 miles to the summit of the mountain for an unforgettable 360-degree view.

The day ends at Nehalem Bay State Park, where long, sandy beaches provide an excellent opportunity to take a relaxing sunset stroll or a bike ride on a paved path out onto a long sand spit.

Mileage Log

0.0 (mp 0.0) Enter Oregon by following US 101 across the 4.2-mile-long Astoria Bridge over the mighty Columbia River. The Oregon Coast ride starts 0.5 mile from the north end of the bridge, where you officially leave Washington and enter Oregon.

3.7 (mp 3.7) A stoplight marks the end of the bridge and the entrance to Astoria. The bike route heads right, following US 101 south across Youngs Bay. *Side Trip* to Astoria: To visit the Astoria Column, the Maritime Museum of the Columbia River, one of Astoria's grocery stores, or the bicycle shop, turn left (east) when you exit the bridge and follow US 30 for 1 mile into town. The road divides and becomes one way. To reach the Astoria Column, take the first left, on Commercial St., to 16th St., then turn right and head steeply up to the column. A left on 17th St. leads down to the Maritime Museum and the dock of the old lightship *Columbia*.

The bicycle shop is located at the eastern end of town, and markets and grocery stores are found throughout.

4.5 (mp 4.5) Youngs Bay Bridge. Traffic is heavy; however, the shoulder is spacious.

6.3 (mp 6.3) Leave Youngs Bay. For the next 18.4 miles, US 101 travels over gently rolling terrain covered with large pastures and stud-

A ball and musket demonstration takes place at Fort Clatsop National Memorial.

ded with small towns. A roomy shoulder provides relief from a constant flow of traffic.

6.5 (mp 6.5) First turnoff to Fort Stevens State Park; continue on US 101.

7.0 (mp 7.0) ***Side Trip*** to Fort Clatsop National Memorial: Exit left (south) off US 101. Cycle 0.3 mile to intersect US 101 Business, then turn left (east). After 1.9 miles, turn right on an unnamed road for the final 1.6 miles to the fort site. A fee is charged to enter the visitor center and reconstructed fort. Watch the movie, then wander through the interactive displays. Live demonstrations are conducted throughout the fort and the surrounding woods on weekends year round and every day during the summer season. The flintlock demonstration is particularly fun. Other monument amenities include a nature trail, a picnic area, restrooms, and running water.

Side Trip to Fort Stevens State Park: For a visit to Fort Stevens State Park, turn right off US 101 and cycle northwest 1.1 miles to Warrenton. Continue straight 2.3 miles to Hammond and a stop sign. Turn left on Lake Dr. and follow it south, passing two well-signed park roads before reaching the campground entrance at 0.8 mile. Here you will find hiker-biker sites, yurts, beach access, a nature trail, 9 miles of hiking trails, an 8.5-mile bike path, and a lot of mosquitoes. Explore the park, hike, bike, swim in the lake, watch the sunset over the wreck of the *Peter Iredale,* wander through the old fort historic area, or browse the military museum. Maps of the park are available at the entrance booth.

16.1 (mp 18.3) Gearhart; motels.

17.3 (mp 19.5) Seaside; bike shop, several supermarkets, and surf shops. A side trip into this resort town leads to museums and several historic sites, such as the end of the Lewis and Clark Trail and location of the salt works historical site. Directions to historic sites are well signed from US 101.

23.6 (mp 25) Junction of US 101 and US 26. Stay right on US 101 as it heads up a 2.2-mile hill. Once at the top, it's a downhill glide to Cannon Beach.

26.9 (mp 28.1) Turn right, leaving US 101 at the Cannon Beach exit. Continue downhill on Beach Loop Rd. for a scenic tour through Cannon Beach, one of the most photographed areas on Oregon's Coast. On weekends the roads through town are congested.

27.3 *Side Trip* to Ecola State Park: Two miles of steeply winding, narrow road through beautiful coastal forest lead to Ecola State Park, where you will be treated to fantastic views of Cannon Beach and Tillamook Head Lighthouse. Picnic tables, restrooms, and running water are available. It takes all day to thoroughly explore the long, sandy beaches and forested trails of the park. Unfortunately, no camping is allowed. A state park day-use fee is charged.

27.7 Cannon Beach, a very popular resort area with beaches, grocery stores, delis, and restaurants. Strolling on the beach and digging toes into the sand are the two most popular activities. As you ride through

Fort Stevens

This historic fort was commissioned in 1863 during the Civil War to protect the Pacific Coast from the threat of a Confederate invasion. The fort was again heavily staffed during WWI, but saw no action. However, during WWII, on June 21, 1942, a Japanese submarine crept in close enough to shell the beach. Despite the almost overwhelming demands of the enlisted men to fire back, the fort commander elected to hold fire. A total of seventeen shells were fired by the submarine before it departed, never to return, and an armed battle on the Pacific Coast was avoided.

town, Beach Loop Rd. becomes South Hemlock. Continue south.

29.6 Tolovana Park; a small community with a store, beach access, restrooms, and water. Return to US 101 here. Heading south, the shoulders are moderate and the occasional ocean views excellent.

30.6 (mp 32.4) Arcadia State Park; beach access, ocean views, running water, and restrooms.

31.8 (mp 33.6) Hug Point State Park. A short, steep descent leads to restrooms, running water, picnic tables, and beach access. Walk the beach 0.5 mile north to a waterfall and small cave, then climb over a low headland on the remains of the original Coast Highway.

33.8 (mp 35.7) Cape Arch Tunnel runs uphill and bends to the left. Before entering, activate the flashing signal by pushing the button. At the south end, a turnout provides an opportunity to catch your breath while you enjoy the view. After the tunnel, the highway continues to gain elevation for several miles.

33.9 (mp 35.8) Enter Oswald West State Park. Campground, picnic area, and beach access are 4.3 miles south.

35.2 (mp 37.1) Leave Clatsop County and enter Tillamook County.

38.2 (mp 39.3) Oswald West Campground, a walk-in area reached by a 0.25-mile paved trail (no hiker-biker sites). Wheelbarrows are provided to help campers transport their gear to the tent sites. To reach the picnic area, walk the trail for 0.75 mile to Short Sand Beach. Beyond the trailhead parking area, US 101 climbs steeply over a shoulder of Neahkahnie Mountain.

39.1 (mp 40.2) Neahkahnie Mountain Trail starts on the left (east) side of the highway, opposite a turnout, and is marked by an unobtrusive wooden post. Beyond the trailhead, the shoulder on US 101 is narrow as the road climbs steeply for the next mile. *Side Trip:* Hide the bikes in the bushes and hike the steep 2-mile trail to unsurpassed views from the summit.

39.3 (mp 41.2) Top-of-the-hill viewpoint and start of a steep downhill.

39.8 (mp 41.6) Neahkahnie Mountain Trail, south side. This longer, less-scenic trail also leads to the summit.

41.1 (mp 43.2) Manzanita Market, the last grocery store before Nehalem Bay State Park, is easy to miss when zooming down Neahkahnie Mountain. The next grocery store is located 1 mile beyond the state park turnoff in Nehalem. For northbound riders, little to no shoulder exists for the next 5 miles.

41.9 (mp 43.9) Turn right off US 101 and follow the signs to Nehalem Bay State Park.

43.9 Nehalem Bay State Park; hiker-biker campsite, yurts, hot showers, beach access, and 1.5-mile bike path to the south end of the Nehalem spit.

🚲

Nehalem Bay State Park to Cape Lookout State Park (48.2 Miles)

The route continues south along the coast, following US 101 through small resort towns. The road is near the water's edge and the scenery is good for the first 21 miles. Shortly after passing through Bay City, the broad expanse of Tillamook Bay forces US 101 to turn inland, where it travels over a broad and nearly level plain covered with dairy farms and swamps. Miles are covered quickly, leaving you plenty of time to tour the cheese factory at the outskirts of the town of Tillamook. The self-guided tour leads to large viewing windows overlooking the almost entirely automated cheese-making process. A museum explains the history of cheese making, and a slide show illustrates the process. Finally, a snack bar answers any remaining questions.

At Tillamook, the bicycle route leaves US 101 and heads west on the Three Capes Scenic Route to spectacular ocean views, a lighthouse, and beach trails. (US 101 heads inland here to avoid the rugged coast.)

Most of the ride from Nehalem Bay State Park to Tillamook has ample shoulders. Once on the Three Capes Scenic Route, the shoulders end. The roads on this route are narrow and moderately busy. However, the scenery justifies the inconvenience.

Mileage Log
0.0 From Nehalem Bay State Park, pedal back to US 101.
2.0 (mp 43.9) Rejoin US 101 and head south.
3.1 (mp 45) Nehalem, a small, congested town with knick-knack shops for tourists and restaurants and a grocery store for cyclists. US 101 makes a sharp right, then heads around Nehalem Bay.
3.8 (mp 45.7) Cross the Nehalem River on a bridge with a comfortable shoulder.

Blimps in Tillamook

In the midst of WWII, the Navy decided to station a blimp squadron in Tillamook. The blimps would patrol the Pacific and act as escorts for convoys along the coast. The hangers, when completed in 1943, were huge: 192 feet tall and 1072 feet long. Eight blimps were kept there. They could cruise over 2300 miles without refueling and could travel up to 40 miles per hour.

The base was decommissioned in 1948 and eventually turned over to the town's jurisdiction. The blimp hangers still remain and can be viewed from Highway 101 at the southern end of town.

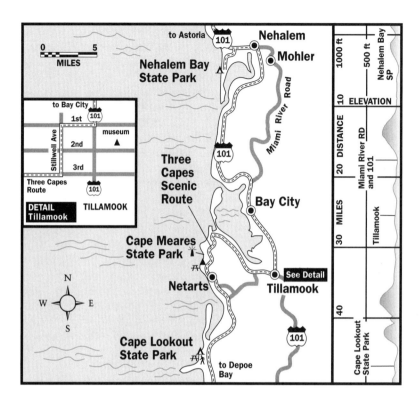

4.0 (mp 46) The road on the right leads to a boat launch with public outhouses.

5.0 (mp 47) Wheeler; small market and tourist shops.

6.7 (mp 48.7) Shoulder narrows as the road enters a slide area. Mileposts are not accurate here.

7.9 (mp 49.9) The shoulder returns to a comfortable width as the highway enters a beach community.

9.6 (mp Z46.9) Start another short section where the shoulder is less than optimal.

11.4 (mp Z48.8) Manhattan Beach Wayside; restrooms, picnic tables, water, and a short trail to a sandy beach. A small market is located just across the road.

11.9 (mp Z49.3) The town of Rockway Beach is entered after crossing a short, shoulderless bridge.

13.1 (mp 50.9) Rockway Beach Public Access; restrooms and beach. US 101 now heads inland, passing several small lakes.

16.1 (mp 53.9) Barview Jetty County Park. This trailer park is located at the North Jetty of Tillamook Bay. There is a small store at the turnoff. Continuing south, the shoulder narrows as US 101 contours around the edge of the bay, passing a couple of small, twisted sea stacks just offshore.

17.0 (mp 54.8) Viewpoint; picnic tables.

17.2 (mp 55.1) Garibaldi; market, Coast Guard station, and an old train on display in Lumbermen's Memorial Park.

19.0 (mp 56.9) Cross the Miami River on a wide bridge.

20.6 (mp 58.5) Viewpoint over Tillamook Bay.

21.4 (mp 59.3) Bay City, a small town with a small market.

26.0 (mp 63.9) Tillamook Cheese Factory, located on the left (east) side of the highway. Signs, several busy parking lots, and a large sailing ship on the front lawn make this an easy attraction to spot. Admission is free; however, free samples are limited and the cheese is cheaper elsewhere. Check out the cheese curd, sold in small bags: It's very affordable and tastes great.

26.4 (mp 64.3) Tillamook; supermarkets, Laundromats, bicycle shops, and shopping malls. The Pioneer Museum is an interesting way to spend a half hour. To reach the museum, pass through the first stoplight, then turn left (east) at the second stoplight. The museum is located 1 block up on 2nd St.

28.5 Go right (west) on 3rd St., following the Three Capes Scenic Route. The narrow road heads west, passing cows busy producing milk for the cheese factory.

30.1 Turn right on the Three Capes Scenic Route. The old, bumpy, shoulderless road hugs the edge of Tillamook Bay. Keep an eye out for a variety of waterfowl.

35.5 Intersection. Following the Three Capes Scenic Route, turn left for a steep, 1.5-mile climb over Cape Meares.

The Glass from Paris

Most West Coast lighthouses originally were equipped with Fresnel lenses, which were manufactured in Paris. These very expensive lenses are made up of as many as a thousand individual prisms. The prisms gather every available bit of light from a source and bend it into a horizontal plane. This allows the lens to concentrate and direct light so that it is visible for up to 20 miles offshore. In order to work properly, these sophisticated lights had to be kept clean, which required frequent hand washing and polishing.

Most of the Fresnel lenses have been replaced by airport-type beacons, which are cheaper and easier to maintain. The remaining Fresnel lenses are treated with great care; if damaged by storms or vandalism, they could never be replaced.

37.7 Cape Meares State Park; picnic tables, restrooms, and water. Descend a short, steep road to the Octopus Tree, a large Sitka spruce, and the lighthouse. Once you have parked your bicycle, grab the binoculars for viewing birds nesting on the rocky cliffs as you walk 0.1 mile down to the lighthouse. You may climb the stairway to the top of the tower for a firsthand look at the prisms. The lighthouse is open daily during the summer from 11:00 A.M. to 5:00 P.M.

40.2 Oceanside State Park Beach; beach access and picnic tables.

42.2 Netarts. If spending the night at Cape Lookout State Park, this is your last chance to replenish your food supplies.

42.8 Turn right, following the Three Capes Scenic Route, and descend to the water's edge. The road then follows the shore of Netarts Bay. The road remains narrow. Traffic is heavy on weekends.

42.9 Netarts Bay Recreation Area; picnic tables and restrooms.

44.3 Stop sign and junction. Continue straight, south along the water, still on the Three Capes Scenic Route.

48.2 Cape Lookout State Park; hiker-biker campsite, yurts, hot showers, picnic area, beaches, 0.25-mile self-guided nature loop, and hiking trails. If time allows, hike the trail to the end of Cape Lookout for terrific views of the coast.

This Fresnel lens, at Cape Meares Lighthouse, has to be washed inside and out frequently to properly refract light.

🚲

Cape Lookout State Park to Beverly Beach State Park (57.5 Miles)

This ride is dominated by three major climbs over three capes. The first climb, over Cape Lookout, begins as soon as you leave the campground. The second climb, over Cascade Head, occurs near the midpoint of the ride. The third climb, over the aptly named Cape Foulweather, awaits you at the end of the day. All three capes are forested and views are hard to come by. However, numerous highlights along the other sections of the ride ensure that you will not miss this area's outstanding scenery.

Plan an early start to allow extra time for a stop at Cape Kiwanda (the third cape on the Three Capes Scenic Route). The cape is a fascinating place; boats are launched directly into the surf, hang gliders take off from the sand dunes, and surfers challenge the waves. From the parking lot, a short walk over sand dunes leads to one of the greatest photography spots on the Oregon Coast.

After Cape Kiwanda, the road heads over several short hills before beginning the long, steep ascent of Cascade Head. You will return to the beach again at Lincoln City (a very congested area). The coast becomes wilder as you head south through Depoe Bay, a famous whale-watching area. The last major climb for the day is over Cape Foulweather. The top of the cape may be very windy, but the view is excellent.

The day ends at Beverly Beach State Park. The camp area is in the forest with access to a long, sandy beach. The best stores are located in Lincoln City.

Mileage Log

0.0 Heading south from Cape Lookout State Park on Three Capes Scenic Route, the day begins with a steep 2.7-mile climb over Cape Lookout.

1.1 Andersons viewpoint. The turnout overlooks Netarts Spit and Bay.

2.7 Top of Cape Lookout (elevation 550 feet) and access to Cape Lookout Trail, a 5-mile round-trip hike through lush rain forest to a beautiful end-of-the-cape viewpoint. As the shoulderless road heads down, watch for several sections of sunken road grade and broken pavement.

6.1 Junction. At the base of Cape Lookout, take the first right (south) to the community of Sand Lake, passing peaceful pastures, sleepy beach homes, and one small store. The lake is visible through the trees on the west side of the road. Beyond the intersection, the terrain varies from level to rolling. The road is narrow and traffic moderate, except on weekends, when thousands of dune-buggy riders and tourists in huge vacation vehicles invade the area.

12.1 Unmarked junction. Stay right (west), paralleling the ocean.

13.6 Cape Kiwanda State Park; running water, restrooms, and beach access. Plan to stop here. The park is the scene of constant activity: dories launching directly into the surf from the beach, hang gliders, surfers, skim boarders, kayakers, sunbathers, children and adults sliding on sand dunes, cameras clicking and whirring. The

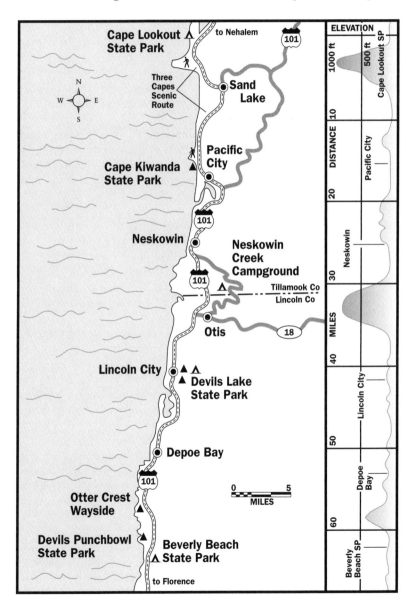

famous photo spot can be reached by a short hike north. Climb a sand ridge to the viewing area. In fall and winter, people come from all over the world to photograph the waves as they crash against the sculptured cliffs. The summer visitor can enjoy a colorful display of layered sandstone as well as sliding on the steep sand dunes.

14.6 Intersection; the bike route turns left (east) and crosses the Nestucca River Bridge. *Side Trip* to Bob Straub State Park: Turn right at the intersection and pedal 0.5 mile south to a parking lot. Beach access.

14.7 Pacific City; several small stores. To continue, after crossing the bridge turn right (south) and follow the Nestucca River back to US 101. The road is rough and narrow.

17.4 (mp 90.4) Return to US 101 and ride south. The traffic is heavy and the shoulders wide. After several level miles over open plain, the highway enters a small valley, climbs over a small headland, and then returns to the coast. This is a very scenic but often windy area.

20.5 (mp 93.5) Oretown; no services.

21.6 (mp 94.6) Viewpoint.

24.4 (mp 97.4) Neskowin, a small town specializing in hotels and motels. A state park wayside gives access to a sandy beach.

25.9 (mp 98.9) The official Oregon Coast Bike Route turns left here and follows forest roads over Cascade Head. This is a delightful alternative route. However, the rarely used road is in poor condition.

26.1 (mp 99.1) US 101 begins to climb over Cascade Head. The shoulder narrows.

28.3 (mp 101.3) Forested summit of Cascade Head (elevation 704 feet).

30.0 (mp 103) Tillamook County–Lincoln County line.

32.0 (mp 105) Junction of State Route 18 and US 101. Use caution at the freeway-type intersections. Continuing south, the road is busy but has a good shoulder. Roadside development increases as you near Lincoln City. Mileposts make a mighty jump and resume some accuracy in town.

34.2 (mp 112) Cross the 45th parallel. You're halfway to the equator.

35.2 (mp 113) Enter Lincoln City, one of the Oregon Coast's chief tourist towns, with innumerable hotels, motels, restaurants, bakeries, curio shops, supermarkets, state parks, and state beaches. Traffic is heavy in the city area, and shoulders disappear in several sections of this very built-up, 5-mile-long strip.

35.9 (mp 113.7) Turnoff to Roads End Wayside State Park, accessed by a mile-long road that terminates in a steep descent to picnic tables and beach access. A large supermarket, located near the turnoff, offers a good opportunity to shop for the night.

37.9 (mp 114.7) Devils Lake State Park campground, on the east side of

This weathered sandstone formation lies atop a cliff that attracts photographers from around the world. The broad, sandy beach to the south is known for its excellent dory fishing, hand gliding, and surfing.

US 101. The hiker-biker area is located on the left, just past the entrance booth, and is divided into two levels, forest and open grass.

38.1 (mp 114.9) "D" River Beach Wayside State Park, a popular area for kite flying. Restrooms and water. Take a quick look at "D" River, claimed to be the world's shortest.

38.8 (mp 115.5) Turnoff to Devils Lake State Park picnic area. Picnic area, boat launch, restrooms, and water are located on Devils Lake, 2 miles east of US 101.

41.8 (mp 118.5) Siletz Bay Park; picnic tables. This area is part of the Siletz Bay National Wildlife Estuary. The shoulder along US 101 is wide in this section, except on some of the older bridges.

46.0 (mp 122.7) Turnoff to Gleneden Beach Wayside State Park. A 0.2-mile access road leads to picnic tables, restrooms, water, and a trail to a long, sandy beach. Several small markets are located along US 101 near the park turnoff.

47.3 (mp 124) Lincoln Beach.

47.8 (mp 124.5) Fogerty Beach State Park on the left; picnic area, restrooms, water, and beach access. The park has two accesses off US 101, one on each side of a small creek. The two parking lots are joined by a paved path.

48.5 (mp 126.2) Boiler Bay Wayside State Park gets its name from the old ship's boiler that is visible at low tide. Restrooms, water, and picnic tables are available at this scenic overlook. This is a popular whale-watching area in season (see next mileage point).

49.6 (mp 127.3) Enter Depoe Bay, whose claim to fame is the world's smallest harbor. The bay is a popular whale-watching area from December through May. (Whales may occasionally be seen through the end of July.) Calm, cloudy days are the best for sighting whales.

52.0 (mp 129.5) Rocky Creek Wayside State Park, another popular whale-watching area; restrooms, water, picnic tables. Views from the park extend north over Whale Bay and south to Cape Foulweather.

52.2 (mp 129.7) Begin climb over Cape Foulweather. Shoulder is good in this section.

53.8 (mp 131.1) Turnoff to restaurant and gift shop located on the old road over Cape Foulweather. Hold on tight to bicycles; winds of up to 60 miles per hour are common.

54.0 (mp 131.4) Otter Crest viewpoint. If you skipped the last turnoff, stop here and check out the view.

55.6 (mp 133) *Side Trip* to Devils Punchbowl State Park and Marine Gardens: Go right on the 0.6-mile access road to a natural punchbowl that churns best at high tide, and a beach, where shellfish gathering is prohibited to preserve the ecosystem.

57.5 (mp 135.1) Beverly Beach State Park campground, located on the left (east) side of US 101. The campground has a hiker-biker camp (located on the hillside beyond the group area), yurts, hot showers, and access to long, sandy Beverly Beach. Some groceries may be purchased near the park entrance. If you are looking for something to do at the end of the day, consider a ride to Yaquina Lighthouse. See the next section for details.

Beverly Beach State Park to Jessie M. Honeyman Memorial State Park (60.3 Miles)

With so much to see in the next 60.3 miles, expect travel time to be long and distances between stops very short. The first stop, Yaquina Lighthouse National Wildlife Refuge, lies just 3.5 miles south of Beverly Beach State Park. The obvious attraction here is the tall, white lookout tower on the windswept point, visible for miles up and down the coast. However, the real attention-getters are the birds, nesting on rocky offshore islands clearly visible from a viewing platform at the lighthouse. Check out the visitor center and the tide pools of Lower Quarry Beach, then watch the surfers (long boarders mostly) take in the low, lazy waves. Avoid the temptation to linger; many other distractions lie ahead.

In Newport, the route leaves US 101 and heads through scenic residential streets along the coast to avoid downtown congestion and endless stoplights. The route returns to US 101 in time for a side trip to the Newport Marina as well as the Oregon State University's Henry O. Hatfield Marine Science Center. The science center features fascinating

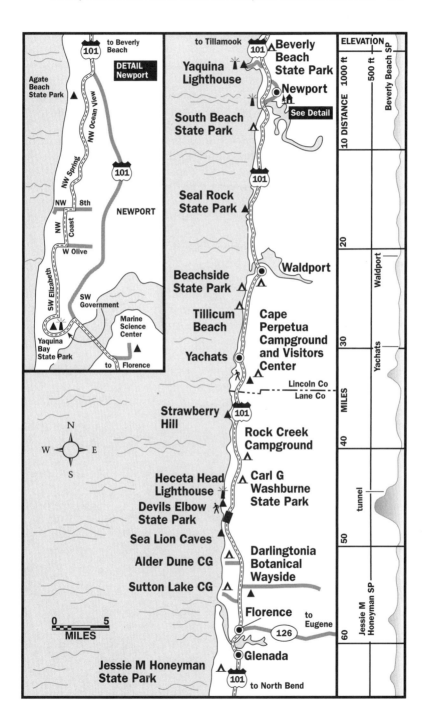

interactive learning displays and specializes in the economical and environmental aspects of the ocean. From sound waves to natural disasters to a computer game that sends you deep-sea fishing for a season, this is an extremely educational facility.

At Sea Gulch, stop and gawk at the world's largest collection of chainsaw woodcarvings. Artists often work along the side of the road. Their delicate expertise with a chainsaw is amazing to watch.

Among the many parks and waysides along the route, Cape Perpetua is the most popular. Trails lead to the Devils Churn, tide pools, an old native American camping ground, and a panoramic viewpoint. The visitor center offers displays and a movie on the area's history. A steep, 1.5-mile side road beckons cyclists up to one of the best views on the coast.

Sea lions are common along the coast but not always easy to spot. However, south of Cape Perpetua, at the Strawberry Hill turnout, you have an excellent chance of seeing these mammals take their daily sunbath on rocks just 100 feet offshore.

Farther south, the route passes Devils Elbow State Park, location of the much-photographed Heceta Head Lighthouse. The park is near the Sea Lion Caves, a popular private enterprise where, for a price, you can ride an elevator down the cliffs to a colony of sea lions.

Probably the most amazing sight on the entire coast is seen at the

Sea lions are frequently seen sunbathing on rocky outcroppings along the shoreline at Strawberry Point.

Darlingtonia Botanical Wayside, home of a group of very pretty and very carnivorous California pitcher plants.

The day's ride ends just south of Florence at Jessie M. Honeyman Memorial State Park. This park is located several miles inland from the ocean, separated from the beach by a broad expanse of sand dunes. In recognition of its uniqueness, the area has been designated as the Oregon Dunes National Recreation Area. Despite the large amount of motorized use on the dunes, this is a great place to spend an evening. The top of Honeyman Dune is an ideal location for watching the sunset, and an even better location to forget about the sunset and spend an hour sliding and climbing on the sand.

This section of the coast includes some of the best scenery and some of the narrowest sections of US 101. The shoulder disappears in the Cape Perpetua and Devils Elbow areas. Southbound travelers also meet the challenge of the second and last tunnel on the Pacific Coast Bicycle Route.

Mileage Log

0.0 (mp 134.3) South of Beverly Beach State Park, US 101 parallels the ocean. A wide shoulder provides a comfortable buffer from the traffic. Yaquina Head Lighthouse is visible ahead. Moolack Beach parking area provides access to the beach.

2.5 (mp 136.8) Newport city limits; bike shop, supermarkets, restaurants, motels, youth hostel.

3.5 (mp 137.8) *Side Trip* to Yaquina Head Lighthouse: The access road is 1.5 miles long and a fee must be paid at the entrance station before proceeding to the visitor center, lighthouse, and beaches. At the lighthouse, walk to the viewing platform to look for cormorants, common murres, tufted puffins, and gulls nesting on the offshore islands. Whales are occasionally spotted in the bay below. A road descends to the shore, where tide pools may be explored and sea lions sunbathe on the rocks. Restrooms are available. The lighthouse is open for limited hours during the summer.

4.1 (mp 138.3) Start the Newport bypass by exiting US 101 at Ocean Bay Dr. Cyclists looking for supermarkets or the bike shop must leave the posted bike route and brave the endless stoplights of the city.

5.6 NW Ocean View Dr. becomes NW Spring St. in a quiet residential neighborhood.

5.9 NW Spring St. ends; turn right (west) on NW 8th St.

6.0 NW 8th St. ends; turn left (south) on NW Coast St.

6.4 Turn right (west) on W. Olive St., which, in a few blocks, becomes SW Elizabeth St. Head south past summer houses, motels, and small shops. The City of Newport has built a small park along the headland overlooking the beach. The best feature of the Donald

A. Davis Park is the small gazebo, where you can temporarily escape the rain if needed.

7.3 When SW Elizabeth St. ends, turn right (west) on SW Government St. and follow it into Yaquina Bay State Park; restrooms, water, picnic tables, beach access, and a haunted lighthouse that may be toured for a small fee from May through September, 11:00 A.M. to 5:00 P.M. daily. Follow the road as it loops through the park, then returns to US 101.

7.8 (mp 141.4) Back on US 101, head south across the 0.5-mile-long Newport Bridge. Use the sidewalk when bridge traffic is heavy.

8.5 (mp 142.1) *Side Trip* to Newport Marina and the Marine Science Center: Take the first right (west) off US 101 after crossing the bridge. Northbound riders also exit right (east). Follow signs 1 mile to the huge marina parking lot (fee charged), then on to the science center (donations gratefully accepted); open daily 10:00 A.M. to 6:00 P.M. during the summer, and 10:00 A.M. to 4:00 P.M. the rest of the year.

9.7 (mp 143.3) South Beach State Park; hiker-biker sites, yurts, hot showers, beach access, 0.75-mile self-guided nature trail, hiking trail, and horse rentals.

13.5 (mp 147.1) Lost Creek State Park; picnicking and access to a sandy beach.

15.3 (mp 149.0) Ona Beach State Park; restrooms, water, and beach access. Stop and enjoy a shady picnic on a grassy lawn. Beyond the park, US 101 runs along the coast with glimpses of sandy beaches. Shoulder width is moderate.

16.6 (mp 150.3) Sea Gulch, the chainsaw art center, is on the east side of the highway.

17.0 (mp 150.7) Seal Rock State Park; restrooms, water, and beach access. Walk to the cliff's edge and watch the surf pound against a giant rib of rock. Despite the name, seals are rarely spotted.

19.2 (mp 152.9) Driftwood State Park; restrooms, water, picnicking, and a beach access.

21.0 (mp 154.7) Alsea Bay North Wayside; an off-the-road viewpoint of the bridge.

21.5 (mp 155.2) Enter Waldport at the southern end of a 0.5-mile-long bridge with a good shoulder. The town offers grocery stores, tourist facilities, and a private campground.

23.4 (mp 157.1) Governor I. L. Patterson State Park; restrooms, water, and a sandy beach.

25.3 (mp 159.0) Beachside State Park; a small campground with a hiker-biker camp, yurts, showers, and easy access to sandy beaches.

26.6 (mp 160.3) Tillicum Beach Campground, operated by the U.S. Forest Service. No hiker-biker site.

29.6 (mp 163.4) Enter Yachats. Every year in early July, the world's largest smelt fish fry is held here—perfect for hungry cyclists. Much of the smelt fishing takes place in the center of town at Yachats State Park. If you miss the fish fry, there are grocery stores nearby.

29.7 (mp 163.5) Smelt Sands State Park, as the name suggests, is a popular smelt-fishing area. The fishing is exciting to watch in the early months of summer.

30.9 (mp 164.7) Yachats Oceanic Wayside, a favorite beach spot for the locals; restrooms and running water. Some of the Oregon Coast's most spectacular scenery and steepest hills lie just ahead. Shift to low gear and pedal slowly to enjoy every possible view. The next 20 miles are the windiest on the coast; expect gusts up to 60 or more miles per hour. The shoulder width is narrow to nonexistent for southbound riders, and even less for northbound riders.

32.5 (mp 166.3) Cape Perpetua.

33.0 (mp 166.8) Devils Churn Wayside. At high tide, rushing waves are forced into a narrow channel, where they churn into a white foam.

33.1 (mp 167.0) Cape Perpetua Campground and **Side Trip** to Cape Perpetua viewpoint: This forest service campground has restrooms, running water, and walk-in campsites, as well as trails to the viewpoint, visitor center, and beach. The side trip to Cape Perpetua viewpoint involves a very steep, 1.8-mile ride to the top of the cape, where you are treated to a spectacular panoramic view over 150 miles of coast. The viewpoint may also be reached by a hiking trail from the campground or visitor center. (If you don't wish to tackle the steep viewpoint road, check out the photographs at the visitor center.)

33.4 (mp 167.3) Cape Perpetua Visitor Center, open 9:00 A.M. to 5:00 P.M. daily, has restrooms and running water. The visitor center has many displays, including a 15-minute movie explaining the area's natural history. Trails lead to viewpoints and tide pools.

33.7 (mp 167.6) Leave Lincoln County, enter Lane County, and pass another nameless wayside.

34.5 (mp 168.4) Neptune State Park; restrooms, water, and picnic tables.

35.3 (mp 169.2) Strawberry Hill turnout. View sea lions and harbor seals on rocks just a few feet offshore.

35.9 (mp 169.8) Bob Creek Wayside; beach access.

37.0 (mp 170.5) Commercial campground and small market.

37.5 (mp 171.0) Stonefield Beach Wayside; picnic area and beach access. As the name implies, an intriguing stone-covered beach.

39.4 (mp 172.9) This is the halfway point between Washington and California.

40.1 (mp 173.6) Ocean Beach Picnic Area; picnic tables, beach access. No bathrooms.

40.5 (mp 174.1) Rock Creek Campground, a forest service facility open summer months only. Exit left (east) to reach the hiker-biker area. No hot showers.

41.6 (mp 175.2) Muriel O. Ponsler Memorial Wayside, another scenic wayside with beach access.

42.3 (mp 175.9) Carl G. Washburne Memorial State Park. Exit left (east) off US 101 for camping with hiker-biker sites and hot showers.

44.5 (mp 178.1) Devils Elbow State Park; picnicking, restrooms, water, and beach access. Descend a short, steep road to the park, then walk the scenic path to the much-photographed Heceta Head Lighthouse.

44.6 (mp 178.2) A short, shoulderless, uphill bridge with no sidewalk.

44.7 (mp 178.3) Enter Cape Creek Tunnel, the second and last tunnel for riders heading south on the Coast Route. The tunnel has an uphill grade, so strap on a bicycle light and activate the warning signal before entering. After the tunnel, the highway narrows, climbing steeply over a barren, windswept headland. The shoulder is narrow on the southbound side and nonexistent northbound. Check out the scenic turnouts with views of Heceta Head Lighthouse.

45.6 (mp 179.3) Sea Lion Caves. An admission fee covers the cost of an elevator ride down to a large cave inhabited by a colony of sea lions. Beyond the caves, the road winds over a second headland, then glides downhill for several miles with sweeping views over the coast.

50.1 (mp 183.5) Alder Dune Campground, a forest service area with restrooms and water but no hiker-biker sites. US 101 soon widens to include a comfortable bike lane.

51.8 (mp 185.2) Darlingtonia Botanical Wayside; picnic tables, restrooms, and water. Approximately 100 yards to the left (east) off US 101, a short path leads to a small marsh, where the rare and unusual California pitcher plants (*Darlingtonia californica*) flourish. These carnivorous plants thrive in nutrient-deficient soil by devouring insects.

52.0 (mp 185.4) Sutton Lake Campground, a forest service facility with restrooms and water but no hiker-biker sites.

54.2 (mp 187.6) Florence. Supermarkets large enough to feed the hungriest of cyclists are located here, as well as a bike shop for those in need of repairs. Expect considerable traffic and stoplights.

56.8 (mp 190.2) Junction of US 101 and State Route 126 (to Eugene and points far east). Continue straight on US 101.

57.8 (mp 191.2) Bridge with a slippery steel-grate decking. Cyclists are advised to use the sidewalk.

58.0 (mp 191.3) Glenada. This is your last chance to purchase groceries before Jessie M. Honeyman Memorial State Park.

60.3 (mp 193.7) Jessie M. Honeyman Memorial State Park; hot showers,

hiker-biker camp, a small lake for swimming, a small store and restaurant, boat rentals, and access to the sand dunes. Try the short
trail opposite site 11 in Loop I for easy access to Honeyman Dune.

Jessie M. Honeyman Memorial State Park to Sunset Bay State Park (54.9 Miles)

Miles of soft sand contoured by the wind and accented with ripple marks
border the road from Florence to North Bend. Lie on it, walk through it,
run over it, or slide down it; no matter how, take time to get to know
this beautiful sea of sand known as the Oregon Dunes National Recreation Area. Very little of this fascinating area can be viewed from US
101, so plan one or more short side trips. For cyclists, the most convenient dune accesses and viewpoints are at Jessie M. Honeyman Memorial State Park and the Oregon Dunes Overlook. For a greater wilderness
feel, try one of the short trails from Carter Lake, Tahkenitch, or Eel
Creek Campgrounds. These trails are particularly attractive in May and
June, when the native rhododendrons are in bloom.

After sticking with US 101 for the first 20 miles of the day's ride, get
set for a brief tour of Winchester Bay, where back roads lead you past a
busy marina, Umpqua Lighthouse, a state park campground, and a picnic
area. The bicycle route leaves US 101 for a second time at North Bend for
a tour of Coos Bay and Charleston, then ends the day at Cape Arago.

Cape Arago is magnificent. This unique area has three state parks
along a 2.5-mile section of road. The first is Sunset Bay Campground,
located on a broad bay with a narrow neck. The second park is Shore
Acres Botanical Gardens, formerly a lumber baron's estate. The formal
gardens, set on the lip of sculptured sandstone cliffs, are still beautifully
maintained. The third park is Cape Arago, a picnic area next to knife-
edged Simpson Reef. Background music for picnickers is provided by a
noisy colony of sea lions living on the rocks. Trails from the park lead to
nearby beaches and coves.

Mileage Log

0.0 (mp 193.7) From Jessie M. Honeyman Memorial State Park, follow US 101 south through forested countryside. The shoulder varies in width from 2 to 3 feet.

1.0 (mp 194.6) Dune City. Rent your dune buggy here.

3.4 (mp 196.9) Tyee Campground, located on the east side of the highway, is a forest service area with restrooms and running water but
no special hiker-biker facilities.

4.6 (mp 198.2) Turnoff to Siltcoos Dunes and Beach, a popular dune-
buggy area. Siltcoos Dune Rd. passes two forest service campgrounds

and a trail to the beach, 2 miles west of US 101. (A trailhead parking fee is charged.)

5.1 (mp 198.7) Carter Lake Campground, a forest service area situated next to a deep-blue lake. A trail leads through the dunes to the beach. A trailhead fee is charged.

5.5 (mp 199.1) East Carter Lake Campground, another forest service area.

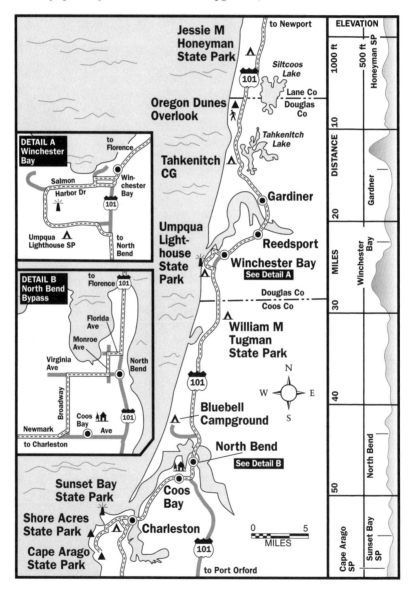

7.3 (mp 200.9) **Side Trip** to Oregon Dunes Overlook: A 0.3-mile road leads to a viewpoint overlooking the dunes, berm, and ocean. If time for dune exploration is limited, this is a choice spot. Just a few feet from the overlook you can take off your shoes and run your toes through the sand. If you have time, hike a trail through the dunes to the ocean, or walk the entire 5-mile loop. The overlook has restrooms, water, and picnic tables.

8.9 (mp 202.5) Tahkenitch Creek Trail. A trailhead fee is charged to explore this interesting area.

10.0 (mp 203.6) Tahkenitch Campground, a forest service area with a 1-mile trail through rhododendron forest to the dunes. A trailhead fee is charged for parking.

14.8 (mp 208.4) Gardiner, a small town with a grocery store and large paper mill. The terrain levels as US 101 curves inland around Winchester Bay, a popular clam-digging area.

An easy stroll from the campground will put you right in the heart of the sand dunes at Jessie M. Honeyman Memorial State Park.

16.6 (mp 210.2) Smith River is crossed on a narrow bridge. Cyclists choose between a narrow sidewalk or a narrower shoulder.

17.4 (mp 210.9) Historical marker dedicated to Jedediah Smith.

17.5 (mp 211) Umpqua River Bridge. Cyclists may use the sidewalk for the 0.3-mile ride into Reedsport.

17.8 (mp 211.3) Reedsport; grocery stores, and headquarters of the Oregon Dunes National Recreation Area. Displays of dune formation and habitat are located on the right side of the highway at the first stoplight after the Umpqua River Bridge. US 101 goes straight through the center of this small, congested town. No shoulders.

Beyond Reedsport, the road climbs a forested hill, then sweeps down to the town of Winchester Bay. Shoulder width varies from 2 to 8 feet.

22.3 (mp 215.8) Winchester Bay; small grocery store. Start the Winchester Bay Scenic Tour. Take the second right (west) off US 101 and cycle the level, shoulderless road past the marina and Windy Cove County Park campground. The park has a nice tent area. When the road divides, stay left.

23.2 Take the first left (south) off Salmon Harbor Dr. and head uphill toward Umpqua Lighthouse State Park, passing the historic Umpqua Lighthouse and a Coast Guard museum. Near the lighthouse is a view over the breakwater and harbor entrance.

24.3 Umpqua Lighthouse State Park campground; hiker-biker area, hot showers, a small lake for swimming, beach access, and picnic area.

24.6 Beyond the park, the road heads up steeply to an intersection. Take the right (uphill) fork.

24.8 (mp 217) Return to US 101. The road climbs to the top of a forested hill, then cruises past Clear Lake.

25.0 (mp 217.2) Viewpoint of lighthouse and jetty.

29.0 (mp 221.2) Leave Douglas County and enter Coos County.

29.3 (mp 221.5) Pass the William M. Tugman State Park campground on the left (east) side of US 101. A hiker-biker camp, located to the left of the entrance booth, has hot showers, lake-side picnicking, and swimming. Nearby food supplies are very limited.

29.5 (mp 221.7) Lakeside, a small tourist town with a small grocery store and commercial campground.

30.3 (mp 222.5) Eel Creek Campground, a forest service area with restrooms, running water, and a trail through the dunes to the beach. Fee charged for parking. Beyond the campground, US 101 runs past a series of small lakes captured between large, forest-covered sand dunes. The road levels at about milepost 230 and swings inland around Coos Bay, where large mud flats attract hundreds of clam diggers.

30.5 (mp 222.7) Umpqua Dunes trailhead; parking fee charged.

32.4 (mp 224.6) Spinreel Campground, a forest service area with running water and restrooms.

40.9 (mp 233) *Side Trip* to Horsfall Dunes, the southern end of the Oregon Dunes National Recreation Area: It's a 2-mile side trip to the forest service's Bluebell Campground and 3 miles to a long, sandy beach. This scenic area is very popular for dune-buggy riding.

41.5 (mp 233.6) Coos Bay Bridge. Ride with caution: The bridge is narrow, traffic is heavy, vehicles are large, and crosswinds are often fierce. An ordinance makes it illegal to hold up traffic as you cross the bridge. This law is obviously aimed at getting cyclists up onto the narrow sidewalk. When crosswinds are strong, consider walking.

42.1 (mp 234.2) Enter North Bend.

42.5 (mp 234.6) South end of Coos Bay Bridge. No shoulder here, so ride with caution. Several lumber mills offer tours during the summer months in North Bend and its sister city, Coos Bay. Amenities include bike shops and supermarkets.

42.9 (mp 235.0) Tourist information, Pioneer Museum, an old train engine, and a city park lie on the right (west) side of US 101. Running water and restrooms.

43.4 (mp 235.5) Turn right (west) off US 101 at Florida Ave. Cycle 1 block uphill, halfway around a large traffic circle, then continue down Florida Ave.

43.6 Turn left on Monroe Ave.

43.7 Go right on Virginia Ave., a broad road without a shoulder. Watch for road signs to Charleston and state parks. Several large grocery stores are passed.

44.3 Turn left (south) on Broadway and ride 0.9 mile.

45.2 Go right (west), up a freeway-type ramp to Newmark Ave. A bike lane starts in 0.5 mile when the road enters the town of Coos Bay.

47.0 At the end of Newmark Ave., turn left (south) on Empire and follow it to Charleston. The bike lane is good in this section.

51.9 Cross South Slough on a wide bridge.

52.2 Charleston; two small grocery stores, the last until Bandon, 20 miles south.

52.4 Leaving Charleston, the road climbs a short, steep hill to an intersection. Stay right for Sunset Beach. The left fork climbs steeply up toward Seven Devils and Bandon. (You will return to this intersection in the next section.)

53.8 Turnoff to Bastendorf County RV Park; campsites, hot showers, and beach access.

54.6 The bike lane ends and road narrows; travel with caution.

54.9 Sunset Bay State Park; campground, hiker-biker sites, hot showers, hiking trails, picnicking, and swimming next to a bay that is almost enclosed by rock walls. This is also the starting point for the side trip to the tip of Cape Arago. Set up camp, then continue on along the narrow road for 1.1 miles to reach Shore Acres State Park, with its scenic overlooks, botanical gardens, picnicking, running water, and restrooms. Then ride on for another mile to Simpson Reef viewpoint, where sea lions are often spotted sunning on the rocks. At the end of the road are picnic tables and a trail to the beach.

Sunset Bay State Park to Humbug Mountain State Park (57 Miles)

Leaving Sunset Bay State Park, the route heads away from the coast and climbs to the ridge tops to catch sweeping views of Oregon's coastal forest and South Slough Estuary. The tranquility of the ridge crest is followed by a screaming descent back to sea level, where the route returns to US 101 after 18.9 peaceful miles—but not for long. The bike route sticks with US 101 for just 2.7 miles before heading off again, this time for a tour along a spectacular section of sea stack–dotted coast at Bandon. Overlooks, state parks, and numerous access points to this unusual beach tempt riders to abandon their journey and explore.

Beyond Bandon, the bike route returns to US 101 and follows it over rolling, grassy hills miles inland from the coast. This is prime rangeland for cows, horses, sheep, goats, and even llamas. It's also excellent riding country, and miles fly by without the distraction of waysides and scenic overlooks.

Humbug Mountain State Park, the day's destination, has a treat for saddle-sore cyclists: a 2.5-mile hiking trail up Humbug Mountain. This trail is an excellent afternoon walk and the destination is a high vantage point with views south along the coast. Or you may walk north from the park on an abandoned portion of the Old Coast Highway. The road climbs up a small hill to a viewpoint of the coast and US 101, a great place to watch the sunset.

If you have any spare time during the day, consider a stop at Bullards Beach State Park, a tour of the old town of Bandon, or a visit to the cheese factory. The state park features a lighthouse and museum located on a long, sandy spit at the mouth of the Coquille River, and excellent views of Bandon and the fishing marina. The old section of Bandon has a delightful selection of shops designed to please a starving cyclist, such as a bakery, fudge factory, and restaurants. The cheese factory, the Coquille Valley Dairy Co-op, is located on the north end of Bandon at 680 US 101 (2 blocks north of the old town) and is open to visitors from 8:00 A.M. to 5:00 P.M., Monday through Friday.

If you have a lot of extra energy, take a side trip (5 miles each way)

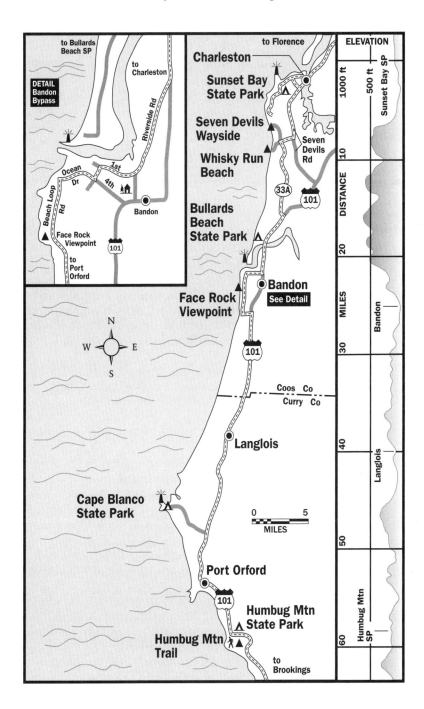

Surf fishermen line the shore, braving the chilly waters in search of dinner at Bullards Beach State Park, north of Bandon.

out to Cape Blanco State Park, a lighthouse, and 100-year-old Hughes House (open Thursday through Monday, May through September). The cape is such a beautiful, secluded area that, once there, you may be tempted to stay.

Mileage Log

0.0 Leaving Sunset Bay State Park, ride back toward Charleston.

2.5 At the intersection just above Charleston, turn right (east) on Seven Devils Rd. (County Rd. 208). The road is steep for the first mile, steeper than most in Oregon, after which it levels off on a rolling ridge top.

7.5 South Slough National Estuarine Reserve; interpretive center, views, nature trail, estuary trail, restrooms, and water. The South Slough cannot be properly explored without spending time hiking or boating the area; however, if your exposure to sloughs and estuaries has been slim or nonexistent, the displays here illustrate the ecology and history.

13.3 Junction with unnamed road signed to Whisky Run Beach and Seven Devils Wayside. Turn right (west) and begin an exhilarating descent.

16.1 Junction with County Rd. 33A. The bike route turns left (south), heading back to US 101. ***Side Trip:*** To the right (north), County Rd. 33A descends 2 miles to Seven Devils Wayside: restrooms, running water, picnic tables, and a long, lonely beach. ***Side Trip:*** Straight ahead (west), an unnamed road descends 1 mile to Whisky Run Beach; no facilities, just a sandy beach for strolling and beachcombing and views of huge wind turbines perched on a hill above. Just before the beach, a narrow dirt road branches off on the right, leading 0.25 mile to a small interpretive center and viewpoint. (Unless you have a mountain bike, it's best to skip the interpretive center.)

18.9 (mp 257.4) Junction of County Rd. 33A and US 101. Turn right (south) on US 101 and start a long glide to Bandon. Shoulders are wide, making the brisk ride enjoyable.

20.8 (mp 259.3) Bullards Beach State Park; hiker-biker area, yurts, hot showers, 1.5-mile hiking trail, beach access, and lighthouse with a museum featuring pictures of local shipwrecks (open summer months only). The nearest grocery stores are 1 mile south, off the main route, on US 101.

20.9 (mp 259.4) Narrow, shoulderless bridge over the Coquille River.

21.5 (mp 260.1) Start Bandon scenic route. Turn right (west) off US 101 on Riverside Rd.

22.1 Enter Bandon.

23.0 Turn right (west) on 1st St. and cycle past the marina. Views extend across the Coquille River to the lighthouse at Bullards Beach State Park. For grocery stores or a visit to the cheese factory, ride to the marina, then return to US 101 and go left (north). Sea Star Traveler's Hostel is located on 2nd St., just off US 101.

23.5 After passing several factories, 1st St. bends left (south) and becomes Edison Rd., then climbs steeply for 1 block.

23.8 Turn right (west) on 4th St. SW and ride through a quiet residential area. Before long, 4th St. becomes Ocean Dr., and soon after becomes 743rd. After a few more blocks the road bends left and becomes Beach Loop.

24.4 Coquille Point; viewpoint, nature trail, and beach access. Go left off Beach Loop to the large parking area with a view of the seastack-studded bay. This is a bird-watching area, one of the most popular varieties for the layman being the tufted puffin.

25.2 Face Rock viewpoint; restrooms and running water. Large sea stacks decorate the beach below. A trail descends to the beach, inviting exploration of these gigantic monoliths.

26.8 State park beach access; picnic tables and ocean view.

27.3 State park beach access; picnic tables and running water.

27.5 State park picnic area; no running water.

28.4 (mp 277.6) Junction of Beach Loop and US 101. Turn right (south), leaving the coast behind and exchanging the smell of salt for the scent of pine and grass. The shoulder is narrow but adequate.

31.1 (mp 280.3) A market is passed on the left.

36.6 (mp 285.8) Leave Coos County and enter Curry County.

38.7 (mp 287.9) Langlois; a small market and art shops.

39.2 (mp 288.4) Turnoff to Floras Lake County Park. Ignore bike route signs to the park, which is many miles off the main road.

40.2 (mp 290.2) Denmark; commercial campground but no other facilities.

40.5 (mp 290.5) Second turnoff to Floras Lake and Boice Cope Park; restrooms, picnic tables, and lake access.

46.4 (mp 296.4) *Side Trip* to Cape Blanco State Park, lighthouse, and Hughes House: The park is 5 miles west of US 101 on a steep, narrow, rough road. The motorhome-oriented campground, situated on a bluff above Cape Blanco Lighthouse, has hot showers as well as a hiker-biker area. Because of the park's isolation, buy food in Langlois or Port Orford. A small market at Sixes, 0.3 mile before the turnoff, can supply the basics when open.

49.7 (mp 299.7) Port Orford; last stores before Humbug Mountain State Park.

51.3 (mp 301.3) Battle Rock Historical Wayside; restrooms, ocean views, beach access, and picnicking. An information board explains the history of the area. Heading south, the road is carved along the steep hillside. Shoulder width varies radically with the condition of the road. Watch for sunken grades and nonexistent shoulders.

57.0 (mp 307) Turn left to Humbug Mountain State Park; hiker-biker sites, hot showers, hiking trails, and beach access. (The hiker-biker site is in the forest. It is very cool and full of bugs. If the park is not already full, you may want to join up with other bicyclists and share a regular campsite.) The trail up Humbug Mountain starts at the southwest corner of the park in the lower camping loop. The Old Coast Highway Trail starts to the right of the pay booth.

Humbug Mountain State Park to the California Border
(56.2 Miles)

Saving the best for last, the Oregon Coast section of your tour ends with breathtaking scenery: long, sandy beaches, rocks carved into graceful arches, jagged sea stacks, and sheer cliffs. US 101 is etched on hillsides that drop nearly straight to the ocean. These wind-blasted hillsides are dotted with viewpoints, parks, and beach accesses. Highly recommended stops are Arch Rock, Thunder Rock Cove, Natural Bridges Cove, Whalehead Beach, and Harris Beach State Park. In late spring and early summer, flower-lovers should not miss Azalea State Park, in Brookings.

The ride is relatively easy, with only one steep climb. You'll have more trouble with the level areas, which tend to be windy in the afternoons. Early morning starts are recommended to avoid the winds, logging trucks, and tourist traffic.

There is only one (short) opportunity to escape the noise of US 101 on this ride. This not-to-be-missed escape is on a section of the Old Coast Highway where the narrow and rarely used road winds along the coast through pastures and a small beach community.

Brookings, 6 miles north of the California border, is the logical end point for Oregon Coast bicycle tours. The chief source of transportation out of town is the Greyhound bus. All bicycles must be boxed for shipping.

Cyclists continuing south into California will find Harris Beach State Park a convenient and beautiful spot for an overnight stop. The next campground lies 27 miles south of the California border.

Mileage Log

0.0 (mp 307) From Humbug Mountain State Park, return to US 101. The road is narrow as it snakes its way over a shoulder of Humbug Mountain. Watch for rocks on the road.

0.7 (mp 307.7) Humbug Mountain State Park picnic area; restrooms, tables, and running water.

3.0 (mp 310) US 101 turns toward the ocean, with views of the broken coastline. Humbug Mountain dominates the northern horizon.

4.7 (mp 311.7) The shoulder disappears, marking the start of a slide area. For the next 5 miles the road is rough, and, depending on how the repair crew is doing, the shoulder may appear and disappear several times.

6.2 (mp 313.2) Dinosaurs leer at travelers from the side of the road, heralding a commercial campground and the Prehistoric Gardens. Admission is charged.

12.1 (mp 319.1) Ophir Rest Area; beach access, restrooms, and running water.

15.2 (mp 322.3) Geisel Monument State Park, a small wayside built to commemorate the burial site of the Geisel family, four of whom were killed by natives.

17.1 (mp 324.1) Watch closely, or you may miss the start of the escape from US 101. Turn right (west) on the Old Coast Highway. The road is narrow, little–used, and very scenic. Pass several beach access trails and cross two cattle guards. Imagine what it was like when this was the main route along the coast.

17.3 Otter Point State Park. A 0.2-mile descent on a dirt road leads to beautiful beach with Coast Trail access.

19.0 The road improves.

19.8 (mp 326.3) Return to US 101 at the small community of Agate Beach.

21.0 (mp 327.5) Cross the Rogue River on a shoulderless bridge. Cyclists may use the narrow sidewalk.

21.3 (mp 327.8) Gold Beach, best known as the starting point for tours of the Rogue River. Billboards advertising jet-boat rides assault the

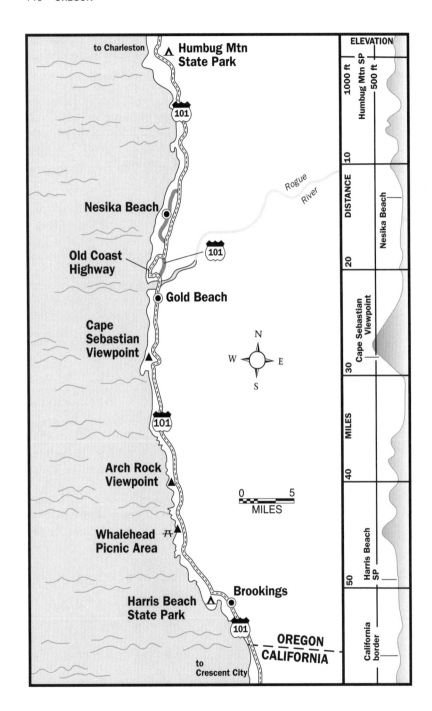

to Charleston

Humbug Mtn
State Park

101

ELEVATION

1000 ft

Humbug Mtn SP

500 ft

Rogue River

10

DISTANCE

Nesika Beach

101

Nesika Beach

20

Old Coast
Highway

Gold Beach

Cape
Sebastian
Viewpoint

Cape Sebastian Viewpoint

30

N

W   E

S

101

40

MILES

Arch Rock
Viewpoint

0   5
MILES

Whalehead
Picnic Area

Harris Beach SP

50

Brookings

Harris Beach
State Park

101

OREGON
CALIFORNIA

California border

to
Crescent City

Harris Beach is fun to explore at low tide. The sea stack-dotted shoreline is a great place to look for starfish and other intertidal dwellers.

senses as you approach town. Other features include an attractive boat harbor, a large grocery store at the south end of town, and the Curry County Museum, featuring local history. Beyond Gold Beach, US 101 starts its climb over Cape Sebastian. This is a slide area, and shoulder width varies from comfortable to nonexistent. Northbound travelers have even less shoulder.

27.4 (mp 333.9) Summit of Cape Sebastian (elevation 712 feet).

28.6 (mp 335.1) Cape Sebastian Historical Marker describes the origin of the name.

28.7 (mp 335.2) Turnoff to Cape Sebastian viewpoint. The viewpoint, reached by a very steep 0.5-mile access road, is somewhat overgrown.

30.9 (mp 337.4) Myers Creek bridge, short but lacking shoulders or sidewalk. Use caution when crossing this and subsequent bridges. US 101 is once again near sea level, and massive sea stacks dot the shoreline.

32.7 (mp 339.2) Pistol River State Park; beach access but no facilities.

37.1 (mp 344.1) Boardman State Park. This long, narrow park has three picnic areas, numerous viewpoints, beach accesses, and pullouts.

37.7 (mp 344.7) Arch Rock viewpoint.

37.9 (mp 344.9) Arch Rock Picnic Area; views of the arch, picnic tables, and toilets. No water or beach access.

38.9 (mp 345.9) Thunder Rock Cove: Awesome!

39.0 (mp 346) Natural Bridges Cove. Water enters this cove through rock arches. The area is exceptional when the tide is coming in. North Island Trail starts here and descends to the beach.

41.4 (mp 348.4) Thomas Creek Bridge is 345 feet high, making it the highest bridge on the Oregon Coast. At the south end is a turnout and bridge viewpoint.

41.7 (mp 348.7) Indian Sand Trail viewpoint. The viewpoint is overgrown. However, the trail leads to an elegant view of arched rocks.

42.2 (mp 349.2) Whalehead Beach Picnic Area; restrooms, picnic tables, running water, and beach access. The beach is reached by a steep, 0.2-mile descent.

42.8 (mp 349.8) Whalehead Trail viewpoint.

44.3 (mp 351.3) Turnoff to House Rock viewpoint.

45.2 (mp 352.2) Cape Ferrelo viewpoint access.

45.9 (mp 352.9) Lone Ranch Picnic Area, reached by a very steep 0.3-mile descent; restrooms, water, and tables. The scenic picnic area is located next to a sandy beach. The ocean is peppered with sea stacks.

46.9 (mp 353.9) Rainbow Rock viewpoint.

47.4 (mp 354.4) Enter Brookings. The commercial section lies 3 miles south.

48.7 (mp 355.7) Turn right (west) for Harris Beach State Park and left (east) for the Oregon Tourist Information Center and Rest Area. The state park has complete facilities for day use and camping. The hiker-biker area is located behind the trailer dump station; the showers are really hot and the yurts really dry. A visit to the beach is a must. There are sea stacks of all sizes to climb, explore, and sit on while watching a lingering sunset. The nearest stores are 1.5 miles south, in Brookings.

50.0 (mp 357) Downtown Brookings; large supermarkets, and a bus station on Pacific St.

50.8 (mp 357.8) Azalea State Park turnoff; picnic area, restrooms, water, and azalea garden. To reach the park, turn left (east) off US 101 at North Bend Rd. and follow the signs.

50.9 (mp 357.9) US 101 crosses the Chetco River Bridge, marking the start of 5 nearly level miles through open country on an excellent shoulder.

56.2 (mp 363.3) California.

Opposite: *Easter lilies grow wild on the Monterey coast south of Carmel.*

The California Coast covers 1038 miles, which is over half the length of the entire Pacific Coast Bicycle Route. The scenery is richly varied, with cool, foggy redwood forests in the north and massive urban areas bordered by inviting palm-lined beaches in the south. Except in the larger cities, riding along the California Coast is addicting. Some sections are ideal for easy riding and you can log impressive daily totals. Other roads are steep and winding, the magic kind of roads where bicycles can safely travel faster than cars. However, the California Coast offers more to the bicycle traveler than just good riding. Historic missions, lighthouses, marinas, beaches, and famous California ambiance will distract even the most determined riders from logging too many impressive mileage totals.

When considering topography and roads, the California Coast just seems to naturally divide into three distinct sections: north, central, and south. The northern section follows US 101 (the Redwood Highway) south 208.9 miles from the Oregon border to Leggett. Much of the riding is inland from the coast, with several sections traversing beautiful redwood forests. Average yearly rainfall is high, up to 70 inches at Crescent City. October and November are usually the wettest, but you can get rained on in northern California any month of the year. During the summer months, this portion of the coast is often shrouded in fog for several weeks at a time. The fog can be almost as wet as a rainstorm. Raingear should be carried in this section, and fenders will sure save you from a lot of water and dirt if you do get caught in a storm or a wet fog. Temperatures are moderate along the northern portions of the coast, warming as you approach Leggett. The north has several sections of hazardous highway—fast, busy, and shoulderless—as well as long, steep hills, making the northern section most enjoyable for cyclists with considerable road riding experience.

The central section of the California Coast Route follows Highway 1 for 492.7 miles, from Leggett to Pismo Beach. Except for a day spent riding through the San Francisco Bay Area, this portion of the state is typified by lonely stretches of two-lane highway etched into cliffs overlooking the coast. The grades are frequently steep, the riding often demanding, the countryside beautiful, and the views outstanding—all in all, some of the best cycling on the entire coast. Traffic on Highway 1 is generally light, composed principally of vacationers. To avoid some of the traffic, early morning starts are recommended. The chance of rain is minimal in June, July, and August; however, fog is likely, often lingering until noon. On warm days, temperatures rise to the 70s or low 80s. As you prepare for a ride along the central coast of California, remember the famous observation attributed to Mark Twain, "The coldest winter I ever spent, was a summer in San Francisco."

The central section of California is recommended for cyclists who have previous touring experience and who are in good shape.

If looking for the California mystique—beach boys, bikini-clad girls, surfers, suntans, palm trees, large cities, Mexican food, and Spanish architecture—the 336.4-mile-long southern section is the place to ride. The

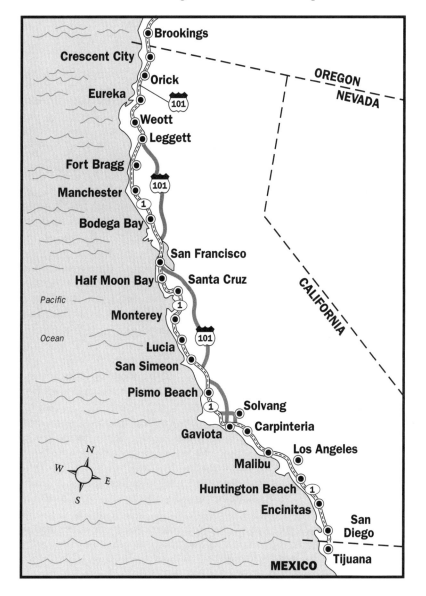

Coast Route loses its isolated feeling as it passes through a long series of resort towns and massive, sprawling cities south of Pismo Beach. The terrain levels, and the need for strength is replaced by a need for navigational skills to wind through a network of city streets. Bicycles are a common mode of transport here, and motorists are the most courteous on the coast. Weather conditions for riding are good from April to mid-November. The southern section of the California Coast can be completed by all strong cyclists with city commuting experience.

For budget-minded cyclists, camping and lodging can be problematic south of Los Angeles. At Newport Beach, a youth hostel is the recommended overnight stop. However, no matter whether you choose to stay in a hostel or a hotel, you will need to plan ahead. The southern coast of California is a popular vacation destination, and lodging may be difficult or impossible to find without reservations. If the hassles seem more than you can handle, consider making Los Angeles International Airport (LAX) the end point of your ride south.

Taken as a whole, some generalities can be made for the entire California Coast. One generality concerns the fog. No matter where you are on the California Coast, be prepared for dense, wet blankets of fog that can last for several days. All riders should have bright, visible clothing and carry lights.

The Bicentennial Route, established in 1976, is followed along the California Coast. When the route was first launched, Caltrans (California Transit) signed most of the key intersections throughout the state; however, signs have been stolen, roads have changed, and a shopping mall was built in the middle of the route, so keep your book and maps handy and do not rely on Bicentennial Route signs to get you through the major urban areas. Mileposts in California show the miles from the nearest county line. The numbers decrease from north to south, reaching zero at the south end of the county. Each milepost notes at least three points of information: the road number, the county name (abbreviated), and the mileage to the hundredth.

Almost every winter, the California Coast is plagued by landslides, making Highway 1 the most costly road in the nation to maintain. Caltrans sets up alternate routes whenever this occurs, creating very scenic, but sometimes long and arduous, detours. If in doubt about the route, contact the California Highway Patrol. The best source of information is other cyclists and tourists traveling up the coast on bikes or in cars. Ask around.

The California Coast has only one tunnel, and it's for northbound cyclists only. The tunnel, on US 101 north of Gaviota State Park, is 0.3 mile long, with an uphill grade and an 18-inch shoulder; expect a strong head wind.

The state and county park systems provide forty-six hiker-biker camps along the coast for cyclists. They generally are small and may be very crowded. No reservations are required. Large groups (eight or more cyclists) are required to camp in regular sites, which should be reserved ahead of time. Contact the state parks for details. Most state parks on the coast remain open year round. Only Mill Creek Campground, in Del Norte Coast Redwoods State Park, the farthest north, is closed after Labor Day. Future budget cuts may result in more closures; if planning an off-season tour, check ahead.

Campgrounds are not spaced evenly along the coast. In the northern and southern sections, long distances are covered between public campgrounds. In several areas, private campgrounds, and in one case a youth hostel, were chosen to fill in the gaps between the state parks. The strength of the group should be the deciding factor when determining whether the distance between campgrounds is too far. The rides through San Francisco and the Los Angeles area are extremely demanding. Plan ahead and use one of the many hostels, hotels, motels, and privately operated campgrounds along the coast if necessary. You may also shorten your city rides by calling a taxi or riding a bus across town.

In several locations, advance reservations are a necessity. Call ahead and reserve your campsites as soon as you feel certain about your itinerary. Campsites that must be reserved ahead of time are the hiker-biker site on the Marin Headlands overlooking the Golden Gate Bridge

Hiker-biker sites such as this one at Manchester State Beach are great places to meet other cyclists and share stories of the road.

(see Samuel P. Taylor State Park to Half Moon Bay State Beach), Malibu Beach RV, Colonial Inn Hostel at Huntington Beach, and Newport Dunes Aquatic Park in the Los Angeles area.

South of Santa Barbara, transients pose a major problem at all the state park campgrounds; this has forced many to close their hiker-biker sites. You will not be turned away from any state park campground; however, you may be required to pay full price for your site or end up sharing a site with the campground hosts.

The closest city to the northern California border is Brookings, Oregon (6 miles north). Greyhound bus, from Portland, San Francisco, or Eugene, is the only form of public transportation. Crescent City (21 miles south of the California–Oregon border) is the first major city on the California Coast. It can be reached by Greyhound bus or small commuter airplane. Eureka is the first city with train access.

An easy escape from the maze of city streets that make up southern California is LAX. The bike route passes right by the end of the airport runway.

At the true southern end of California, San Diego International Airport and the Amtrak station lie right on the bike route, and the bus station is only a few blocks away.

Oregon Border to Elk Prairie Campground (61.8 Miles)

Crossing the California state line may remind you of entering a foreign country. However, what initially appears to be an international customs station is simply an agricultural inspection center. Instead of pulling out a passport, you are required to pull out all fruit and vegetables from your touring bags and pockets. Any produce that might contaminate the native crops will be confiscated.

Once past the inspection station, the bicycle route escapes the busy and occasionally shoulderless US 101 and follows rural roads for the next 20 miles through Crescent City. You will pedal around farm fields, cattle ranches, a state penitentiary, and dense forests, and finally along a section of wild and beautiful coast.

At Crescent City, the route follows the rock-studded coast, passing one scenic vista after another, but missing the main shopping area. Potential stops include a visit to Battery Point Lighthouse, accessible at low tide only, and to the very small Redwood National Park Visitor Center for an introduction to the country ahead, home of some of the tallest trees in the world. The route then heads out of town past the fishing docks, where occasionally you can watch fishermen unload the heavily laden fishing boats.

South of Crescent City, ocean views give way to massive trees as the road climbs 1,100 feet over the triple summit of the Crescent City Hills. The road is narrow, truck traffic heavy, and shoulders nonexistent. Early mornings and weekends are best for traveling. To add a little melodrama and a lot of danger to the ride, the hills are frequently swathed in fog. Dress brightly and ride with a great deal of caution and courtesy.

After zooming down from the last summit of the Crescent City Hills, glide south past the Trees of Mystery, where an oversize Paul Bunyan and Babe, his giant blue ox, welcome visitors to the world's largest collection of redwood carvings.

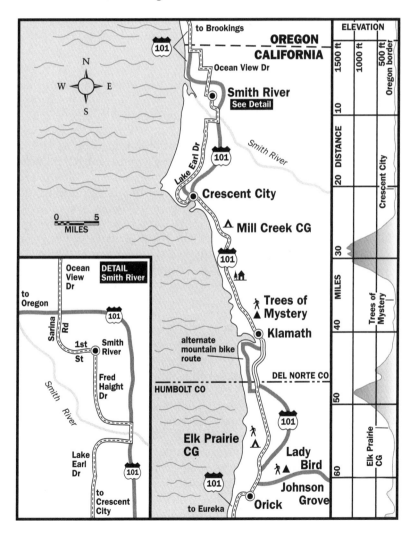

After several short miles of level travel, the highway climbs steeply over another hill, gaining nearly 900 feet in elevation. In the middle of this climb, the bike route leaves US 101 for a tour through the majestic redwood groves of Prairie Creek Redwoods State Park. Plan a stroll through this venerable forest before ending the day at Elk Prairie Campground, where a herd of Roosevelt elk grazes year round, occasionally wandering through the hiker-biker site. The elk may be there at any time, but are best viewed in the early morning and late afternoon when they are grazing. The park also has numerous hiking and mountain bike trails through the redwood forest, short trails to fern groves, longer trails to some of the world's tallest trees, and a 4-mile trail to a fern-covered canyon on the coast.

Mileage Log

0.0 (mp 46.49) Oregon–California border. Enter Del Norte County on US 101.

0.2 (mp 46.29) California fruit inspection. Cooperate, and help protect California agriculture.

0.4 (mp 46.09) Take the first left after the fruit inspection on Ocean View Dr. (County Rd. D5). Shoulders are nonexistent, but traffic is light and travel pleasant.

6.1 Cross US 101 and continue straight on the nearly level Sarina Rd., passing small cattle ranches and large lily fields.

6.6 Intersection; bend left on 1st St.

7.3 Enter the small community of Smith River. Smith River lies at the heart of Del Norte dairy country and is also known as the Easter Lily Capital of the World. The surrounding fields produce over 90 percent of the nation's Easter lily bulbs. In July, a festival celebrates the harvest.

7.7 Turn right on Fred Haight Dr. (County Rd. D4).

10.8 Turn right (south) on US 101. Cross the Smith River on a shoulderless bridge, then take the first right.

11.2 (mp 36.00) Exit right (west) off US 101 on Lake Earl Dr. (County Rd. D3), passing a small gas station and grocery store on the right. Follow Lake Earl Dr. to Crescent City. Traffic is light, and there is a good shoulder for over half the distance.

11.6 At an unmarked intersection, the route bends left and then heads past an old barn.

12.0 Cycle through the one-store town of Fort Dick.

12.5 Begin wide shoulder.

13.7 Pass a state penitentiary on the left; do not pick up hitchhikers in this area.

14.5 Pass a road to Kellogg Beach Coast Access on the right.

20.6 Major intersection; turn right (south) and ride the wide shoulder along Washington Blvd., beginning a scenic loop around the commercial center of Crescent City.

22.3 Turn left on Pebble Beach Rd. and ride along the coast. The shoulder is intermittent in the residential area.

23.8 Pebble Beach; beach access. Picnic tables are located at the next turnout.

24.3 Crescent City limits; supermarkets, campground, motels, and restaurants.

24.5 Coast access road descends to a rocky outcropping.

24.6 Brother Jonathan Vista Point overlooking a rock-studded bay to Battery Point Lighthouse. A city park with a bathroom is located just across the road.

24.9 Follow the coast road as it heads left up 5th St. for 1 block.

25.0 Go right on A St.

25.2 Cross Front St.

25.3 Turn left on Battery St. and ride through Crescent Park; covered picnic tables, restrooms, and a hollow redwood tree. *Side Trip:* Before turning left on Battery St., go straight 0.2 mile to the often-photographed Battery Point Vista and Lighthouse. Admission is charged to enter the lighthouse.

25.9 Turn left on H St.

26.0 Go right on Front St. and follow it to US 101. *Side Trip* to Redwood National Park Visitor Center and supermarkets: Follow Front St. for 3 blocks, then go left on K St. for 1 block to the visitor center. They can answer questions and suggest hikes through the giant trees. Supermarkets are found by continuing up K St. for 2 more blocks before heading right until you reach the store and laundry facilities.

27.1 (mp 26.20) Turn right on US 101.

27.6 (mp 25.80) Turnoff to the Citizens Dock on the right. When the fish are running, the area bustles with activity. US 101 widens to include a shoulder as the highway heads out of town.

29.8 (mp 23.60) Base of the Crescent City Hills. Fog often engulfs these hills, so wear bright clothing and strap on a light that is visible to cars coming up from behind. Southbound travelers have two lanes (no shoulder) on the climb; northbound travelers have only a single lane.

30.8 (mp 22.70) Crescent City Vista Point offers a grandstand view of the city before the road enters Del Norte Coast Redwoods State Park. Although the road passes some magnificent trees, the ride is too hectic to really enjoy their grandeur.

33.3 (mp 20.31) After a short descent, pass the turnoff to Del Norte Coast Redwoods State Park's Mill Creek Campground. A steep, 2.2-mile road descends over 600 feet to a quiet campground nestled at the base of some giant redwoods; hiker-biker sites and hot showers. Food supplies must be brought from Crescent City. This campground is open from early May to the end of September.

34.6 (mp 19.00) Summit of the first and highest of the Crescent City Hills, approximately 1,200 feet. Southbound traffic merges into a single lane for a quick descent. The passing lane reappears when the road begins to climb again.

35.9 (mp 17.70) Summit of second hill; only one more to go.

37.3 (mp 16.22) Top of the third and last summit. It's all downhill for the next 3.5 miles. Sliding and slumping of the roadway has created some very challenging riding in this area. Stay alert.

37.7 (mp 15.80) Damnation Creek trailhead; a scenic 4-mile hike to the beach.

40.1 (mp 13.4) Vista point with a view south.

40.9 (mp 12.53) The southern end of the Crescent City Hills is marked by a nice picnic area and sandy beach for relaxing. A narrow shoulder begins as the road skirts along a bay. On the left side of the highway is the Redwoods Hostel. The hostel is open March through November before 10:00 A.M. and after 5:00 P.M. For information or reservations call (707) 464-6101.

41.6 (mp 11.88) Coastal Trail access; restrooms and running water. The trail follows the coastline through Redwood National Park. The shoulder disappears.

42.6 (mp 10.86) Trees of Mystery and Klamath city limits. Good, rideable shoulders begin as you enter Klamath; grocery stores, fast food, and a commercial campground that accepts tents are just ahead.

45.5 (mp 8.15) Coast Trail Access; the trail, picnic area, and scenic vista are reached by a steep road.

48.3 (mp 5.36) Klamath shopping center is located left of US 101 and has the best food selection for miles.

49.3 (mp 4.42) Golden Bear Bridge. Two golden grizzly bears, California's state symbol, stand guard at the entrance of a pair of shoulderless bridges over the Klamath River. After the second bridge, the good shoulders return as US 101 climbs over another major set of hills. Coast Road *Alternate Route:* Cyclists touring on mountain bikes may be interested in a 14-mile tour along the coast (8 miles are gravel). The road starts at the southern end of the Klamath River bridges and follows the river to the coast, then swings south to loop back to US 101. This route is only mildly scenic.

52.4 (mp 1.20) Top of the first summit, approximately 500 feet in elevation.

53.4 (mp 0.0 and 134.89) Turn off US 101 on Newton B. Drury Scenic

Elk are commonly viewed lounging in the meadow during the morning and evening hours at the aptly named Elk Prairie Campground, in Prairie Creek Redwoods State Park.

Parkway, a Scenic Byway through the redwoods. At the base of the highway exit, go right and head uphill on a good shoulder. Leave Del Norte County and enter Humboldt County. Across the county line, the highway climbs uphill for several more miles to an elevation of 900 feet.

54.4 (mp 134.29) The Coast Road Alternate Route loops back to the bike route.

54.6 (mp 134.19) Enter Prairie Creek Redwoods State Park. Continuing uphill, the shoulder narrows as the heavily shaded highway passes under towering redwood groves.

55.1 (mp 133.67) Summit; it's all downhill to Elk Prairie Campground. The road passes several memorial groves with short (0.5 mile or less) trails into the forest. Stop at least once to look at the trees.

60.7 (mp 128.40) Cork Screw Tree turnout. Follow a short path to a twisted and deformed tree standing tall and proud.

61.1 (mp 127.96) Big Tree. Exit left (east) off US 101 to a parking lot and walk to a tree over 300 feet tall and 17.7 feet in diameter.

61.8 (mp 127.24) Elk Prairie Campground; hiker-biker sites, warm showers, roaming elk, visitor center, and trails through the redwoods to the beach. The hiker-biker site has food storage boxes to protect your food and loose gear from curious bears and marauding raccoons. If time allows, take an extra day to explore the park. The trail to the beach and fern canyon is a must. Elk may be seen on the beach in the mornings and late afternoons.

Elk Prairie Campground to Eureka KOA (46.3 Miles)

With the first major set of California hills behind you, the ride from Prairie Creek Redwoods State Park to Eureka will seem relatively easy. This should leave you plenty of time for side trips, exploring, or bicycle maintenance at the excellent repair shops in Arcata or Eureka.

This section sees the evolution of US 101 from a narrow country road into a busy four-lane freeway. Riding on the freeway is legal (unless otherwise posted), and, thanks to a wide shoulder, generally very safe. However, the noise and dirt are fatiguing, so be sure to take advantage

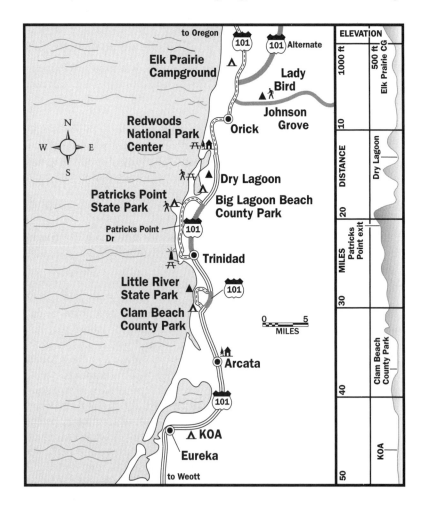

of the two scenic escape routes off the freeway, and all the side trips. The first suggested side trip is to the beautiful Lady Bird Johnson Grove. The grove has a mile-long loop trail through a forest of ferns and mammoth redwoods. The access road to the grove is very steep; hide the touring bags at the bottom, if possible.

The second stop of the day is at the Redwoods National Park Center, located just south of Orick. The displays are interesting, the building well heated, and the local population of banana slugs simply amazing.

Beyond the National Park Center, US 101 heads around Stone Lagoon and Dry Lagoon (part of Humboldt Lagoons State Park). Winter storms can cause the lagoons to overflow and create deep channels where they empty into the ocean. To date, the surf has always repaired the lagoons. This is a very scenic section of highway.

Near Patricks Point, US 101 widens into a freeway with broad shoulders and noisy traffic. After a couple of miles on the freeway, the bike route escapes to back roads and parallels the coast to the next "must" stop, at Patricks Point State Park. The park is situated on a rugged point overlooking the ocean. Trails crisscross the bluffs and climb to breathtaking views from sheer cliffs. The driftwood-covered beaches are fun to explore. Seals and sea lions live on offshore sea stacks; their constant barking echoes throughout the park.

In Trinidad, visit the Trinidad Memorial Lighthouse with its giant two-ton fog bell before heading south on US 101 to more excellent views of the coast. Leave the freeway (US 101) for a second time at Little River State Beach and cycle along the beach road for a peaceful 1.8 miles before returning to the hectic rush of the highway. When riding on the freeway, use extra caution at the busy exits and entrances as you near Arcata and Eureka.

The day's ride ends a couple of miles north of Eureka at the KOA, the only campground in the area with a special site just for cyclists. Although a discount fee is offered to cyclists, it still isn't cheap. However, most other campgrounds in the Eureka area are designed for trailers; the managers generally do not accept tents. Alternate options include hotels and numerous bed and breakfasts.

Mileage Log

0.0 Head south from Elk Prairie Campground on the Newton B. Drury Scenic Parkway. Elk can be spotted grazing in the open fields or resting under crab apple trees in the morning.

1.1 (mp 126.25) Newton B. Drury Scenic Parkway ends. Go right and return to US 101.

2.9 (mp 124.4) Lost Man Creek Mountain Bike Trail access on left.

5.1 (mp 122.31) *Side Trip* to Lady Bird Johnson Grove (and restrooms):

Lady Bird Johnson Grove is truly stunning all the time, but it is exceptionally beautiful on foggy mornings.

Turn left (east) off US 101 and cycle 2.3 miles up a narrow and very steep road to the 1-mile nature loop trail. This side trip is a must in May and early June when the rhododendrons are in bloom.

5.6 (mp 121.87) Enter the town of Orick. Grocery stores (the last before Patricks Point State Park), restaurants, motels, and an assortment of tourist shops.

8.3 (mp 119.17) ***Side Trip*** to the Redwoods National Park Center and picnic area: The center, located 0.2 mile off the highway, has heated restrooms, warm water, beach access, and information. Beyond the park center, US 101 returns to its typical up-and-down motion, with little to no shoulder. The highway crosses a narrow sandspit between the ocean and Freshwater Lagoon, where the county provides a large parking area on the west side of the road. A tents-only area is located at the south end; no water.

10.2 (mp 117.38) Turnoff to Stone Lagoon, part of Humboldt Lagoons State Park.

12.3 (mp 115.28) Humboldt Lagoons State Park Visitor Center; a small building with camping information. The tables outside offer an opportunity to picnic along the shores of Stone Lagoon. The shoulder ends here, and riders should give themselves a generous amount of room to keep cars and trucks from trying to squeeze by on this narrow, rough road.

13.3 (mp 114.28) Turnoff to Dry Lagoon; beach access, restrooms, a lot of driftwood, but no water. Located 1 mile west of US 101. Beyond the park access, US 101 climbs over two small hills and then descends to parallel Big Lagoon before widening into a four-lane freeway with wide shoulders.

19.6 (mp 108.00) Big Lagoon Beach County Park exit; scenic campsites near the beach, water, and restrooms. No hiker-biker campsites.

21.3 (mp 106.30) Exit US 101 on Patricks Point Dr. The road is narrow and shoulderless but has less traffic than US 101. Watch for sections of rough road and occasional short, steep pitches. After passing motels and an RV campground, the road slips along steep, open hillsides overlooking the ocean.

24.0 Patricks Point State Park entrance; hiker-biker sites, hot showers, beach access, and hiking trails. *Side Trip:* To visit the park, take a right at the entrance and descend to the tollbooth. Purchase an inexpensive park map, then follow the road toward Agate Beach. (To reach the hiker-biker site, take a left turn off Agate Beach Rd. toward Wedding Rock and follow that road to its end.)

27.5 Trinidad, a small town with a grocery store and fast-food restaurants. *Side Trip:* Before returning to US 101, make a short 0.5-mile side trip to Trinidad Memorial Lighthouse. Follow Main St. to its end, then turn left on Trinity St. for 0.2 mile. A state beach with picnic tables, restroom, running water, and beach access is located off Stage Coach Rd.

27.6 (mp 100.50) At Trinidad, return to US 101. Shoulders disappear on bridges.

31.5 (mp 97.13) Exit US 101, following signs to Little River State Beach for the second scenic escape. This is a confusing exit; watch for the truck weight station, then take the road that goes above it. At the end of the exit, go right and follow the state park road, which parallels US 101 for 2.3 miles, passing several beach access areas. Return to US 101 at Clam Beach County Park; camping, restrooms, no water.

33.3 (mp 95.70) Little River State Beach Rd. returns to US 101.

34.6 (mp 94.38) Vista Point, overlooking the Clam Beach-Little River area; no facilities, and no access for northbound travelers.

39.5 (mp 89.77) Mad River Bridge; little shoulder and no sidewalk.

40.4 (mp 89.00) Arcata. US 101 hurries riders through town; use extreme caution at all exits and entrances. Those wishing to visit stores, a bike shop, or Humboldt State University, or simply to escape the hassles and dangers of riding a freeway through town, should exit the freeway here. As a bonus, riders who go through town will see some carefully maintained Victorian buildings.

42.1 (mp 87.30) Humboldt State University and City Center exit. Once past the center of Arcata, US 101 swings around Arcata Bay. Be prepared for strong winds as the level road sweeps across the open countryside.

46.3 (mp 83.40) The KOA campground lies on the left (east) side of US 101, requiring a hazardous crossing of this busy highway. Be patient and wait for a break in the traffic. The campground has a small store, endless hot water for showers, small cabins to rent if the weather is bad, and laundry facilities. Call ahead for information or reservations: (707) 822-4243.

Eureka KOA to Marine Garden Club Grove (51.2 Miles)

The day begins with a tour through Eureka. This is a beautiful old Victorian town with meticulously tended period buildings. The bike route leaves US 101 at the entrance to the central business corridor and follows a route through a residential area, passing fifty or more masterpieces of Victorian design. If that's not enough, you can take a short side trip to the ornate Carson Mansion and the Old Town area. Fort Humboldt, at the southern end of town, has an excellent indoor and outdoor logging museum.

Beyond Eureka, the route rejoins US 101, which returns to its freeway status at the southern end of town. The shoulder is wide, the road nearly level, and miles speed by. If freeway riding is not your idea of a good way to see the country, take advantage of three alternate routes. The first alternate route is a loop through the town of Loleta, where you may want to stop at the Loleta cheese factory and try a sample or two. The second alternate route swings out to the Victorian tourist town of Ferndale and then follows farm roads back to the freeway. This variation will add 11 extra miles to the day's total. The little town of Scotia provides the third escape. In Scotia, visit the Pacific Lumber Company Museum. While there, pick up a free pass for a self-guided walking tour through the lumber mill and factory, which takes you on a catwalk over-

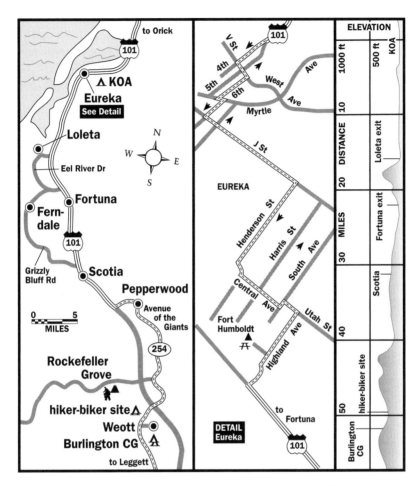

looking the largest redwood mill in the world (open weekdays only).

The scenic portion of the ride begins when the route exits the freeway at the start of the Avenue of the Giants. This road is a section of the Old Coast Highway, which winds through a narrow corridor of majestic redwoods. Explore the numerous groves, hike the trails, and spend some time pondering these magnificent trees. The avenue is narrow and generally deeply shaded. Wear bright, visible clothing.

The day ends at the Burlington Campground hiker-biker site, located 1.8 miles south of the main camp area among the giant redwoods of the Marine Garden Club Grove. The site is primitive, without hot water or showers, but the scenic layout more than compensates for any inconveniences. (Showers may be taken at the campground.)

Mileage Log

0.0 (mp 83.40) Starting at the Eureka KOA, the first challenge of the day is to cross the northbound side of the freeway to rejoin the southbound traffic on the west side. Once across US 101, head south over a level plain along the edge of Arcata Bay. Riding is easy on the wide shoulder.

2.4 (mp 81.1) Enter Eureka.

3.6 (mp 79.95) The narrow bridge over Eureka Slough, with sidewalks but no shoulders, marks the entrance to downtown Eureka. Once across the bridge, the freeway ends and the bike route bypass of Eureka begins. Eureka has a supermarket and bike shop located near the bike route at the south side of town.

4.1 (mp 79.45) Turn left (east) on V St. for 2 blocks to 6th St. **Side Trip** to Carson Mansion and Old Town: Take 6th St. to M St. and head right (west) for 3 blocks to the mansion. Cyclists must be content with viewing the structure from the outside; the mansion is now an exclusive men's club. You can begin a tour of the Old Town from the mansion. Cycle west on 2nd St. to C. St., go left for 1 block, and head back up 3rd St. to M St.

5.0 Turn left on J St. and follow it for 1.3 miles to Henderson St.

6.3 Go right on Henderson St. for 1.4 miles through a commercial section of town. Look for the bike shop in this area. Eureka has spent time and money making this road appealing to cyclists; a bike triggers the stoplights as easily as a car.

7.4 When Henderson bends, take a left on Central Ave.

7.7 Jog left to Utah St. for 0.1 mile.

7.8 Turn right on Highland Ave. and continue straight to US 101.

8.3 Fort Humboldt State Historic Park, a highly recommended stop. Restrooms, running water, and picnic tables, as well as an indoor/outdoor logging museum and excellent views of Eureka from the old fort site.

8.4 Go left on US 101 (known as Broadway in this section of town).

9.0 (mp 75.5) Freeway and good shoulder resume as US 101 leaves Eureka and heads through open country along Humboldt Bay. Use considerable caution when cycling past the exits and entrances to this busy freeway.

11.9 (mp 72.5) Fields Landing exit. On the east side of the freeway is a commercial area with a grocery store.

13.4 (mp 71.02) College of the Redwoods exit.

16.4 (mp 68.0) First Loleta exit, and start of the first alternate route. Beyond the exit, the freeway spends the next 1.4 miles climbing a steep hill. The road broadens into three lanes with no shoulders. **Alternate Route** through Loleta: At the end of the off ramp, turn right (west) on Hookton Rd., then take the first left on Eel River Dr. If the Loleta cheese factory is on your itinerary, turn off Eel River Dr. at Main St. and ride through the center of town. Go left on Loleta Dr. and ride over the railroad tracks. The alternate route returns to the freeway at the Ferndale exit.

18.2 (mp 65.8) Top of the hill; freeway narrows to two lanes, with a shoulder on the southbound side. The northbound corridor widens to three lanes without shoulders.

19.6 (mp 64.59) Ferndale exit. ***Alternate Route*** through Ferndale begins here. From the exit, go straight on a shoulderless road. In 0.7 mile go right and cross the narrow Eel River Bridge. Once across, the road widens to include a shoulder as it heads south through farmlands. At 4.7 miles from US 101 reach Ferndale. Ride through town and explore (on foot or wheels) some of the side streets to

Carson Mansion, in Eureka, is the most famous of the many examples of ornate Victorian architecture found along this section of the Redwood Coast.

see the showpiece houses that have made this area famous. When you are ready to continue, head east from the town center on Washington St. After 0.5 mile, take a right on Lincoln St. for 0.4 mile to Grizzly Bluff Rd. Head east through the farm fields, where there are more dogs and chickens than cars on the road. Climb a steep bluff 7 miles from Ferndale and at 12.9 miles return to US 101.

21.6 (mp 62.6) This is the halfway point between Vancouver, British Columbia, and the Mexican border.

22.2 (mp 62.0) Fortuna exit. US 101 passes the west edge of town; the supermarkets are 1 mile east of the freeway.

27.2 (mp 57.0) Van Duzen River Bridge marks the start of the gradual ascent to the redwood forests. The bridge is narrow, with little shoulder and no sidewalk.

30.4 (mp 53.80) Rio Dell exit; a readily accessible market is located on the east side of the freeway. Ferndale Alternate Route returns to US 101 here.

32.2 (mp 51.97) Scotia exit and the third opportunity to briefly escape the freeway. Scotia is a company town and the company is the Pacific Lumber mill, which claims to be the largest redwood mill in the world. Summer visitors may tour the mill and factory, or browse through the logging museum (weekdays only, closed daily from 10:30 A.M. to 1:00 P.M.). Off-season visitors may view the outdoor park section of the museum and stock up on food at the grocery store. To continue south, parallel the freeway, cycling past the lumberyard, and return to the freeway when the road enters Pacific Lumber land.

37.1 (mp 47.0) Vista Point exit. Gaze over the Eel River from a large parking area.

38.1 (mp 46.0) Exit US 101 and go left to ride the Avenue of the Giants, a narrow and winding road with no shoulder. Traffic varies from moderate to heavy. **Side Trip** to the Pacific Lumber Demonstration Forest: At the base of the freeway exit, go right for 0.2 mile to the parking area: water, restrooms, picnic tables, and nature trail. This is a great chance to compare a logged redwood forest with the trees on the Avenue of the Giants.

38.2 Enter Humboldt Redwoods State Park. Don't strain your neck looking up at all the trees. Pick up an Auto Tour map on the right side of the road.

40.1 Enter Pepperwood; small tourist shops but no grocery store. Just south of town two short nature trails, Drury Trail and Percy French Loop, wander through redwood groves.

43.2 Immortal Tree, growing on the east side of the highway, shows marks of floods, fire, ax, and wind. The tree is a testimonial to the incredible ability of redwoods to survive.

44.7 Redcrest; a small tourist town whose principal attraction is the Eternal Tree House. In the tree house (which is actually a hollowed stump) is a register where you can check the number of international visitors this area receives. Restaurant but no grocery store.

48.6 No. 8 on the Auto Tour is a rest area with picnic tables and chemical toilets.

48.7 Avenue of the Giants brushes along the edge of US 101. *Side Trip:* Take Bull Creek Flats Rd., which branches right and ducks under the freeway. This road offers an excellent ride through tall stands of ivy-wrapped trees. At 1.3 miles, take a short walk through Rockefeller Grove before heading back the way you came.

48.9 Turnoff to Founders Grove. The grove and 0.5-mile nature loop are located just 200 feet left (east) of the Avenue of the Giants. They provide an excellent introduction to the life of the forest. Giant redwoods, notably the Foundation Tree and fallen Dyerville Giant, are located only minutes from the road.

51.2 Marine Garden Club Grove of Humboldt Redwoods State Park and hiker-biker camp; picnic tables, running water, restrooms, tall trees, and great swimming holes in the Eel River. A grocery store is located 0.2 mile south at the small town of Weott. Showers for the camp are located 1.7 miles south at Burlington Campground.

Marine Garden Club Grove to Standish–Hickey State Recreation Area (48 Miles)

South of Marine Garden Club Grove, the impressive grandeur of the Avenue of the Giants continues as you cycle through beautiful stands of redwood, such as the Garden Club of America Grove, where you may quietly enjoy some of nature's most regal handiwork. Along with the natural wonders are the manmade "attractions," such as a drive-through tree and one-log house.

At the end of the Avenue of the Giants you must leave the quiet and shade and return to US 101. This busy highway is followed through the narrow South Fork Eel River Valley. Redwood groves disappear immediately and are soon replaced by dry, open hillsides. Temperatures soar, rising as much as 15 degrees away from the protective shade of the redwoods. Be sure water bottles are full and sunglasses handy.

The Avenue of the Giants is not the end of the redwoods. Just 14 miles south lies Richardson Grove State Park. This narrow band of redwoods grows in an area otherwise bare of the tall trees. Trails in the park climb from cool redwood groves to sun-dried ridge tops and open viewpoints. For a quick introduction to the park, a short nature trail provides insight to the life cycle of the redwoods and their ability to survive through infestation, fire, and flood.

Beyond Richardson Grove, the South Fork Eel River Valley widens and then narrows again, with forested hillsides and an occasional redwood grove. The road twists and rolls, passing right over Confusion Hill, an area of unexplained mysteries that can be viewed for a small fee.

This short day ends at Standish-Hickey State Park Recreation Area, a delightful place to spend an afternoon swimming, hiking, or exploring redwood groves.

Only one alternate route on this portion of the ride offers relief from the noise and dirt of US 101. This alternate route follows Percey Cook Valley Rd. (Highway 271) for 5.7 miles, paralleling the hot and dry US

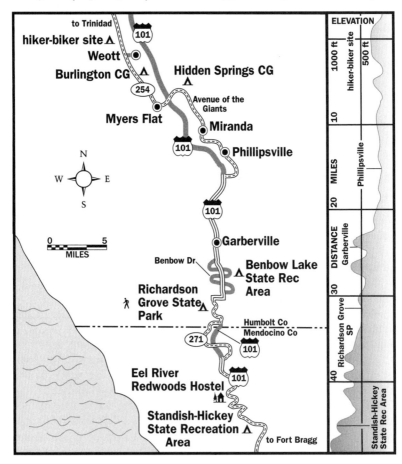

101 under the partial shade of deciduous trees.

Throughout this section, US 101 is very busy, with a seemingly end-less stream of trucks, cars, and oversize tourist vehicles. For most of the distance, the highway is wide—almost a freeway—with broad shoulders. Unfortunately, the road narrows in several sections, and four lanes of traffic squeeze onto an appallingly narrow, shoulderless, two-lane road that twists and bends with the narrow valley. Trucks and cars rarely slow down when the road narrows and cyclists are forced to fend for themselves. To be on the safe side, start this ride early in the morning and ride defensively. When you have to share the road with large ve-hicles in both lanes, take the coward's way out, pull over to the side, wait for a break in the traffic, and live to tell about it.

Mileage Log

0.0 From the hiker-biker camp at the Marine Garden Club Grove of Humboldt Redwoods State Park, cycle south on the Avenue of the Giants.

1.7 Pass Burlington Campground on the left (east); water, showers, and a small visitor center.

3.5 Garden Club of America Grove; restrooms and running water. A short path and a bridge lead across the South Fork of the Eel River to a large redwood grove on the opposite side.

4.7 Williams Grove day-use area; picnic tables, restrooms, running water, giant trees, and river access. Open summer only. Williams Grove has free admission for cyclists (but not for cars). Overnight camping is allowed—for self-contained RVs only.

5.4 Myers Flat. Like all towns along the Avenue of the Giants, this one has a touch of tinsel in its rustic setting. Myers Flat's main attraction, besides grocery stores, cafes, and Laundromats, is a drive- or ride-through tree. Admission is charged.

6.7 Turnoff to Hidden Springs Campground; hiker-biker area, hot show-ers, and trails through the redwoods. Open summer only.

11.4 Leave Humboldt Redwoods State Park.

11.7 Miranda; groceries and fast food.

15.4 Franklin K. Lane Grove; picnic area, shady trees, running water, and restrooms.

15.6 Phillipsville; grocery store and restaurants. If intrigued, visit a house made from a single log.

18.5 Avenue of the Giants (Highway 254) ends. Return to US 101, a four-laner. Shoulders vary from several feet wide to nonexistent for the next 10 miles as the highway climbs two distinct hills. North-bound cyclists exit US 101 here (mp 17.5) to follow the Avenue of the Giants.

Towering redwood trees cast deep shadows across the narrow road through the Avenue of the Giants.

23.8 (mp 13.30) First Garberville exit. If looking for food and groceries, continue on to the second exit.

24.7 (mp 11.29) Second Garberville exit; grocery stores.

26.7 (mp 8.58) Benbow Lake State Recreation Area exit. Benbow Lake Campground is located 1.1 miles from the exit; hiker-biker campsite, running water, swimming, hiking trails, boat rentals, and ranger-led "hikes" in canoes. No hot showers.

28.6 (mp 5.22) US 101 narrows to a two-lane highway here, and shoulders disappear.

32.5 (mp 2.03) Enter Richardson Grove State Park, a welcome refuge from the hot, dry surrounding countryside. US 101 narrows a bit more.

32.8 (mp 1.73) Richardson Grove State Park campground entrance; hiker-biker area, hot showers, hiking trails, nature loop, small store, and swimming holes in the South Fork Eel River. A small grocery store is located 1 mile south.

33.4 (mp 1.18) Leave Richardson Grove State Park and the shaded coolness of the redwoods as US 101 returns to a wide, fast-moving, four-lane highway. Shoulders return to a comfortable size, but not for long.

33.9 (mp 0.68) Pass a private campground and small grocery store.

34.3 (mp 0.35) Percey Cook Valley *Alternate Route:* Exit US 101 on Highway 271 and pedal south for the next 3.4 miles along the South Fork of the Eel River. When the road divides, go left under the freeway, then right for another 2.3 miles before returning to US 101.

34.7 (mp 0.0 and 104.2) Leave Humboldt County and enter Mendocino County.

37.7 (mp 101.47) Highway 271 passes under US 101, providing a second access to the alternate route.

40.1 (mp 99.1) Highway 271 returns to US 101 as the road enters a narrow section of the valley. The steep hillsides slide frequently. Most of the shoulders have been carried off downhill somewhere. (Shoulders come and go until approximately 0.5 mile before Standish-Hickey State Park Recreation Area.)

42.5 (mp 99.45) Confusion Hill. Strange magnetic forces cause unexplained mysteries. For a small fee you can view these phenomena. (The forces may have affected the mileposts in this area).

42.9 (mp 99.1) Treehouse and small cafe. Last chance to see a hollowed-out, but still living, redwood tree.

45.3 (mp 96.42) Frankland and Bess Smith Redwood Grove; running water and restrooms. A small oasis of cool shade in an otherwise hot river valley.

48.0 (mp 94.00) Standish-Hickey State Recreational Area. Everything for the cyclist—hiker-biker campsite, hot showers, a lake for swimming, and trails for hiking. Groceries are available at the small store and deli across US 101, or 1 mile south in Leggett.

Standish–Hickey State Recreation Area to MacKerricher Beach State Park (39.4 Miles)

Just south of Standish-Hickey State Recreation Area, the bicycle route leaves US 101 and heads back to the coast on California's famous Highway 1. The highway starts out by climbing over the much-maligned Leggett Hill, which, at nearly 2,000 feet, is the highest point on the Pacific Coast Bike Route. Cyclists talk about Leggett Hill up and down the coast, increasing its proportions as they go. Contrary to popular rumor, abandoned touring bags do not line the road, nor are there graves of cyclists who did not make it.

From the summit of Leggett Hill, gaze out over the miles of forested hills and deep valleys where US 101 can be seen rushing south toward San Francisco. To the west lies the Pacific Ocean, sometimes shimmering in the sun but, more often, shrouded in a thick cover of fog.

The descent from Leggett Hill is exhilarating and much too short. The road almost reaches sea level before beginning another steep climb over 690-foot Rockport Hill. The descent of this second hill leads to the ocean and stunning viewpoints of a coastline studded with sea stacks, which look more like giant fangs than the friendly, offshore bird rookeries they are.

The day ends at MacKerricher Beach State Park. This is a wonderful place to explore, with fascinating tide pools, harbor seals sunbathing on offshore rocks, a small lake for swimming, and an abandoned log-haul route for riding or walking right on the shore.

Standish-Hickey State Park Recreation Area to MacKerricher Beach State Park is a section of changes. When the Coast Bike Route leaves US

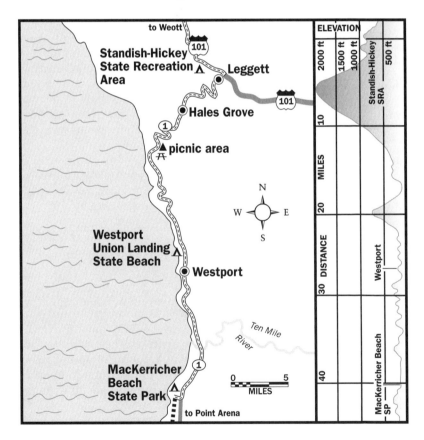

101, it also leaves behind the drier inland climate, where summer temperatures average from 80 to 100 degrees. (On the coast, summer temperatures average between 50 and 60 degrees.) Vegetation changes from forest to windswept grasslands. Much of the commercial traffic is left behind, and road quality changes from quasi-freeway to a uniformly narrow two lanes, with little or no shoulder.

Riding on narrow, winding roads is hazardous. It's important to ride in single file and to always stay on the correct (right) side of the road. Never climb by switchbacking. Never cut corners when descending. Wear bright clothing, and be conscious of the motorists coming up from behind.

Between Standish-Hickey State Park Recreation Area and MacKerricher Beach State Park, stores and restaurants are few, so plan food stops ahead. Small grocery stores may be found in Leggett, in Westport, and just before MacKerricher Beach State Park.

Mileage Log

0.0 (mp 93.87) Leaving Standish-Hickey State Recreation Area, follow US 101 south. The two-lane highway is narrow with a variable shoulder of up to 2 feet. Terrain is rolling, mountainous, and dry.

1.5 (mp 91.20 and mp 105.21) Exit US 101 onto Highway 1.

1.6 (mp 105.11) Leggett; the grocery store is located 0.1 mile left (south) on Drive Through Tree Rd.; 0.2 mile south on the same road is the Drive Through Tree. Admission is charged. After Leggett, Highway 1 descends rapidly 0.3 mile to cross the South Fork Eel River. Expect some logging truck traffic.

2.1 (mp 104.61) The ascent of Leggett Hill begins at 1100 feet. You see, it is not so hard.

5.6 (mp 101.10) Leggett Hill summit, elevation 1950 feet. The road traverses the ridge crest for 0.8 mile and then drops steeply through heavy forest. This is a great descent, but don't get too enthusiastic. Large potholes are often hidden in deep shade at the corners.

9.4 (mp 97.32) Hales Grove. The road levels for a mile, then resumes its descent.

15.2 (mp 90.87) Highway 1 takes the name of Shoreline Highway as it heads south.

15.4 (mp 90.60) Cottoneva Creek marks the end of Leggett Hill.

17.0 (mp 88.95) Louisiana-Pacific Picnic Area; tables, restrooms, and a small demonstration forest with a short nature walk.

18.2 (mp 87.85) Recross Cottoneva Creek and pass the abandoned community of Rockport, tucked around the base of Rockport Hill. Beyond the creek, the road climbs steeply. The highway is narrow, the hillsides clearcut.

19.7 (mp 86.38) Rockport Hill summit, elevation 690 feet. No views or turnouts, just a wonderful descent.

21.5 (mp 84.59) The crossing of Hardy Creek marks the end of Rockport Hill.

21.7 (mp 84.39) A small gravel turnout is the first of many spectacular vantage points overlooking the Pacific Ocean. Sea stacks, arch rocks, nesting birds, and barking seals may be seen and heard. Shortly after returning to the coast, the road broadens to include a 2- to 3-foot shoulder.

23.5 (mp 82.59) Vista Point.

23.9 (mp 82.10) Westport Union Landing State Beach and viewpoint; restrooms, ocean views, camping, and water (not potable). Beach access and picnic tables are located at the south end of the park. The highway parallels the state beach for the next mile.

25.4 (mp 80.70) Dehaven Creek day-use parking area; picnic tables and pit toilets.

Highway 1 south of Westport weaves its way along steep hillsides to magnificent views of rolling meadows and a turbulent coastline.

25.7 (mp 80.40) The shoulder ends, marking the start of a 16-mile section of narrow, winding road. On foggy or rainy days, wear bright clothing and use blinking lights to increase your visibility.

26.2 (mp 79.90) Wages Beach Creek Camp (private).

27.3 (mp 77.71) Westport, a small town with a grocery store and restaurant. Beyond town, Highway 1 traverses grassy hillsides overlooking the ocean. The hills give way to steep cliffs and the road clings to the scenic coastline, exposed to the wind and elements, occasionally dipping into small coves and then climbing steeply back to the open cliffs.

30.1 (mp 74.01) Vista Point; just a parking lot.

35.1 (mp 68.85) Ten Mile River Bridge ushers in a 0.5-mile section of good shoulder.

39.1 (mp 64.87) Two small grocery stores, the last before MacKerricher Beach State Park and Fort Bragg.

39.4 (mp 64.67) MacKerricher Beach State Park; hiker-biker site, running water, and hot showers. From December through April, this is an excellent place to watch migrating gray whales. Large grocery stores are available 2.7 miles south in Fort Bragg, which is reached by a scenic ride along the beach on the old logging haul road.

MacKerricher Beach State Park to Manchester State Beach
(42.1 Miles)

Although short, this very scenic ride is strenuous. Highway 1 hugs the rugged coastline, dropping in and then climbing out of the many narrow canyons that cut the steep cliffs. Some sections of the road are without shoulders. Traffic is generally light, except on midsummer weekends.

Although this is a short ride, you can easily devote an entire day to exploring this section of the coast. The day starts with a ride through Fort Bragg, a lumber town whose main attraction is the Skunk Railroad. The not-so-charming name of "Skunk" was derived from the smell of the original engines, which have been replaced with a less pungent variety. The train travels east through farmlands and redwood country to end at the town of Willits. Also in Fort Bragg are a large logging museum, a tree nursery, and Noyo Harbor, which is the largest working harbor between Eureka and San Francisco. During the Fourth of July weekend, the harbor is home of the world's largest salmon barbecue.

A few miles south, at Jughandle State Reserve, you can study a half-million years of the earth's history by walking a nature trail up an ecological staircase with five distinct terraces, each about 100 feet higher and 100,000 years older than the last. From the ocean's edge, the nature trail heads inland through changing vegetation, starting with north coastal prairie, moving into coast redwood and Douglas fir forests, and ending near a pygmy forest. The entire 500,000 years is covered in a 5-mile round trip. A shorter 0.5-mile loop covers the most recent history—about 100,000 years worth.

Continuing south, the route passes Mendocino, a quaint New England–style village perched on a cliff overlooking the Pacific Ocean. The village was founded in 1852 and has been beautifully maintained ever since.

Russian Gulch and Van Damme State Parks north and south of

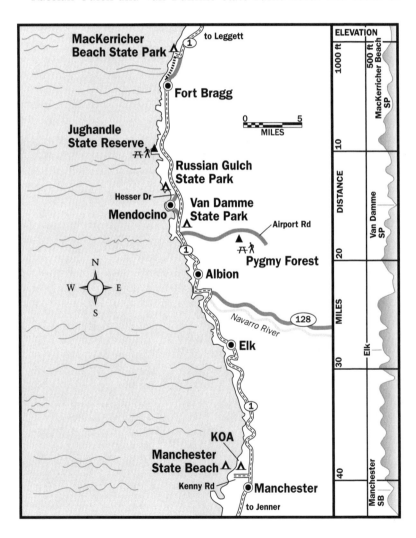

Mendocino offer camping with hiker-biker sites, trails to a couple of waterfalls at Russian Gulch, and a pygmy forest at Van Damme. The pygmy forest, where 70-year-old trees are barely knee-high, can also be reached by a side trip off Highway 1.

Mileage Log

0.0 Leaving MacKerricher Beach State Park, do not return to Highway 1. Instead, descend toward the beach, passing a small lake. Cycle under an overpass, then immediately turn left and head up the gravel access to an old logging haul road. Head south on the haul route, passing two gates. The road is rough, but the views are excellent as you parallel the coast for the next 2 miles.

2.2 Bridge ahead is closed. Return to Highway 1 by riding through a public parking lot located next to a band of tall, wind-swept trees. Back on Highway 1, head right on the busy road, which descends to cross Pudding Creek, then climbs to enter Fort Bragg. The large lumber mill located in town explains the thundering truck traffic. The largest attraction in Fort Bragg is the Skunk Railroad. For rates and schedules, turn right (west) on Laurel St. to the station. The redwood museum (free) is adjacent to the Skunk Railroad. A large supermarket and well-stocked bike shop are located at the southern end of town on the east side of Highway 1.

4.4 (mp 60.48) Noyo Harbor, to the left (east) of Highway 1.

5.8 (mp 59.08) Mendocino Coast Botanical Gardens. For a fee, you may walk down paths lined with rhododendrons and through a fern canyon.

7.9 (mp 56.00) Jughandle State Reserve; restrooms, picnic tables, water, beach access, and nature trail through the ecological staircase.

8.8 (mp 55.10) Vista point with a view of the coast and the Casper Creek Bridge. This bridge, like most on Highway 1, has no shoulder.

10.8 (mp 53.2) Russian Gulch State Park; hiker-biker sites and hot showers. A 2.5-mile bicycle path up a narrow gulch leads to a 1.5-mile loop hiking trail to the Russian Gulch Falls. On the beach is a spectacular "Punch Bowl."

12.5 (mp 51.5) Mendocino Headlands State Park exit and start of a scenic **Alternate Route** along the ocean's edge through the state park and the tourist town of Mendocino. Exit Highway 1. After 0.5 mile turn right on Hesser Dr. for a quiet ride along the rocky cliffs. The wide-open state park makes a nice lunch stop; watch for seals bobbing in the surf. Continue to follow the coastline through the quaint town of Mendocino, with its grocery stores, delis, bakeries, craft shops, art galleries, and bookstores. The road will return you to Highway 1.

13.0 (mp 50.50) Mendocino Headlands State Park scenic Alternate Route rejoins Highway 1.

13.2 (mp 50.37) Big River State Beach; beach access only.

13.5 (mp 50.00) Commercial campground on the left.

13.7 (mp 49.84) Vista point. The best way to savor the New England flavor of Mendocino is to look at it from a distance.

15.2 (mp 48.34) Town of Little River; grocery stores.

15.5 (mp 48.03) Van Damme Beach State Park; hiker-biker sites, water, beach access, and hiking and biking trails to a fern canyon and pygmy forest. (The forest may also be reached by road as described below.) To reach the park, you must make a left (east) turn across Highway 1.

16.0 (mp 48.55) Highway 1 becomes narrow and winding with a minimal shoulder that occasionally disappears altogether. *Side Trip* to a pygmy forest: Exit left (east) off Highway 1 on Airport Rd. A

After turning off Highway 1, Kenny Road is followed past open pastures to Manchester State Beach Campground.

moderately steep climb of 2.7 miles leads to a nature loop, located on the left (north) side of the road.

19.3 (mp 44.07) Albion; last grocery stores for 10 miles. Highway 1 heads through open coastal grasslands. At about the 22-mile point, the road descends steeply, with some tight corners, along the canyon walls of the Navarro River.

23.1 (mp 40.28) Intersection of Highway 1 and Highway 128. Turn right on Highway 1 and cross the Navarro River (Highway 128 heads east to Cloverdale and US 101). Shift to your lowest gear and wish for a lower one. The mile-long ascent out of the river valley is steep and hot. A sign along the road reading NARROW WINDING ROAD FOR THE NEXT 21 MILES indicates that road conditions will remain the same for some time to come.

28.7 (mp 34.05) Enter the town of Elk, the last chance to pick up groceries before Manchester State Beach. Beyond Elk, the road descends to cross a small creek and then climbs back up with a series of tight, steep switchbacks. Take heart; this short climb is probably the steepest on the entire Pacific Coast.

37.5 (mp 25.27) Vista point with ocean views.

41.4 (mp 21.4) Manchester State Beach turnoff. Follow Kenny Rd. right (west) past a private KOA campground with hot tub, swimming pool, camping cabins, and hot showers.

42.1 Manchester State Beach; hiker-biker camp, water, 4.5 miles of beach, and views from a windswept bluff of the ocean and Point Arena Lighthouse. No showers. Nearest grocery store is in Manchester, 1 mile south on Highway 1.

Manchester State Beach to Bodega Dunes State Beach (65.4 Miles)

Grass-covered hills, miles of traditional wooden fences, surf-battered cliffs, sheltered coves, and a wide array of weathered sea stacks provide an awe-inspiring backdrop for the ride from Manchester State Beach to Bodega Dunes State Beach.

And, as if the scenery weren't enough of a distraction, Salt Point State Park has numerous trails to lure you off your bike for quiet walks to sheltered coves, fern canyons, tall timber, and large rhododendron trees. Farther south, bikes may again be set aside for a tour of Fort Ross Historical Park. The fort was built by a group of Russians and Eskimos who were sent south in the early 1800s to grow grain for Alaskan settlements. The fort has been reconstructed and is open to visitors. There is also a visitor center that offers a slide show and historical notes describing the fate of these little-known pioneers.

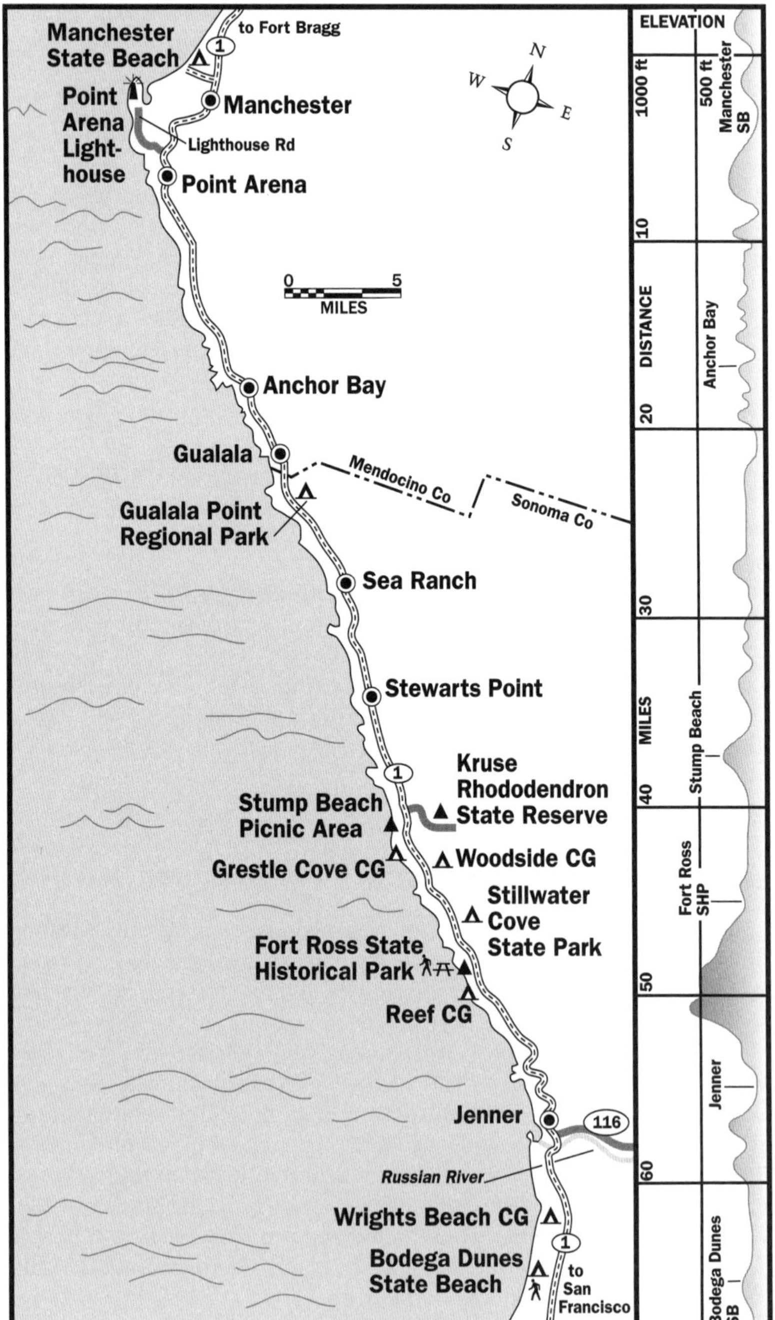

Manchester
State Beach
to Fort Bragg
1
Point
Arena
Light-
house
Manchester
Lighthouse Rd
Point Arena

N
W   E
S

0   5
MILES

Anchor Bay

Gualala
Gualala Point
Regional Park
Mendocino Co
Sonoma Co

Sea Ranch

Stewarts Point

1
Kruse
Rhododendron
State Reserve
Stump Beach
Picnic Area
Grestle Cove CG
Woodside CG
Stillwater
Cove
State Park
Fort Ross State
Historical Park
Reef CG

Jenner
116
Russian River
Wrights Beach CG
Bodega Dunes
State Beach
1
to
San
Francisco

ELEVATION
1000 ft
500 ft
Manchester
SB
10
DISTANCE
Anchor Bay
20
30
MILES
Stump Beach
40
Fort Ross
SHP
50
Jenner
60
Bodega Dunes
SB

The day ends at Bodega Dunes State Park. This is a large park set on Bodega Bay, at the edge of the sand dunes. Hours can be spent here, wandering over the dunes.

The ride from Manchester State Beach to Bodega Dunes State Beach is long and demanding. The road is narrow, winding, and steep. Traffic is light, except on summer weekends. Wandering sheep and cattle, and the cattle guards that are supposed to keep the sheep and cattle from wandering too far, add an extra challenge to the 5-mile section south of Fort Ross. It is best to approach the guards straight on, at a moderate pace.

As there are numerous campgrounds along this section of coast, it is easy to stop and linger if you desire. Beyond Bodega Dunes, campgrounds are few and far between, and the pace becomes hectic as the route heads into the Bay Area.

Mileage Log

0.0 From Manchester State Beach, go left on Kenny Rd., and return to Highway 1.

0.7 (mp 21.40) Head right (south) on Highway 1, passing numerous coastal access points.

1.1 (mp 20.90) Manchester city limits; two grocery stores. Beyond Manchester, the road continues to be steep and narrow. Sheep and cows graze on the open hillsides and, in search of greener grass, occasionally wander out onto the road.

4.9 (mp 17.00) Pass a commercial campground. *Side Trip* to Point Arena Lighthouse and museum: The lighthouse, located 2.3 miles off Highway 1, has a distinctive, tall, slender tower visible for many miles along the coast. It is now a museum and open to the public from 11:00 A.M. to 2:30 P.M. on weekdays and 10:00 A.M. to 3:30 P.M. on weekends. Admission is charged. Even if you don't go inside, the ride is rewardingly scenic. Once at the lighthouse, you are standing at the closest point on the West Coast to Hawaii.

5.7 (mp 16.20) Point Arena; complete tourist facilities, including grocery stores. Highway 1 parallels the coast with occasional views.

16.4 (mp 4.71) Anchor Bay; a minute-sized town with a small grocery, private campground, and restaurant.

19.5 (mp 1.31) Gualala; many amenities dear to the heart of a touring cyclist—grocery stores, delis, restaurants, ice creameries, and motels are found here. Watch out—you may ride completely through this small town before you figure out how to pronounce it.

20.9 (mp 0.00 and 58.68) Leave Mendocino County, enter Sonoma County at Gualala River Bridge.

21.3 (mp 58.20) Gualala Point Regional Park. The campground is on the east side of Highway 1; hiker-biker area, running water, no showers. The day-use area on the west side of Highway 1 has a visitor center with restrooms, running water, and beach access. Beyond the park, Highway 1 enters Sea Ranch, a long rambling community of expensive beach houses. The area is generally quiet during the week until Friday afternoon, when there is a mass migration up from the San Francisco Bay Area. On Sunday afternoon, the process is reversed as everyone dashes south. All side roads through Sea Ranch are private. The state park system has set up four coastal access parking areas where you can leave your bike and walk to the beach; restrooms but no water.

29.6 (mp 49.64) Leave Sea Ranch and return to the cow- and sheep-dotted landscapes.

31.3 (mp 48.1) Stewarts Point; a small tourist-oriented community. The grocery store has limited hours of operation. Beyond Stewarts Point, the road remains narrow, winding, and steep, with several short, tantalizing sections of shoulder.

34.7 (mp 44.48) Enter Salt Water State Park.

36.3 (mp 42.75) *Side Trip* to Kruse Rhododendron State Reserve: Turn left (east) off Highway 1 and cycle up Kruse Ranch Rd. to the end of the pavement and an intersection. Walk or ride the right fork

Russian Settlement in California

In 1806, when Nikolai Resanov arrived in Sitka, Alaska, to take over the Russian-American fur trading company, he found the residents of this prosperous outpost on the verge of starvation. This man of action immediately sailed south to California for supplies. The Spanish were reluctant to deal with him, so he married the San Francisco commander's daughter. Once he became part of the commander's family, he was allowed to trade for the supplies he needed and soon headed back to Sitka.

While in the south, Nikolai Resanov determined that a permanent settlement needed to be established in California to keep the Sitka hunters supplied with food. In 1812, when most of Europe and America were involved in war, Ivan Kuskov was sent to build a fort and base for Russian activities north of San Francisco. Fort Ross was built rapidly and with great skill. By the time the Spanish learned of its existence, it was too well established to be removed easily. The skillful Eskimo hunters brought south by the Russians nearly wiped out the otter and seal population along the northern California coast during the next twenty-nine years before the fort was sold to the Americans.

0.4 mile to the reserve. Trails vary from 0.2 mile to 5 miles in length. The forested area is at its best from late April through mid-June, when the rhododendrons are in bloom.

36.4 (mp 42.63) Fisk Cove; restrooms, beach access, and picnic tables.

37.8 (mp 41.22) Stump Beach picnic area; restrooms and access to a sandy cove. No running water.

38.9 (mp 39.90) Grestle Cove Campground; campsites, beach access, and running water. Hiker-biker site is located 50 feet south on the left side of the road at Woodside Campground.

39.0 (mp 39.89) Woodside Campground; hiker-biker site, water, and many miles of trails to the beach, along the bluffs, up the hills to vista points, and to a pygmy forest behind the park. No showers.

40.7 (mp 38.2) Ocean Cove; a tourist community with a very small grocery store and a commercial campground.

41.6 (mp 37.02) Stillwater Cove State Park; hiker-biker site, running water, showers, and beach access. This small park is popular with skin divers.

44.8 (mp 33.83) Fort Ross store; limited groceries.

The reconstructed buildings from an old Russian settlement are open to the public at Fort Ross State Historic Park.

45.4 (mp 33.00) Fort Ross State Historic Park; fort, visitor center, slide show, historical displays, restrooms, water, picnic facilities, and a grassy bluff for strolling. Fort Ross marks the start of 10 strenuous and scenic miles as Highway 1 climbs over headlands and drops into deep coves. The highway becomes a bare etching across the steep, unstable cliffs ahead. Caltrans has installed a gate that will be closed when the road or hillsides ahead are deemed unstable.

46.5 (mp 31.90) The first of many cattle guards to be crossed in the next 4 miles.

46.9 (mp 31.37) Reef Campground. This primitive facility is located in a sheltered little valley; pit toilets and beach access.

51.6 (mp 26.50) Long, moderate ascent leads to the top of a 520-foot hill and the end of the cattle guards. A steep road on the right climbs to the Vista Trail and a scenic view along the hillcrest. Highway 1 sweeps back to sea level with an exhilarating switchback. Watch out for slow-moving cars as you go down—this is definitely a better road for cycling than driving.

53.1 (mp 24.40) Russian Gulch Bridge marks the end of the descent and the start of another steep, though lesser, climb.

55.6 (mp 21.5) Jenner, a small town perched on a steep hillside overlooking the Russian River and a long sandspit. A small gas station/convenience store on the left side of the road is your last chance to purchase groceries before Bodega Dunes.

57.3 (mp 20.28) Junction of Highway 1 and Highway 116. Highway 1 continues south, while Highway 116 heads east to California's famous wine country.

57.4 (mp 20.00) Cross the Russian River. A restaurant, occasionally open, is located on the left at the south end of the bridge. A commercial campground is located on the right.

58.3 (mp 18.6) Turnoff to Goat Rock State Beach, the first of a series of Sonoma Coast State Beaches. Goat Rock State Beach has two access roads. The first access descends 0.8 mile; the second is a steep 2-mile descent. Restrooms and water at both access points.

59.2 (mp 18.2) Shell Beach; tide pool exploration and surf fishing. No facilities.

60.6 (mp 16.77) Wrights Beach, a small campground; restrooms and running water. No showers or hiker-biker sites.

61.1 (mp 16.35) Duncans Landing Beach, historical loading area for old coastal trading ships. The rocky headland next to the beach earned the name of Death Rock among sailors.

62.7 (mp 14.68) Portuguese Beach, a popular day-use area. No facilities.

63.0 (mp 14.33) Schoolhouse Beach; restrooms and tide pools to explore.

64.4 (mp 12.90) North Salmon Beach; sandy beaches, surf fishing, and restrooms. Highway 1 is lined with ice plant along this section of the coast, painting the sides of the road with exuberant colors.

65.4 (mp 11.67) Bodega Dunes State Beach campground; hot showers, restrooms, and a sandy hiker-biker area. A hiking trail through the dunes leads to a sandy beach. The nearest grocery store is 1.2 miles south, in Bodega Bay.

Bodega Dunes State Beach to Samuel P. Taylor State Park
(40.6 Miles)

Three large bays—Estro Americano, Tomales Bay, and San Francisco Bay—cut deep into the coastline between Bodega Bay and San Francisco. Highway 1 turns inland to bypass Estro Americano and then skirts along the edge of Tomales Bay before heading east around the Marin Headlands to cross San Francisco Bay at the Golden Gate Bridge.

The main point of interest on this ride is Point Reyes National Seashore, a beautiful 64,000-acre park with more than 70 miles of coastline. This unique area, geographically isolated from the mainland by the San Andreas Fault, is habitat for several hundred species of birds and seventy kinds of mammals. Trails are the only access to many of the park's beaches, sand dunes, and lakes, making it a difficult area to explore on a bicycle. The best place to begin is at the visitor center, which has displays, movies, a nature trail along the San Andreas Fault, and an authentic replica of a native American village. To fully explore the park requires several days—or weeks—to hike or ride the mountain bike trails and tour the paved road to the lighthouse. Camping is permitted at a hiker-biker site in Tomales State Park (adjoining the national seashore). The Point Reyes Youth Hostel, located off Limantour Rd., is another great place to spend a day or two. If touring with fat tires, you can take advantage of the park's backcountry campsite system, accessed by well-maintained, vehicle-driven, double-track trails.

Beyond Tomales Bay, the route leaves Highway 1 and heads inland to the San Francisco Bay Area. Although Highway 1 appears tempting on the map, it's considered extremely hazardous south of Olema—narrow, winding, shoulderless, and busy.

Inland from coastal breezes, the temperatures rise—quite a surprise, especially to those with empty water bottles. But that is not the end of the surprises; once past the first set of hot, dry hills, the route abandons the road in favor of a well-shaded bicycle path through the redwoods, ending at Samuel P. Taylor State Park.

Samuel P. Taylor State Park was one of the first areas in the United States where outdoor camping was promoted as a recreational pursuit.

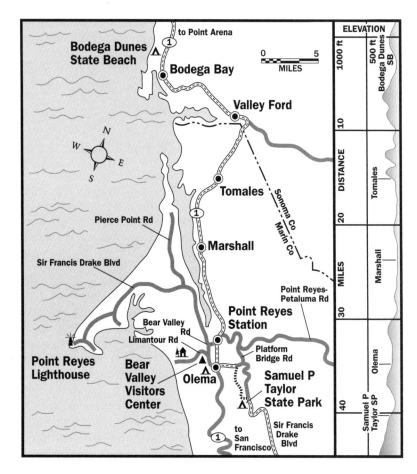

The park has numerous trails, and, time and energy permitting, you can hike or ride your mountain bike to a fire lookout or to the foundations of a paper mill, where the first square-bottomed paper bags were made in the late 1800s.

If you are lucky enough to secure a reservation, you may opt to pass up Samuel P. Taylor State Park in favor of a fantastic campsite 30 miles south of the state park at Marin Headlands, in the Golden Gate National Recreation Area. This extraordinary hiker-biker site has a stunning view overlooking San Francisco and the Golden Gate Bridge. Space is limited and advance reservations are required, so call the visitor center: (415) 331-1540. (If possible, call several days ahead.)

To reach the Marin Headlands, it is necessary to negotiate a fair amount of city traffic, a very slow process. See the next section for details.

Mileage Log

0.0 (mp 11.67) From Bodega Dunes State Beach, head south on Highway 1.

0.5 (mp 11.17) Fast-food heaven, an excellent spot to fill those empty stomachs with an All-American diet of greasy carbs.

1.2 (mp 10.47) Town of Bodega Bay; adequate facilities to feed the hungriest cyclist, as well as motels, restaurants, a grocery store, and a Laundromat. From the center of town, look across Bodega Harbor to the large fishing fleet. Keep an eye out for brown pelicans and other aquatic life. Beyond Bodega Bay, the shoulders are excellent as Highway 1 heads inland, climbing over grass-covered hills.

9.5 (mp 2.10) Valley Ford; grocery stores, restaurants. Shoulders end here.

11.3 (mp 0.18) Junction of Highway 1 and Valley Ford Rd. Turn right (south) on Highway 1. Valley Ford Rd. heads inland to Petaluma and US 101.

11.5 (mp 0.0 and 50.5) Leave Sonoma County and enter Marin County. The highway rolls over short, steep hills with unobstructed views of the countryside. Shoulders are infrequent and, when present, usually very narrow. Traffic is moderate. Cattle ranches appear. Redwood groves give way to eucalyptus trees.

16.0 (mp 46.00) Tomales; limited groceries and a few bed-and-breakfast inns. Leaving town, Highway 1 descends, twisting with little shoulder, to parallel Tomales Bay for the next 19 miles.

21.7 (mp 40.11) Popular windsurfing area.

23.1 (mp 38.41) Marshall; restaurants and a grocery store.

28.2 (mp 33.65) Coastal Access; parking lot, restrooms, and bay access.

31.5 (mp 30.65) Parking area with trail access to Tomales Bay.

32.4 (mp 29.28) Sharp corner and intersection. Go right and follow Highway 1 toward Point Reyes Station and two grocery stores.

32.8 (mp 28.94) First turnoff to Point Reyes National Seashore; do not turn here.

32.9 (mp 28.77) Point Reyes Station; purchase groceries for the night here. This small town has numerous restaurants and coffee shops.

34.3 (mp 27.37) Turnoff for Point Reyes National Seashore. (For side trip details, see end of this mileage log.) Just before the turnoff is Olama Ranch Campground, a commercial facility with grocery store, restaurant, showers, water, and laundry facilities. (This campground can be used as an alternate when Samual P. Taylor runs out of water and closes, as happens occasionally in the late summer and fall.)

34.6 (mp 26.76) Olema; limited groceries. The route leaves Highway 1 here and heads left (east) up Sir Francis Drake Blvd. Climb a steep

A short walk takes you to the flower-covered headlands at Chimney Rock Point, near Point Reyes Lighthouse.

hill, then descend into a narrow valley.

37.1 (mp 20.54) Just before crossing a short bridge over Lagunitas Creek, go right and descend a gravel trail to the paved Marin Bicycle Trail. Go left and parallel Sir Francis Drake Blvd. as it heads along Lagunitas Creek.

38.5 Jewell Trail branches off to the right. Continue straight, paralleling the creek into the state park.

40.6 Cycle through the camp area to an intersection. Go right, crossing the creek to reach the entrance booth for Samuel P. Taylor State Park and register; hiker-biker site and hot showers under the deep shade of the redwood forest.

Point Reyes National Seashore Side Trip

Turn right (west) on Bear Valley Rd. At 0.5 mile, go left to the information center for a park map, movie, slide show, restrooms, water, picnic tables, San Andreas Fault Trail, Indian village, beach trails, and backcountry campsite reservations. To reach the Point Reyes Youth Hostel, it is necessary to ride up Limantour Rd. (2.1 miles north of the information center), gaining 1,400 feet before descending back to sea level. Call ahead for reservations: (415) 663-8811.

The hiker-biker campsite at Tomales State Park is a pleasant place to stay and very easy to reach. Cycle north from the information center on Bear Valley Rd., which merges with Sir Francis Drake Blvd. At 8.2 miles, go right (north) on Pierce Point Rd. for 1 mile to the park. Follow the signs to the hiker-biker site (the only camping allowed in the park). If you ride the entire 21.1 miles to the end of Sir Francis Drake Blvd. you'll reach the famous Point Reyes Lighthouse. Visitors descend 300 steps to the light and an impressive view of the surrounding coast, including sea lions on the offshore rocks.

Samuel P. Taylor State Park to Half Moon Bay State Beach
(58.1 Miles)

Between Samuel P. Taylor State Park and Half Moon Bay State Park sprawls the Bay Area, a dizzying conglomeration of cities that includes San Francisco and a dozen satellites. As this is the first major urban center on the Pacific Coast Bike Route since Vancouver, British Columbia, take advantage of its numerous services and repair any mechanical or gear problems you might be having with your equipment.

The Bay Area is ideal for cycling, if you know where you are going or if you can take it at a leisurely pace. Bike paths crisscross the cities, connecting parks, viewpoints, and beaches. However, if you are planning to traverse this large metropolitan area in a single day, even an early start will leave little time for exploration. Winding through residential streets and stopping for lights and stops signs makes for slow going, requiring any number of extra hours.

Much of the route through the Bay Area is delineated by green and white city bike route signs and an occasional Bicentennial or Pacific Coast Bicycle Route marker. Some riders find it helpful to buy a city street map and trace the route on it before starting. You may also find it useful to make a copy of the Mileage Log or tear it out of the book and keep it handy.

The route through the Bay Area is very scenic, with views of San Francisco Bay, Alcatraz, the Golden Gate Bridge, classic residential areas, sandy beaches, and the precipitous Devils Slide. Close to—but not on—the route are the famous Marin Headlands, Fort Point, and Golden Gate Park. Marin Headlands are part of the Golden Gate National Recreation Area, with a magnificent view of San Francisco and the Golden Gate Bridge. For anyone who would like to linger and explore this wildly scenic area, there is a youth hostel, hiker-biker site, beach access, a lighthouse accessed by bridges, and hiking trails over the rolling coastal hills. Fort Point is a classic brick fortress that was outdated almost before it was completed in 1861, and Golden Gate Park is a beautiful island of green in the middle of San Francisco with lakes, botanical and Japanese gardens, a buffalo paddock, museums, the Academy of Science, and quiet groves of trees.

Cyclists spending time in San Francisco can stay at any number of places in or near the city: on the Marin Headlands (hiker-biker campsites and a 300-person hostel, reservations strongly recommended: (800) 909-4776 hostel code 73); in San Francisco at one of three hostels or hundreds of hotels; or at the Montara Lighthouse Hostel (20 miles south of San Francisco but on a main bus route to town; get your reservations ahead of time by calling (800) 909-4776 hostel code 153).

If planning to end your ride in San Francisco, check at the end of the Mileage Log for routes to the airport and railroad station.

South of San Francisco, the route returns to Highway 1 just in time to

The bike route passes through traditional upscale neighborhoods near Golden Gate Park, in San Francisco.

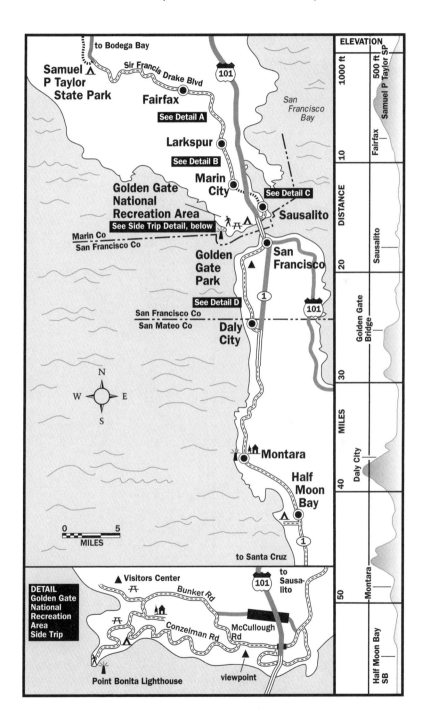

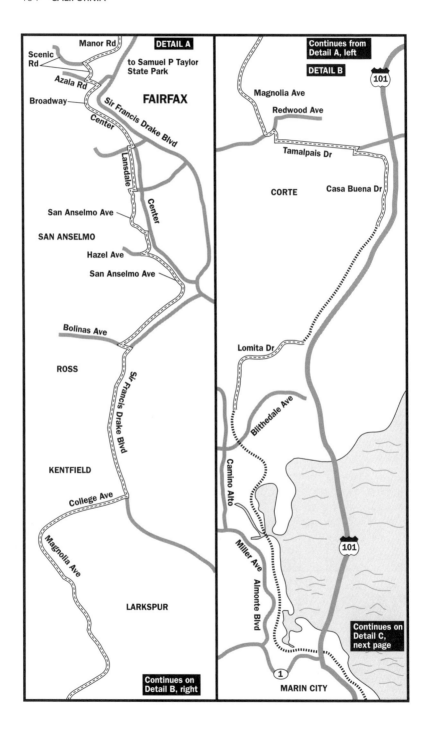

Manor Rd

Scenic Rd

DETAIL A

to Samuel P Taylor State Park

Azala Rd

Broadway

FAIRFAX

Sir Francis Drake Blvd

Center

Lansdale

Center

San Anselmo Ave

SAN ANSELMO

Hazel Ave

San Anselmo Ave

Bolinas Ave

ROSS

Sir Francis Drake Blvd

KENTFIELD

College Ave

Magnolia Ave

LARKSPUR

Continues on Detail B, right

Continues from Detail A, left

DETAIL B

101

Magnolia Ave

Redwood Ave

Tamalpais Dr

CORTE

Casa Buena Dr

Lomita Dr

Blithedale Ave

Camino Alto

Miller Ave

Almonte Blvd

101

Continues on Detail C, next page

1

MARIN CITY

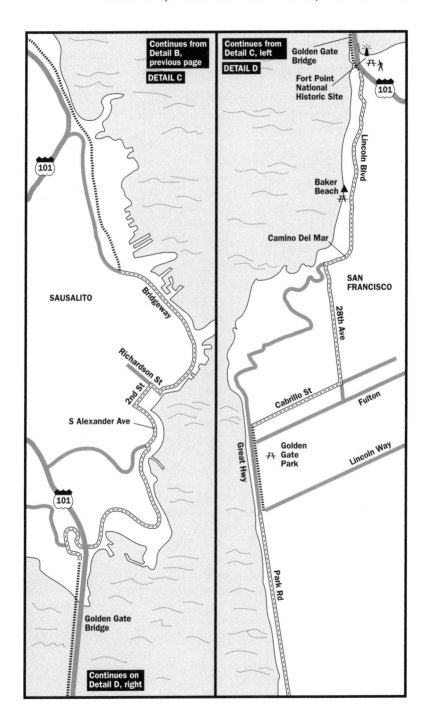

Continues from
Detail B,
previous page
DETAIL C

Continues from
Detail C, left
DETAIL D

Golden Gate
Bridge

Fort Point
National
Historic Site

101

Lincoln Blvd

Baker
Beach

Camino Del Mar

SAN
FRANCISCO

28th Ave

101

SAUSALITO

Bridgeway

Richardson St

2nd St

S Alexander Ave

Cabrillo St

Fulton

Great Hwy

Golden
Gate
Park

Lincoln Way

101

Golden Gate
Bridge

Park Rd

Continues on
Detail D, right

tackle the slide-prone Devils Headland. The road is very narrow. Try to reach this area as early as possible to avoid the afternoon traffic. Detours are common, especially in the spring.

Mileage Log

0.0 Leaving Samuel P. Taylor State Park Campground, head southeast on Sir Francis Drake Blvd. The shoulderless road is narrow and winding, shaded by dense foliage, and full of potholes.

1.7 Leave Samuel P. Taylor State Park.

2.4 Lagunitas; a small town with a grocery store. The road widens as it leaves the redwoods to include a shoulder.

3.0 Forest Knolls; a sprawling residential community with a small store. Head out into the open countryside for 5 miles of straightforward riding. Use caution as you descend the steep hill into Fairfax; large water drains make riding on the shoulder hazardous.

8.4 At the entrance to Fairfax, go right on Olema Rd. and follow city bike route signs through town. The next 35 miles are on city streets.

8.9 Pass a second sign announcing Fairfax city limits.

9.2 Go right on Manor Rd. When Manor Rd. divides, stay left.

9.4 Take a left on Scenic Rd.

9.6 Turn left on Azala and almost immediately after go right on Broadway. Ride through the town center, passing numerous small businesses and specialty restaurants.

10.0 Broadway becomes Center Blvd.

10.2 Jog right on Lansdale, a narrow road—almost an alley—that parallels Center Blvd.

10.4 Enter San Anselmo.

10.6 Jog to the right again on San Anselmo Ave. and continue following bike route signs through quiet residential streets.

10.9 Arrive at a T intersection and go left.

11.2 Go left again on Hazel Ave., once again paralleling Center Blvd.

11.3 Intersection; a jog to the left puts you back on San Anselmo Ave.

11.5 Go right, still on San Anselmo Ave., and head through the town center.

12.1 Go left on Bolinas Ave.

12.2 A right turn returns you to Sir Francis Drake Blvd., which is now a busy road with a very minor shoulder. Before long you will pass the Kentfield city limits.

13.4 Go right on College Ave. Follow it as it turns into Magnolia Ave. at the Larkspur city limits. Mount Tamalpais, the birthplace of mountain biking, is on the right.

15.5 Pass Oliver Park on the right; restrooms.

16.1 Turn left on Redwood Ave. Descend 1 block, then go right on

Tamalpais Dr. Continue straight for 0.5 mile.

16.7 At the second-to-the-last stoplight before the US 101 freeway entrance, turn right on Casa Buena Dr. Climb a steep hill, which parallels US 101.

17.6 At the top of the second of two steep rises, the road bends sharply uphill. Go straight ahead on a bike path, paralleling the freeway.

18.1 The bike path ends on Lomita Dr. Follow Lomita Dr. as it bends to the right and stay with it to an old elementary school-turned-business center.

18.6 When Lomita Dr. bends left, go straight ahead on a narrow, gravel-surfaced bike path. After a short 0.1 mile, go left again on a paved path that heads up the hill to a wide bikeway.

19.1 Bikeway crosses Blithedale Ave. Continue straight, following the bikeway over a marsh and past a small lagoon. The bikeway takes you under US 101 and then parallels the boat harbor.

21.5 Bikeway ends. (This is a very confusing area. If you suddenly find yourself riding on a sidewalk, turn around and go back to the last intersection.) Cross Bridgeway, which is a major four-lane highway in this area. Once across the intersection, go left. Ride south on Bridgeway until it ends.

23.9 Bridgeway ends. Turn right and pedal up Richardson St. At the

The wide bicycle and pedestrian lane on the Golden Gate Bridge allows you to pull off to the side and gawk at the view.

first intersection, turn left on 2nd St. and follow it through a congested area of small shops, then up a steep hill.

24.1 As 2nd St. ends, turn left on South St.

24.2 South St. bends right and becomes S. Alexander Ave.

25.2 Continue straight, ignoring a city bike route sign pointing to the left, and ride through an underpass of US 101.

25.4 Go right at the freeway interchange and head uphill, following, briefly, signs to Marin Headlands and Golden Gate National Recreation Area. Take the first left, which leads to a parking lot. Ride across the parking lot to find the entrance to the west-side Golden Gate Bridge Pedestrian Way. For details of the Headlands side trip, see end of this Mileage Log.

25.6 Head across the Golden Gate Bridge, beautiful in sun, fog, or smog.

26.0 Leave Marin County; enter San Francisco County.

27.6 Follow the bike path as it loops around and then under US 101 to the east side of the bridge. Unless shrouded in fog, take the time to visit the Vista Point for a long look over San Francisco Bay.

27.7 Ride as straight as possible through the busy parking area to reach Lincoln Blvd.

27.8 Turn right on Lincoln Blvd. **Side Trip** to Fort Point: Go left (east) on Lincoln Blvd. for 0.5 mile to the fort access road. The fort has been turned into a military museum.

28.5 Pass an unsigned turnoff to Baker Beach; restrooms, picnic tables, water, and a sandy beach.

28.9 Lincoln Blvd. becomes Camino Del Mar. Continue straight for 3 more blocks.

29.1 Turn left on 28th Ave. and ride up and over a hill through a tightly packed and beautifully maintained residential area of San Francisco.

30.1 At Cabrillo St. go right. (If you are heading for the Amtrak station, check directions at the end of this Mileage Log.)

31.4 Cabrillo St. ends; go left on a bike path paralleling the busy Great Highway (also called Park Rd.).

31.5 Intersection. Southbound travelers should cross Park Rd. here, then go left either on the wide shoulder or on the beachside bike path. The tops of two windmills can be seen over the crest of the trees marking the famous Golden Gate Park to the left. The park makes an excellent side trip or a lunch stop.

34.3 Bike path ends. All riders must now return to the shoulder of the highway.

35.1 Skyline Blvd. joins Park Rd. from the left and the combined road (which is now also called Highway 35) continues south with a broad bicycle lane on the shoulder.

36.1 Pass two accesses to Fort Funston on the right; beach access.

36.4 Leave San Francisco County; enter San Mateo County.

36.8 (mp 31.00) Daly City; fast food and supermarkets.

38.2 (mp 29.80) Begin Daly City Bypass Route. At the false summit of a steep hill, leave Highway 35 and go right on Westmoor Ave. After 1 block, bear left on Skyline Dr. Pedal up a rather steep hill through a residential area. Once up, go very steeply down and do not allow the excellent view south over the coast to distract you. (If heading to the San Francisco International Airport, leave the bike route here. See end of this Mileage Log for details.)

40.0 While still descending steeply, pass a school on the right, then take the first left on Crenshaw Dr. In 1 block, go right on Palmetto Ave. and stay with it as it parallels Highway 1 past freeway entrances and a shopping center.

42.5 At the end of Palmetto Ave., go left on Clarendon, then immediately right on Lakeside Ave.

42.7 Lakeside Ave. exits onto Francisco Blvd. Continue south, passing along the right side of Sharp Park; picnic tables, restrooms, and water.

43.3 Francisco Blvd. turns into Bradford Way; continue straight. Circumnavigate around the left side of a Moose Lodge. On the far side of the lodge, the road divides; stay left. Just before reaching Highway 1, go right up a very steep bike path, paralleling the freeway. (Ignore bike path signs pointing away from the road.)

43.8 (mp 42.50) Bike path ends; continue on the shoulder of Highway 1.

45.3 (mp 40.00) Lind Mar Rest Area; a parking lot with restrooms and beach access but no water. No easy access for northbound cyclists.

45.7 (mp 39.63) The highway narrows as it begins its steep climb over the Devils Slide. The shoulder shrinks and then disappears entirely. Note the "Think Tunnel" bumper stickers on cars. If you reached this area during rush hour, you will soon be ready to grab a shovel and help them start digging.

46.6 (mp 38.40) Pass the remains of the first of two old military installations precipitously perched on the headlands. Find a pullout to stop and look at this spectacular area.

49.9 (mp 36.00) Enter Montara, a coastal tourist town with grocery stores and fast food. The route is now on level terrain, and the shoulders are good and remain so for the rest of the day.

50.1 (mp 35.8) Beach access, restrooms, but no water.

50.8 (mp 35.4) Montara Lighthouse Hostel. Advance reservations are highly recommended. This scenic location has excellent beach access.

51.0 (mp 35.42) Enter the small coastal town of Moss Beach; no grocery stores near Highway 1. Pass the turnoff to James Fitzgerald Marine Reserve, where you can explore the marine habitat on a large band of coast rocks. Sea lions are often seen sunbathing on the outer rocks.

53.2 (mp 33.4) El Granada; a small grocery store is 1 block left from Highway 1.

53.8 (mp 32.8) Half Moon Bay city limits.

55.8 (mp 30.6) Access to Dunes Beach, a horse park.

57.5 (mp 28.80) Junction of Highway 1 and Highway 92; a major shopping center and a bike shop are on the east side of the road.

57.8 (mp 28.50) Turnoff to Half Moon Bay State Beach and campground. Turn right on Kelly Rd., opposite a small but adequate convenience store.

58.1 Half Moon Bay State Beach; beach access, restrooms, cold outdoor showers, and a hiker-biker site at the far end of the camping area. For a little end-of-the-day recreation, ride the coast trail along the beach for views and a lovely sunset.

Golden Gate National Recreation Area Side Trip

At the northern entrance to the Golden Gate Bridge, pass the parking area turnoff and continue up the steep grade of Conzelman Rd. Viewpoints are numerous, and, in good weather, so are the automobiles. At 1.2 miles the road divides. Cyclists looking for views should stay left and continue up the final mile to the summit. To reach the hiker-biker camp or hostel, follow the right fork on a 1-mile descent to Bunker Rd., then go left. Follow Bunker Rd. 1.2 miles to a Y intersection. If the hostel is your destination, stay left on Field Rd. for 500 feet, then turn uphill,

══════════ Golden Gate Bridge ══════════

One of the most common misconceptions about the Golden Gate Bridge is that it is painted from end to end every year. This distinctive "International Orange"–colored bridge has only been completely repainted once. Most of the work done on the bridge is simply touch-up painting. However, the touch-up crew is an amazing group consisting of seventeen ironworkers and thirty-eight painters whose job it is to repair and repaint the corroding steel and rivets, often while suspended high above the bridge in wind and rain, fog and sunshine. The ironworkers move ahead of the painters, removing plates and bars to provide access to the interior of the columns for the painters, and then close up when they have completed their work.

following the signs. If the hiker-biker camp is your destination, continue on Bunker Rd. for another 0.8 mile, register at the visitor center, and receive directions to the camp area. Be prepared to put up with some inconveniences—no showers, no running water (it is available nearby)—and enjoy the tremendous view. You must call ahead to the Golden Gate National Recreation Center Visitor Center for reservations: (415) 331-1540.

Amtrak and the Oakland Airport

San Francisco does not have an Amtrak station. The nearest station is located across the bay in Oakland, and the best way to get there is by BART (Bay Area Rapid Transit). Follow the bike route through San Francisco for 30.1 miles to Cabrillo St. Go right on Cabrillo St. to 43rd Ave., then turn left and ride through Golden Gate Park on 37th Ave. At Yorba St., go left then right on Sunset Blvd., which will turn into Lake Merced Blvd. At John Daly Blvd., go left and follow this major street until it crosses a freeway. Exit and go left (north) to BART Station No. 1. Bicycles are allowed on BART from 9:30 A.M. to 3:30 P.M. Monday through Friday and all day on weekends and holidays. Once at the station take the elevator down to the platform, then look for a station agent to let you through the gate. If you cannot find an agent, buy your ticket, go through the gate, then lift your bike over the 4-foot barrier.

San Francisco International Airport

Follow the Mileage Log for the first 38.2 miles. Stay on Highway 35 after the bike route exits in Daly City and follow it to Bruno Ave. Head east. Near the airport you will cross over US 101. Continue straight until Bruno Ave. ends, then go right and follow the busy frontage road to the terminal.

Half Moon Bay State Beach to New Brighton State Beach
(56.5 Miles)

The coast south of San Francisco is a popular vacation getaway. During the summer, this area overflows with tourists from around the world. On weekends, fishermen, surfers, sunbathers, and beachcombers from the Bay Area mob the beaches. Despite its popularity, the coast is remarkably unspoiled, with only a few towns marring the open grasslands and sandy beaches. Where the highway parallels the ocean, an observant cyclist may spot sea lions basking in the sun or otters playing in the surf.

A stop at Año Nuevo State Reserve is highly recommended. From December through April, elephant seals breed and raise their young here. During the summer, they can be spotted sunning themselves on the offshore rocks. Reservations are required for visits during breeding season. If interested, call (800) 444-4445. The rest of the year, visitors are required to have a permit, which can be obtained at the visitor center.

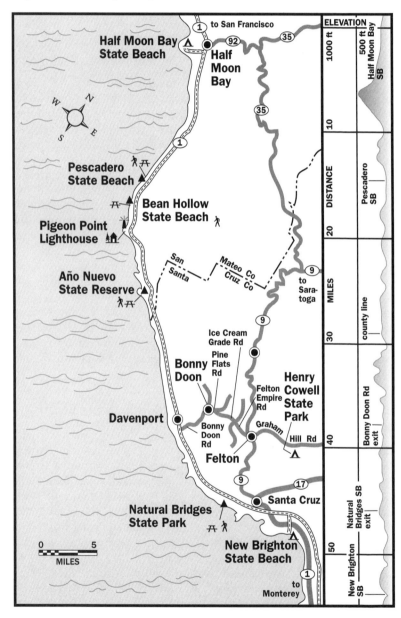

Despite the cold waters, Santa Cruz is the surfing mecca of northern California and attracts enthusiasts from around the world.

Tide pools are excellent in this area. Some of the richest pools are at Bean Hollow and Natural Bridges State Beaches. If you have never explored a tide pool, take this opportunity to do so. The variety of life that survives in the precarious and ever-changing environment of these small pools is amazing.

In Santa Cruz, Highway 1 turns into a busy, congested freeway, and the bike route wisely heads west for a spectacular tour along the coast, passing Natural Bridges State Beach, overlooks, surfing beaches, and a surf museum. The route then follows city streets through town to New Brighton State Beach.

Highway 1 has a good shoulder throughout most of this section, and riding is generally very enjoyable—a marked contrast to the trek through San Francisco. One note of caution: Before leaving Half Moon Bay, be sure to check your food and water supplies. The first water stop is at 27.2 miles, and the first grocery store is 36.9 miles south.

Mileage Log

0.0 From Half Moon Bay State Park, follow Kelly Rd. back to Highway 1.

0.2 (mp 29.10) Kelly Rd. ends at Highway 1. The Pacific Coast Bike Route heads south toward Santa Cruz.

2.9 (26.30) Cowell Ranch beach access; pit toilet, trail to beach, and history information.

10.7 (mp 18.15) San Gregorio State Beach; beach access, toilets, no running water.

12.3 (mp 16.59) Pomponio State Beach; beach access, toilets, no running water.

14.1 (mp 14.65) Pescadero State Beach; beach access, chemical toilets, no running water. Translated, Pescadero means "the fishing place," and is well known for surf fishing. In the next mile, two more Pescadero State Beaches are passed.

15.0 (mp 13.54) Turnoff to the Butano State Park campground, located several miles inland from the coast. The park has some nice redwood groves and mountain biking trails but no hiker-biker sites or showers.

16.6 (mp 12.00) Bean Hollow State Beach, also known as Pebble Beach; beach access, tidal pools, and a mile-long, self-guided nature trail along the bluff. Pebble Beach gets its name from the multicolored gravel that covers the shoreline. Don't mine the beach; leave it for others to enjoy.

17.6 (mp 11.20) A second Bean Hollow State Beach access; restroom, southern end of the nature trail, and beach access.

20.7 (mp 8.00) Turnoff to Pigeon Point Light Station and hostel. This beacon, the second tallest in the nation, is visible from great distances, by land or sea. If spending the night at the hostel, take a walk along the beach to look for whale bones, common here, or watch for live whales on their annual migration. Advance reservations are almost a requirement to stay at this popular hostel, so call ahead: (800) 909-4776 hostel code 73.

22.8 (mp 5.89) Gazos State Beach; beach access, chemical toilets, no water.

27.2 (mp 1.41) Turnoff to Año Nuevo State Reserve, the first watering hole since Half Moon Bay. In winter, this is a very popular area for viewing gray whales and elephant seals. From December through March you may enter the reserve only with a park naturalist. For reservations, call (800) 444-7475. For the remainder of the year, you are free to explore the tide pools while watching for sea otters and harbor seals in the surf.

28.6 (mp 0.0 and 37.5) Leave San Mateo County and enter Santa Cruz County.

29.5 (mp 36.45) Walden Beach; toilets but no running water. On the left, a short dirt road heads into the western tip of Big Basin Redwoods State Park. (No state park facilities here. The main entrance and the redwood giants are accessed from Highway 9.) The shoulder along Highway 1 remains good as you head south past miles of artichoke and Brussels sprout farms.

31.0 (mp 35.0) Greyhound Rock; public fishing access, toilets.

36.9 (mp 29.13) Davenport. At long last—food. The solitary store in this tiny community is very popular among bicyclists. From here to Santa Cruz are numerous beach access points.

44.3 (mp 21.73) Wilder Ranch State Park; water, toilets, visitor center, beach access, mountain bike trails, guided tours to historic buildings.

45.6 (mp 20.42) Santa Cruz; supermarkets, bike shops, beaches, fishing piers, tide pools, and a lot of people. Some tricky navigation is needed to plot a course through this small metropolis; however, Santa Cruz is a college town, and bicycles are an accepted mode of transport.

46.1 (mp 19.92) Turn right off Highway 1 on Western Dr., following Pacific Coast Bicycle Route signs. Go 1 block to the Wrigleys factory, then take a right on Mission St. and head north for 1 block.

46.2 Turn left on Natural Bridges Dr. and ride west toward the coast.

46.6 Go left again at Delaware Ave.

46.7 At Swanton Blvd., turn right and ride along the south side of Natural Bridges State Beach.

47.1 Before taking a left on West Cliff Dr., go right to Natural Bridges State Beach Overlook and descend to the 20-minute parking lot for a cliffs'-edge view over the rocky beach. (The most spectacular natural bridge eroded away several decades ago.) You have already passed several park entrances, and this is yet another chance to visit this interesting day-use area, which features a sandy beach,

Año Nuevo State Reserve

The low, rocky, and often windswept point that is Año Nuevo is the site of the largest mainland breeding colony in the world for the northern elephant seal. Here the males battle for mates and the females give birth to their pups in the protected dune area. By early March, most of the adults head back out to sea, leaving the weaned pups to follow two months later.

This fascinating glimpse at one of life's great continuing circles is pretty much over by the time the touring cyclist heads down the coast. However, if you are willing to spend some time exploring the area, you may be lucky enough to spot an elephant seal resting on shore during the molt. Permits for hiking the state reserve may be picked up at the visitor center. The reserve closes at 5:00 P.M. during the summer and at 4:00 P.M. in September and October.

tide pools, butterfly trees (wintering spot for monarch butterflies), restrooms, picnic tables, running water, and guided walks. After visiting the beach, head southwest along W. Cliff Dr.

49.0 At Lighthouse Field State Beach, look for the Santa Cruz Surfing Museum, located in the old lighthouse on the point. W. Cliff Dr. now heads east around the Santa Cruz Harbor. The waters here are popular with longboard surfers because of the small, slow waves.

49.9 Stay with W. Cliff Dr. as it leaves the harbor just before reaching the pier, casino, boardwalk, and amusement park.

50.1 West Cliff Dr. ends. Ride straight across Washington St. to Pacific Ave. Before long, Pacific Ave. will become Front St.

50.2 Go right on Laurel St. and ride across an overpass.

50.3 Route divides. Pacific Coast Bicycle Route signs indicate that the route should go straight on a very confusing tour through Capitola. We suggest staying left on Laurel St.

50.5 Laurel St. becomes Broadway.

51.7 Broadway ends; turn left on Frederick St.

52.0 Frederick St. ends. Turn right on Soquel Dr. and follow it for the next 4 miles to the New Brighton State Beach turnoff. Purchase food for the night along this section.

56.0 Turnoff to New Brighton State Beach. Go right on Park Ave.

56.5 New Brighton State Beach; hiker-biker site (a one-night limit), hot showers, and beach access. *Side Trip:* After you set up camp, cycle west on Park Ave. to the town of Capitola for a walk on the beach, then follow E. Cliff Dr. back to Santa Cruz and the famous Boardwalk Amusement Park. If leaving your bicycle for even a moment, be sure it is locked.

New Brighton State Beach to Vets Memorial Park (40.8 Miles)

Between New Brighton State Beach and Monterey, the bicycle route spends 32.4 miles on back roads and bike paths, touring through farmlands. Unless you find Brussels sprouts, strawberries, artichokes, and chicken farms to be incredibly enthralling, start your day's ride early and sprint all the way to Monterey, which is a fascinating place for you to explore.

Although completely lacking in scenic interest, this is a great area for riding. Terrain varies from gently rolling to level. The biggest hazard to cyclists, especially in the Monterey area, is dense fog.

The day's ride ends at Vets Memorial Park, a moderate-size city park with a small hiker-biker area. Cyclists are turned away only when the site actually overflows. Arrive early to claim a space for your tent.

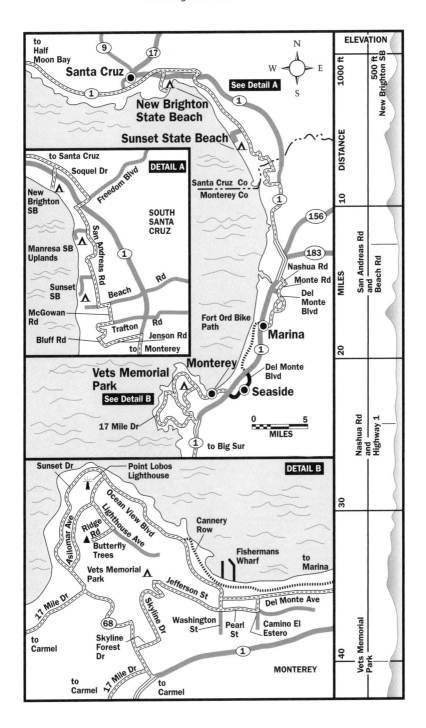

ELEVATION

to Half Moon Bay

9   17

Santa Cruz

1

See Detail A

New Brighton State Beach

Sunset State Beach

1

N
W   E
S

1000 ft
500 ft   New Brighton SB

DISTANCE

DETAIL A

to Santa Cruz
Soquel Dr

New Brighton SB

Freedom Blvd

Santa Cruz Co
Monterey Co

SOUTH SANTA CRUZ

San Andreas Rd

1

Manresa SB Uplands

Sunset SB

Beach   Rd

McGowan Rd

Bluff Rd   Trafton   Rd

Jenson Rd

to   Monterey

156

183

Nashua Rd

Monte Rd

Del Monte Blvd

Fort Ord Bike Path

Marina

1

10

San Andreas Rd and Beach Rd

MILES

Vets Memorial Park

See Detail B

17 Mile Dr

Monterey

1

to Big Sur

Del Monte Blvd

Seaside

0   5
MILES

20

Nashua Rd and Highway 1

DETAIL B

Sunset Dr

Point Lobos Lighthouse

Ocean View Blvd

Lighthouse Ave

Ridge Rd

Asilomar Ave

Butterfly Trees

Vets Memorial Park

17 Mile Dr

68

Skyline Forest Dr

to Carmel

Cannery Row

Fishermans Wharf

to Marina

Jefferson St

Del Monte Ave

Skyline Dr

Washington St   Pearl St   Camino El Estero

1

MONTEREY

30

Vets Memorial Park

40

to Carmel   17 Mile Dr   to Carmel

Monterey attracts visitors from around the world, so expect an international crowd at the campsite.

The Monterey area more than makes up for the uneventful ride, and you can spend the remaining hours of the day enjoying this vibrant town. At the end of the Mileage Log is a special tour of Monterey, including stops at Fisherman's Wharf, Cannery Row ("restored" to an elegance it never had in Steinbeck's famous novel), Point Lobos Light Station (beautifully situated at the edge of the Point Lobos Refuge), and the wintering spot for monarch butterflies (these fragile insects fly all the way down from Alaska). The beautiful 17-Mile Drive (possibly the most famous stretch of road on the entire California Coast) is also included. An afternoon is the absolute minimum amount of time required to see this area. To see it all, an extra day is needed.

The newest addition to this area, an aquarium located at the southern

Brown pelicans and other sea birds are often seen drying their wings on docks and rocks around Monterey Bay.

end of Cannery Row, is a masterpiece. Visitors are taken on a visual journey from the estuary at Elkhorn Slough to the tidelands, then down below the wharf through the kelp beds to the ocean floor. If you enjoy the ocean or just like to space out looking at glowing jellyfish, a trip to the aquarium is a must. Plan to spend 3 or more hours there.

Mileage Log

0.0 From New Brighton State Beach, pedal back up Park Ave.

0.6 Turn right at Soquel Dr., rejoining the Santa Cruz city bike route. Stay on Soquel Dr. for the next 4.8 miles.

2.5 *Side Trip* to Sea Cliffs State Beach: Turn right (west) on State Park Dr. for 0.6 mile to the long, sandy beach, a favorite with sunbathers; picnic tables and restrooms. An old shipwreck has been converted into a pier for fishermen.

4.6 Confusing intersection: After passing Rio Del Mar Blvd., follow Soquel Dr. as it makes a sharp turn to the right.

5.4 Soquel Dr. ends. Turn right on Freedom Blvd.

5.7 Cross Highway 1, then turn left on Bonita Dr. The Santa Cruz city bike route ends.

6.8 Bonita Dr. ends; go right on San Andreas Rd. and follow it for the next 6.1 miles.

8.7 La Selva Beach; a sandy beach popular with surfers. Beyond La Selva Beach, San Andreas Rd. heads inland through farmlands. Traffic varies from light to extremely busy during harvest season.

9.2 Manresa State Beach Uplands Campground; a tents-only area with beach access, water, restrooms, and hot showers. To reach the campground, go right on Sand Dollar Dr., then take a left on Manresa Beach Rd.

11.0 Sunset State Beach turnoff. Cyclists visiting this park must follow Sunset Beach Rd. 2.2 miles past fields of Brussels sprouts and artichokes. The campground offers hiker-biker sites, hot showers, and beach access. If you decide to spend the night at the park, buy food in Santa Cruz—no food or groceries are available near the park. This intersection marks the halfway point of your California Coast tour.

12.9 San Andreas Rd. ends; go left (east) on Beach Rd., then take the first right on McGowan Rd. (not signed). Go straight on McGowan Rd. Cross the Pajaro River bike path (to Watsonville), cycle over a narrow bridge, then cross the Santa Cruz–Monterey county line.

14.1 At the end of McGowan Rd., take a right on Trafton Rd.

15.6 Trafton Rd. ends; turn left on Bluff Rd., cycling through a small residential community, then pass chicken and mushroom farms.

16.4 Bluff Rd. ends at Jensen Rd.; go left (east).

17.1 (mp 100.00) Return to Highway 1 opposite a fruit stand. The highway is busy and has good shoulders.

17.9 (mp 99.10) Moss Landing; a long, narrow town.

18.7 (mp 98.30) Turnoff to Zmudowski State Beach. The beach lies 2 miles west; no facilities.

20.0 (mp 97.00) Moss Landing State Beach turnoff. The beach is located 0.5 mile to the southwest on Jetty Rd.; beach access, views of Moss Landing harbor, and restrooms, but no water.

20.5 (mp 96.60) Cross Elkhorn Slough.

20.9 (mp 96.10) Pass Moss Landing power plant, whose twin towers dominate the skyline. Highway 1 enters the business section of Moss Landing and passes the access to Elkhorn Slough Reserve.

21.7 (mp 95.30) Pass Salinas River State Beach access.

23.0 (mp 94.00) Enter Castroville—Artichoke Capital of the World.

23.5 (mp 93.60) Junction with Highway 156 (heading east) and Highway 183 (heading south). Stay on Highway 1, now a divided freeway.

25.5 (mp 90.20) Nashua Rd.; cyclists must exit Highway 1. At the end of the off ramp, turn right, crossing over the freeway.

25.8 Bicycle path from Castroville joins Nashua Rd. Continue straight.

25.9 Turn right on Monte Rd., paralleling Highway 1. No shoulders; traffic is light (except during harvest season) as you pass large artichoke fields.

27.8 Turn left on Del Monte Blvd. and go 100 feet to a Y intersection. Stay right on Lapis Rd., which rejoins Del Monte Blvd. in 1.3 miles.

29.3 Enter Marina on Del Monte Blvd.; several small grocery stores in this section.

29.7 Start two-way bike path paralleling Del Monte Blvd.

31.4 The bike path passes under Highway 1, then turns left, becoming the Fort Ord Bike Path as it parallels the freeway south through the Fort Ord area.

33.2 Seaside city limits. The bike path continues to parallel the freeway.

35.8 Bike path passes under Highway 1 and ends. The bike route returns to Del Monte Blvd., then heads through a busy business district. Watch for cars parked on the shoulder.

37.3 Busy intersection. Go straight, crossing Cyn Del Rey, then take a right onto a bike path.

37.4 Monterey; supermarkets, restaurants, hotels, and several bike shops.

39.1 Follow the bike path until you are riding along the edge of the beach. Just before it makes a sharp left turn, leave the path and cross Del Monte Ave. Ride up Camino El Estero for 2 blocks.

39.3 Turn right on Pearl St.

39.5 Go straight, following Pearl St. through a confusing intersection with Abrego St. (Even the street signs are confusing; Abrego St.

changes names here, becoming Washington St.)

39.7 Pearl St. becomes Jefferson St. as it heads steeply up.

40.8 Vets Memorial Park; picnic area and campground, hot showers, and hiker-biker camp. No beach access; however, the incessant barking of the sea lions can be heard day and night, keeping campers in tune with the ocean.

Monterey Tour

As mentioned in the introduction, a trip around Monterey is a must. Although you can ride from one attraction to the next, a lot of places cannot truly be explored from the seat of your bicycle. Carry a bike lock and be prepared to walk a little. You can also enjoy the luxury of free bus service (summer only) from Fisherman's Wharf to Cannery Row and the aquarium.

From the intersection of Pearl St. and Washington St., ride down Washington St. to its end at the hotel/convention center. Walk your bike through the plaza to the waterfront and lock it up. Start your tour by exploring the wharf.

Mileage Log

0.0 Fisherman's Wharf is divided into two parts: tourist and commercial. On the commercial wharf, join the pelicans in watching the fishermen unload their catch; on the tourist wharf, purchase a seafood meal for yourself from outdoor vendors. Keep an eye open for sea otters, generally shy, floating on their backs beside the wharfs.

0.4 Leaving Fisherman's Wharf, ride along the waterfront on a wide bike path, watching for harbor seals and otters.

0.9 *Side Trip* to the Coast Guard jetty: Descend from the bike path to the large parking area, then walk out to the end of the jetty, where sea lions nap on the breakwater.

1.1 The bicycle path crosses through the upper portion of Cannery Row, past shops and restaurants located in old buildings made famous by John Steinbeck.

1.6 At the end of Cannery Row, descend 1 block to the Monterey Aquarium, built in an old cannery building. Admission is expensive but worth it. Plan to spend several hours. Continuing south, the path parallels the beautifully sculptured coastline. Watch for sea otters floating on their backs (and hundreds of skin divers floating on their stomachs) in the kelp beds.

2.7 Bike path ends. Go right on Ocean View Blvd. and continue along the coast.

3.9 Go straight through an intersection, entering Point Lobos Refuge.

In the days of John Steinbeck's Cannery Row, this harbor held working fishing boats. The modern-day harbor is filled with pleasure craft.

4.6 Exit Point Lobos Refuge to meet Sunset Dr. Ride along the waterfront past Asilomar State Beach (no facilities) to 17-Mile Drive. **Side Trip** to lighthouse: Turn left on Sunset Dr. for 0.2 mile, then go left again on Asilomar Ave. to the lighthouse entrance (open from 1:00 P.M. to 4:00 P.M. Saturdays and Sundays). Deer often graze near the lighthouse. **Side Trip** to butterfly trees: From September through March, you can take a side trip to the butterfly trees, wintering spot for monarch butterflies. Follow the directions to the lighthouse, except go right on Lighthouse Ave. immediately after turning onto Asilomar Ave. Cycle 0.5 mile to the Butterfly Grove Inn. Walk through the inn's parking area to the trees.

6.2 Turn right on 17-Mile Drive.

6.3 17-Mile Drive entrance station. This is a private road and you must stop here and sign a form waiving your rights to sue should you be run over. You will receive a guide and map of the scenic highlights along the drive. Bike route signs located along the drive make routefinding easy.

16.4 Pass Carmel gate and follow 17-Mile Drive as it climbs steeply through a tree-lined canyon.

17.0 Exit 17-Mile Drive at the Highway 1 gate. Follow Highway 68 back toward Monterey.
17.8 Turn right onto Skyline Forest Dr.
18.0 Turn left on Skyline Dr.
19.1 Vets Memorial Park.

Vets Memorial Park to Kirk Creek Campground (60.2 Miles)

South of Monterey, Highway 1 heads over a wild, undeveloped section of the coast. Rugged cliffs descend at near-vertical angles from the mountains to the pounding surf, leaving little room for man or his roads. As a consequence, Highway 1 is narrow and winding, etched along the hillsides with a shaky hand.

Riding the steeply rolling terrain is strenuous, both physically and mentally. The road is narrow, with little to no shoulder when you need it. Traffic is moderate to heavy, consisting mainly of tourists and tour buses. If you can get yourself moving at dawn, you will have several relatively peaceful hours before the rush of vacationers hits the road around 9:00 to 10:00 A.M. Stores, restaurants, and water stops are few and far between, so plan ahead to avoid shortages.

Between Monterey and Kirk Creek Campground there are only three "must" stops. The first is Point Lobos State Reserve, a Registered National Landmark. Small groves of the nearly extinct Monterey cypress thrive in the harsh environment of the point. The wind has sculptured these trees into graceful shapes, which can be enjoyed by riding the 3 miles of park roads or walking one of the short trails over the headlands and through the groves.

The second stop for the day is Pfeiffer-Big Sur State Park. This park has two distinct parts, an ocean area with a walk-in campground and back-to-nature atmosphere, and the redwoods area with every amenity to pamper the camper. Little of the area's mystique is visible to the passing cyclist. From the highway, it is the commercial aspects, rather than the natural ones, that stand out. To get a better feel of the Big Sur, leave the bikes and spend a day hiking up one of the park trails to high viewpoints, narrow canyons, or ocean beaches, or all the way to the very popular hot springs.

The third stop of special interest is Julia Pfeiffer Burns State Park, where a short trail leads to a spectacular vantage point of a waterfall streaming over the cliffs to the beach.

If a long and difficult ride and three "must" stops are more than you wish to tackle in 1 day, this section divides into perfect halves at Pfeiffer-Big Sur State Park, creating 2 leisurely days, with plenty of time to explore and relax.

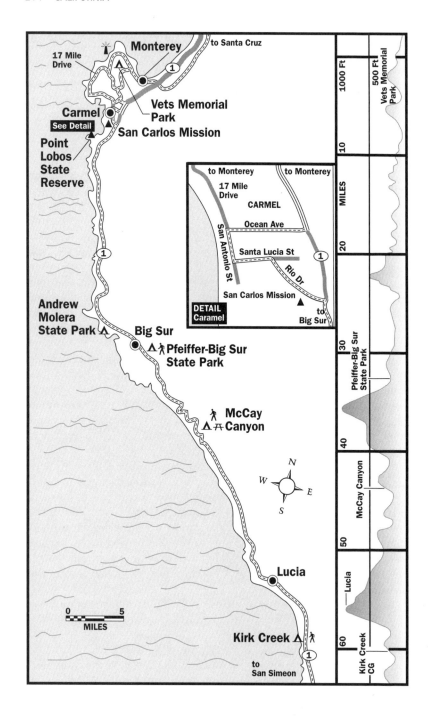

17 Mile Drive

Monterey

to Santa Cruz

Vets Memorial Park

San Carlos Mission

Carmel

See Detail

Point Lobos State Reserve

Andrew Molera State Park

Big Sur

Pfeiffer-Big Sur State Park

McCay Canyon

Lucia

Kirk Creek

to San Simeon

0   5
MILES

to Monterey   to Monterey

17 Mile Drive

CARMEL

Ocean Ave

San Antonio St

Santa Lucia St

Rio Dr

San Carlos Mission

DETAIL
Caramel

to Big Sur

N
W   E
S

1000 Ft

500 Ft
Vets Memorial Park

10

MILES

20

30

Pfeiffer-Big Sur State Park

40

McCay Canyon

50

Lucia

60

Kirk Creek CG

Mileage Log

0.0 Head south from the upper end of Vets Memorial Park on Skyline Dr., which climbs steeply up the forested ridge.

1.1 Turn right on Skyline Forest Dr.

1.4 Take a left on busy Highway 68.

2.3 Pass a 17-Mile Drive entrance, then descend the freeway ramp onto southbound Highway 1. Freeway ends in 0.1 mile. Shoulders are nasty, with dangerous drains.

3.7 Exit right off hectic Highway 1 on Ocean Ave. and descend through Carmel, a tourist-oriented town with small shops, restaurants, and art galleries, including the Weston Gallery, featuring photographs by Edward Weston and Ansel Adams. (If you are short on time you may choose to stay on Highway 1 rather than tour through Carmel.)

4.7 Turn left on San Antonio St. Straight ahead is a large parking area for Carmel Beach.

5.4 San Antonio St. ends; go left on Santa Lucia St.

5.9 Take a right on Rio Rd.

6.0 The grandly restored San Carlos Mission is passed on the right. Visitors are welcome from 9:30 A.M. to 5:00 P.M. for a moderate entrance fee.

6.6 (mp 72.65) Return to Highway 1 and head south. On the east side of the intersection are the last grocery stores before Big Sur. Stock up on food as well as pastries from the bakery.

7.1 (mp 72.30) Cross the shoulderless Carmel River Bridge on Highway 1. The shoulder reappears on the opposite side and remains good, except at slide areas.

8.2 (mp 71.20) Carmel River State Beach; restrooms and beach access. The beach is a popular skin diving area.

9.0 (mp 70.40) Point Lobos State Reserve; restrooms, running water, picnic tables, and trails. Plan to spend as much time here as possible.

9.5 (mp 69.9) Carmel Highlands, a residential area that lasts for several miles. No grocery stores. Highway 1 travels near the coast, climbing over headlands and crossing several slide areas where the shoulder disappears.

19.2 (mp 60.1) Rocky Creek Bridge.

19.7 (mp 59.6) Bixby Creek Bridge.

24.6 (mp 53.7) Pass Point Sur Lighthouse. Visitors are allowed access only in organized groups. If interested in touring the lighthouse, check for times and dates at the Pfeiffer-Big Sur State Park Visitor Center.

28.2 (mp 51.1) Andrew Molera State Park; camping, beach access, and

This famous rocky perch along the Monterey coast is a common stop for tour buses, autos, and cyclists.

hiking trails. The walk-in campground is located 0.3 mile from the road on a trail that is suitable for mountain bikes (bikes with narrow tires should be pushed). The camping is in an open field with pit toilets and water brought in by a tank trailer. No wood may be gathered or purchased for fires. The camp area is 0.2 mile inland from a sandy beach.

30.1 (mp 49.3) Highway 1 heads inland, under the shade of the redwoods.

30.6 (mp 48.8) Enter Big Sur; private campgrounds, grocery stores, motels, and restaurants.

32.1 (mp 47.3) Pfeiffer-Big Sur State Park; a large campground with hiker-biker site, hot showers, wading in the Big Sur River, hiking trails, lodge, restaurant, and grocery store.

33.0 (mp 46.4) Big Sur Station; on the left side of the road is a Forest Service Information Center and a large trailhead parking area with toilets and water. Beyond Big Sur Station, Highway 1 climbs a long hill and then drops back to the coast. Shoulders on the southbound side remain good; views are spectacular.

34.0 (mp 45.2) Last grocery/convenience store for the next 22 miles.

42.3 (mp 36.7) Julia Pfeiffer Burns State Park vista point; view and an information sign that discusses the park as well as the migrations of monarch butterflies and whales.

43.2 (mp 35.8) McCay Canyon day-use area; restrooms, picnic tables, environmental camping (walk-in campsites located 0.2 mile from the road), and a short, 0.25-mile hiking trail to a scenic vantage point overlooking the beach and a waterfall.

51.7 (mp 27.80) Vista point over the rugged coast.

52.7 (mp 26.80) Picnic table on the east side of the highway.

56.1 (mp 23.20) Lucia. This is the last chance to purchase food before Kirk Creek Campground.

58.2 (mp 21.10) Limekiln State Park, a privately operated facility that has been incorporated into the state park system. As of 2004, this park did not accommodate touring cyclists. You cannot even enter the park without paying a fee. No hiker-biker sites. The campground does have hot showers and a trail to some old lime kilns.

60.2 (mp 19.20) Kirk Creek Campground, operated by the Los Padres National Forest; hiker-biker site, running water, beach access, but no electric lights, showers, or hot water.

Kirk Creek Campground to San Simeon State Beach (40 Miles)

From huge hills to nearly level coastal grasslands, the terrain is the key interest along these 40 miles. Leaving Kirk Creek Campground, the route continues to climb and dive its way along the rugged coast for another 22 miles. Then, as if by magic, the hilly countryside is transformed into gentle, low rolling hills.

Once the terrain levels, the miles fly by. While speeding over the lowlands, keep an eye on the tumbling surf; sea otters are often spotted playing just a few yards offshore. Watch the beaches as you go by—sea lions gather by the hundreds in this area for a spot of sunbathing and rolling in the sand.

Near San Simeon, a casual glance east is all that is needed to spot Hearst Castle, perched high on a hill above Highway 1. The massive castle, built by William Randolph Hearst, houses one of the world's largest private collections of art treasures. These treasures may only be viewed by taking one or more of the four organized tours offered by California state parks. Each tour lasts approximately 1 hour and 45 minutes and must be booked in advance by calling (800) 444-4445. Of course, you can always check at the visitor center for unreserved tickets when you arrive.

For the cyclist without extra time or money for a tour, the stop at Hearst Castle Visitor Center allows you a free visit to the museum for insights into the life and times of William Randolph Hearst, as well as information on the designing and building of this massive structure.

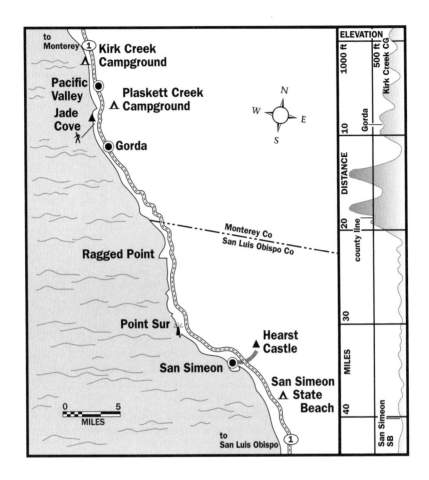

Mileage Log

0.0 (mp 19.10) Leaving Kirk Creek Campground, head south along Highway 1. The shoulder is, at best, whimsical.

0.4 (mp 18.70) Mill Creek picnic area; beach access and restrooms.

5.0 (mp 13.9) Sand Dollar picnic area; picnic tables, running water, and restrooms.

5.3 (mp 13.6) Plaskett Creek Campground on the left (east) side of Highway 1; hiker-biker site, running water, but no showers.

5.4 (mp 13.5) First of two access trails to Jade Cove; a stroll along this beach may turn up bits of jade. Bicycles may be left at Plaskett Creek Campground or at the trailhead.

7.1 (mp 11.90) Willow Creek picnic area and vista point; no facilities.

7.2 (mp 11.80) Picnic table on the left.

Hearst Castle, built high on a hill above San Simeon, was funded by the vast fortune of newspaper mogul William Randolph Hearst.

8.4 (mp 10.30) Gorda; a very small store and restaurant mark the center of this small community.

18.9 (mp 0.0 and 74.32) Leave Monterey County and enter San Luis Obispo County.

20.2 (mp 73.02) Enter Ragged Point. If planning to stop for a bite to eat, start slowing down. When you are flying down the hill, it's easy to miss this small community of fast-food outlets and cliff-hanging houses.

22.2 (mp 70.70) The hill bottoms out and the road heads across a grassy prairie.

29.5 (mp 63.30) Piedras Blancas Light Station. This land was recently turned over to the Bureau of Land Management and is now open for limited tours. As of 2004, tours are offered once a month only and start from the Hearst Castle Visitor Center. For more information, call toll-free: (888) 804-8608. For reservations, call (805) 927-6881.

29.7 (mp 63.03) The road narrows as it skirts the edge of the coast.

30.0 (mp 62.70) A section of blocked-off shoulder signals the next point of interest. Stop and check out the beach below. If it appears to be covered with driftwood, take a closer look. This is a favorite sunning location for sea lions.

31.7 (mp 62.1) Vista point; view of Hearst Castle, beach access, and tide pools. Beyond the vista point, the shoulder returns and remains good for the rest of the ride.

34.8 (mp 58.5) San Simeon city limits.

35.4 (mp 57.9) Turn left (east) for an easy 0.3-mile climb to the Hearst Castle Visitor Center; restrooms, water, tours, museum, gift shop, bike rack, lockers, and snack bar. To the right (west) is the town of San Simeon, which has a small grocery store, and William Randolph Hearst Memorial State Beach; picnic area, fishing pier, restrooms, running water, and beach access.

38.4 (mp 54.9) San Simeon's motel and restaurant row, which includes several small grocery stores.

40.0 (mp 53.2) San Simeon State Beach Campground. Turn left (east) off Highway 1 to reach the campground access. The campground has two parts. The first is San Simeon State Beach, where the small hiker-biker site is right next to the freeway; water, hot showers, and beach access. The second part is Washburn Campground, located on a hill overlooking the beach area. This primitive area has neither hiker-biker site nor showers; however, it is clean, quiet, and scenic. For groups of three or more, this is less expensive than the official hiker-biker site.

If you end the ride with a bit of extra time for exploring, consider taking a hike on the 3.3-mile interpretive trail through the San Simeon Nature Preserve. The main trailhead is located in the Washburn Campground but can be accessed from several other points. Once you have stretched your legs, head down to the sandy beach for a bit of southern California sunbathing and exploration.

San Simeon State Beach to Oceano Campground (52.6 Miles)

The ride from San Simeon State Beach to Pismo State Beach marks the beginning of the transition from central to southern California. The isolation and spectacular scenery of the northern and central coast is replaced by freeways and large urban areas with a Spanish flavor. The very distinctive smell of eucalyptus trees fills the air, beaches are lined with palms, and hillsides are dotted with oaks. Ants are everywhere—so keep the tent door closed and don't leave food out. The ocean is warmer and a swim is a refreshing, rather than a heart-stopping, way to end the day's ride.

Between San Simeon and Pismo Beach is ideal riding country. The terrain is nearly level, the roads are good, and you can cover the miles with time to relax at the end of the day. With the exception of a brief excursion along the coast at Cambria, the first 24.6 miles are spent following Highway 1 (a four-lane highway) south to Morro Bay. The second part of the ride is entirely on quieter back roads through well-developed farmlands. Temperatures in this section may be quite warm, especially in the San Luis Obispo area.

Chief attractions are Morro Bay, a popular beach resort and fishing area known for its distinctive rock, and the sand dunes at Pismo Beach.

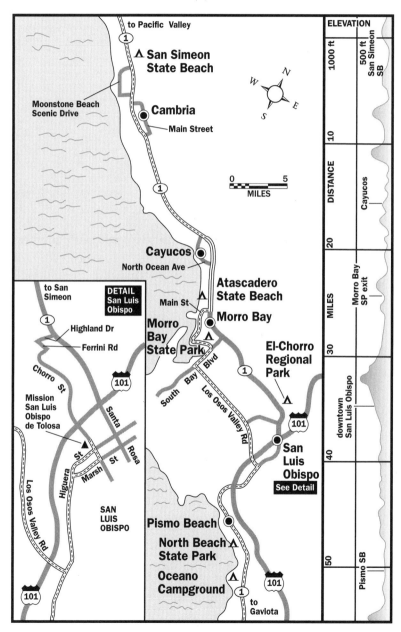

An optional side trip takes you to visit Mission San Luis Obispo, founded in 1772.

The day ends at Oceano Campground in Pismo State Beach. The beach is a popular place, and people drive jeeps and cars to favorite surf-fishing or sunset-watching locations. Inland from the beach is the Sand Dunes Reserve, a natural area closed to motorized vehicles. It's a great place for exploring, sitting, sliding, or just looking.

Mileage Log

0.0 (mp 53.20) Leave San Simeon State Beach on Highway 1. Shoulder width is ample, up to 8 feet wide, except at bridges.

0.4 (mp 52.80) Picnic area and vista point on the right.

0.9 (mp 52.30) At Moonstone Beach Scenic Dr., exit right (west) off Highway 1 for a scenic ride along the coastline. The picnic area at the turnoff has picnic tables and beach access.

1.1 Leffingwell Landing State Beach is a whale-watching area in the winter; picnic tables, water, and restrooms. Continue south, past long, sandy beaches.

2.3 (mp 50.80) Return to Highway 1. *Alternate Route:* Cross to the east side of Highway 1 and follow Main St. south through the center of Cambria past shops and grocery stores. Main St. loops back to Highway 1 in 2.4 miles.

5.0 (mp 48.20) Alternate Route through Cambria returns to Highway 1. Continue inland, traversing sun-baked pastures for the next 10 miles.

16.1 (mp 37.10) Cayucos, a small tourist-oriented town; grocery stores.

16.3 (mp 36.90) *Alternate Route* through Cayucos: Cyclists wishing to shop in Cayucos should exit Highway 1 on N. Ocean Ave. The road parallels the waterfront, passes through town, then returns to Highway 1 in 1.7 miles. Past the Cayucos exit, Highway 1 becomes freeway.

18.3 (mp 34.90) Cayucos Alternate Route returns to Highway 1.

20.5 (mp 32.70) Morro Bay city limits. Markets and shopping centers are visible from the freeway. The town has several state parks, long, sandy beaches, and a wildlife refuge.

21.5 (mp 32.20) Morro Strand State Beach campground; a 3-mile beach, running water, restrooms, many trailer hookups, and cold outdoor showers; no hiker-biker site.

24.6 (mp 28.60) Exit Highway 1 at Main St. Go right on Main St. and follow the signs through town to Morro Bay State Park. The road parallels Morro Bay, winding through a residential district before entering the park, where it turns into State Park Rd. Follow the park road past the golf course, museum, and marina. *Side Trip* to Morro Rock: Go right off Main St. on Beach St. and ride to its end.

Turn left on Embarcadero for 1 mile to Morro Rock and the state park; restrooms, picnic tables, and water.

26.4 Morro Bay State Park campground entrance; hot showers. At the time of this review, the hiker-biker site is located in the picnic area. Tents may not be set up until 5:00 P.M. during the summer and 4:00 P.M. during the winter. Tents must be down by 9:00 A.M. However, the camping situation may change once the scheduled modernization of the campground occurs in 2004 and 2005. If camping at the park, no entrance fee is charged to visit the natural history museum or to enjoy its excellent view of Morro Rock. The rock is a National Preserve and nesting ground for the rare and endangered peregrine falcon. Continue beyond the campground to S. Bay Blvd.

27.0 Turn right (south) on S. Bay Blvd. and continue around Morro Bay. The road starts out narrow and then gradually widens to include a comfortable shoulder.

31.0 Turn left on Los Osos Valley Rd., which heads east away from the ocean. Temperatures soar as the road rolls through open farmlands. (Expect to see numerous cyclists on this road; this is part of a popular training ride.)

31.8 Los Osos Oaks State Reserve; hiking trails through groves of 700-year-old oaks.

37.9 Pass Foothills Blvd., access to Cuesta College. The route continues straight on Los Osos Valley Blvd., entering the residential outskirts of San Luis Obispo.

40.1 Cross over a freeway (US 101 and Highway 1 combined).

40.3 Los Osos Valley Rd. ends; go right on S. Higuera St. *Side Trip* to Mission San Luis Obispo de Tolosa: Go left (north) on S. Higuera

===== Morro Rock and the Nine Sisters =====

Morro Rock, standing sentinel duty in Morro Bay, is actually but one in a chain of volcanic plugs called the Nine Sisters that extends in a near-straight line from San Luis Obispo to Morro Bay. The chain of "Morros" consists of nine major peaks and twelve minor peaks. Some 20 to 25 million years ago there was a line of volcanoes that eroded away, leaving only the harden cores, the "plug" section that we see today. Shortly after the birth of these volcanoes, the forces on the coast changed direction and the volcanoes became extinct. The new pressures along the coast found release in a giant fault system that we know today as the San Andreas.

Pismo Dune Reserve is the only dune area on the California Coast that is not open to motorized use.

St. until the road divides in 2.4 miles. Continue north on Marsh St. (a one-way road) for 0.3 mile, then turn left on Chorro St. and continue 0.2 mile to the mission. Tour the mission, then stroll down to San Luis Obispo Creek. Restaurants, grocery stores, bakeries, and a bike shop are close by. The park has a restroom and water. To return to the route, take Higuera St. (one-way road south) back to S. Higuera St.

42.1 Cross under US 101, staying on S. Higuera St.

42.2 Turn right on Ontario Rd. and parallel the freeway for the next 3 miles. Note the sirens located along the road. If trouble occurs with the nuclear power plant in Diablo Canyon, a warning signal will be heard, lasting from 3 to 5 minutes. The sirens are just one of those little nuisances that must be endured when a nuclear power plant is located on a fault line.

44.3 P G & E Community Center; picnic tables and running water. Before the nuclear reactor was built, the center housed elaborate and expensive displays on energy and conservation.

45.2 When Ontario Rd. ends, turn left on Avila Beach Rd., passing a private campground and pool heated by a hot springs.

45.5 Turn right on Palisades Rd.

45.7 Pismo Beach. Stay on Palisades Rd., sandwiched between the freeway and beach. The road becomes Shell Beach Rd. and then turns into Price St.

49.5 (mp 16.05) When the road divides, descend right on Dolliver St.; you are now back on Highway 1. Ride through the center of Pismo Beach on a wide bike lane.

50.7 (mp 14.70) North Beach campground; hiker-biker site, water, beach access, but no showers in this open-field park.

51.0 (mp 14.40) Grover Beach access.

52.1 (mp 13.24) Oceano city limits.

52.4 (mp 13.00) Turn right on Pier Ave. The small grocery store on the far side of the intersection is the closest store to the campground. Ride Pier Ave. to the state park campground, not to be confused with Oceano County Campground, located on the right side of the road.

52.6 Turn left into Oceano Campground; hiker-biker site complete with bike rack, hot showers, and a trail to the beach. Keep valuables, touring bags, and food stored well out of reach of the flock of marauding ducks and thieving raccoons. *Side Trip* to Pismo Dune Preserve: The sand dunes are located 0.2 mile beyond the campground. Due to the large amount of loose sand, it is best to leave bikes at the campground and walk Pier Ave. or one of the campground trails to the beach. Head south on the beach for another 0.2 mile, cross a creek, then go inland through a low fence designed to keep motor vehicles out of the dunes. Walk beyond the reach of the dune grass to enjoy the sand. This is a great place to watch the sunset. The roads and houses near the Dunes Beach have special problems. In winter, sand tries to engulf the surrounding area. The roads are marked with tall poles, the same as those used in snow-bound mountain passes, to define the roads for the sand plows.

Oceano Campground to Gaviota State Park (61.6 Miles)

For the next 61.6 miles, the huge Vandenburg Air Force Base lies between Highway 1 and the coast. Consequently, the day is spent riding through inland valleys and over rolling hills. Scenery in the valleys ranges from fragrant groves of eucalyptus trees to massive farm fields. To challenge riders, the route crosses two major hills, each about 950 feet in elevation, which have elegant scenery on the long grind up and thrilling descents.

Food and water stops are limited to three towns: Guadalupe, Orcutt, and Lompoc. Temperatures along the route frequently reach 90 degrees during the summer, so start early and carry plenty of water. However, the greatest discomfort comes when the northern trade winds whip across the plowed fields, filling the air with dust.

The day ends at Gaviota State Park. This is a large and very scenic park with beach access and miles of trails to scenic overlooks in the hills above. Unfortunately, the campground, tucked between the base of the Santa Ynez Mountains and the ocean, is small and located near the train tracks and the freeway. There is no hiker-biker site, just first-come campsites. If you arrive late or on a weekend, you may need to continue south another 9.1 miles to the Refugio State Beach hiker-biker site. Gaviota State Park is open Friday through Sunday only from October 1 through March 31.

A highly recommended alternative to the standard Pacific Coast Bicycle Route (and California Bicentennial Route) is the Santa Ynez Valley Alternate Route, starting at Lompoc. The route heads inland to the Danish town of Solvang, through Santa Ynez Valley, then back to the coast at Santa Barbara. Solvang was founded and settled by Danes, who have kept its heritage alive through customs, architecture, and a friendly spirit. One facet of Danish life—cooking—is tastefully represented here. The slightest breeze is filled with tempting aromas from bakeries and fudge factories.

Santa Ynez Valley is scenic country and a superior cycling area, through rolling grass hills dotted with California oak trees. The bright blue sky here is a prime soaring area for hawks and ravens. In the heart of the Santa Ynez Valley is Lake Cachuma County Park, a complete recreation area with everything from camping and swimming to miniature golfing and horseback riding. The Alternate Route makes a long, difficult climb over San Marcos Pass and then descends to Santa Barbara. Views of the coast are outstanding.

In short, the Santa Ynez Valley Alternate Route is a scenic, tasty, and downright enjoyable ride that bypasses a long stretch of riding on US 101 (a busy freeway). The Alternate Route is not recommended in July or August, when temperatures soar into the hundreds.

Mileage Log

0.0 From Oceano Campground, cycle back to Highway 1. Head south through peaceful countryside. Shoulders are narrow and traffic moderate.

2.7 (mp 10.41) Intersection; turn right (south), following Highway 1 toward Guadalupe. After the turn, ascend a short, steep hill.

12.8 (mp 0.0 and 50.6) Leave San Luis Obispo County and enter Santa Barbara County at the city limits of Guadalupe. The first right in town leads 1 block to Le Roy County Park; restrooms, picnic tables,

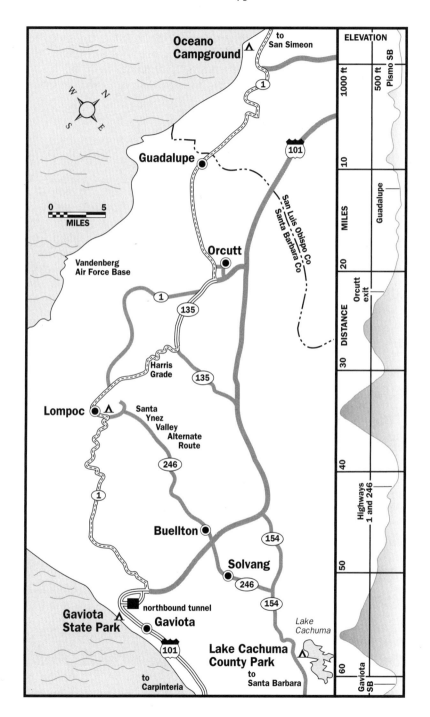

ELEVATION

1000 ft

500 ft Pismo SB

to San Simeon

Oceano Campground

Guadalupe

101

San Luis Obispo Co
Santa Barbara Co

10

MILES

Guadalupe

Orcutt

20

Orcutt exit

Vandenberg Air Force Base

1

135

DISTANCE

30

Harris Grade

135

Lompoc

Santa Ynez Valley Alternate Route

246

1

40

Highways 1 and 246

Buellton

154

Solvang

50

246

154

northbound tunnel

Gaviota State Park

Gaviota

Lake Cachuma

101

Lake Cachuma County Park

to Santa Barbara

Gaviota SB

60

to Carpinteria

0   5
MILES

W N
S E

and water. As you ride through town, you'll notice the signs on grocery stores, restaurants, and bakeries are all in Spanish.

15.1 (mp 48.3) Solomon Canyon Creek. The shoulder narrows.

23.7 (mp 36.05) Intersection; Highway 135 Business branches off to the left, heading into Orcutt.

24.1 (mp 35.0) Highway 1 merges with Highway 135 and becomes a busy four-lane freeway with a wide shoulder.

28.0 (mp R31.50) Highway 1 bears right and heads up a steep hill, climbing into the Vandenburg Air Force Base. Ignore bike signs and leave Highway 1 here. Continue straight ahead on Highway 135. Use caution crossing the Highway 1 exit; most traffic turns off here. ***Alternate Route:*** Highway 1 may be followed to Lompoc. It has steep hills and a lot of traffic.

30.3 The freeway ends. The highway returns to two lanes and a narrow shoulder.

30.8 Turn right (south) on Harris Grade and follow signs to Lompoc. Over 600 feet of elevation are gained in the next 3 miles as the narrow, twisting road climbs over a small band of hills, reaching an elevation of 950 feet. Traffic is light.

After descending Harris Grade, the route levels out for an easy cruise through the city of Lompoc.

34.0 Top of the hill. Enjoy the views across the open farmlands before starting the brisk trip down.

35.9 A roadside marker details the history of the La Purisima Mission.

38.4 (mp 21.80) The bike route rejoins Highway 1; continue straight ahead. Truck traffic increases as the road widens to four lanes with shoulder.

38.5 (mp 21.70) Lompoc; food, Laundromats, bike shops, cafes, hotel, campground, and the last grocery store before Gaviota State Park.

41.1 (mp 19.1) Following Highway 1, turn left (south) on Ocean Ave.

42.4 (mp 20.3) Stay with Highway 1 as it makes a 90-degree turn to the right (south) and begins a 13.5-mile rolling climb to an elevation of over 900 feet. The shoulder is good, except at bridges. Santa Ynez Valley Alternate Route to Santa Barbara starts at this intersection (see details below). *Side Trip* to River Park Campground: When Highway 1 turns right, continue straight on Highway 246 for 0.5 mile. The park entrance is located on the left (north) side of the road; primitive site, picnic area, water, hot showers during daylight hours only.

56.0 (mp 2.6) Summit of hill and start of a fast, 2.5-mile descent to US 101.

58.6 Intersection of Highway 1 and US 101. Take a left turn to head up the US 101 on ramp. US 101 is a freeway with wide shoulders and a lot of noisy traffic. (Northbound travelers, just before the Highway 1 turnoff, must ride through a short tunnel with a very narrow shoulder and, frequently, a very strong head wind. It is like trying to cycle out of a high-suction vacuum hose.) *Side Trip* to Gaviota State Beach Hot Springs: At the junction of Highway 1 and US 101, cross the freeway, then go left on the frontage road to a parking area. A brisk 0.5-mile hike leads to springs and a swimming area. Hide bikes and gear well or take it with you.

60.5 (mp 46.1) Rest area; tourist information, water, restrooms, and cool shade. For southbound travelers only.

61.0 (mp 45.6) Turnoff to Gaviota State Park.

61.6 Gaviota State Park; forty-one first-come campsites, beach access, surfing, swimming, pier fishing, hiking trails into the Santa Ynez Mountains, and a very limited grocery store. No hot showers.

If all campsites are full, or if you simply prefer a campsite on the edge of a palm-lined beach and hot showers, continue south on US 101 for 9.1 miles to Refugio State Beach.

Santa Ynez Valley Alternate Route

0.0 The junction of Highway 1 and Highway 246 marks the start of the Alternate Route through Santa Ynez Valley to Santa Barbara. Follow Highway 246 east over rolling terrain. Shoulders vary from 1 to 8 feet wide, traffic from light to heavy.

0.5 Pass Riverside Campground; primitive area, water, restrooms.

1.9 *Side Trip* to La Purisima Mission State Historical Park: Turn left on Mission Gate Rd. for 0.3 mile, then cross the street to reach the entrance; historic mission, water, bathrooms.

16.0 Enter Buellton, home of Anderson's split pea soup (which, if you like pea soup, is supposed to be the best). Leaving Buellton, continue southeast on Highway 246, crossing US 101 to reach Solvang.

19.5 Solvang; the main road through town is Mission St. (Highway 246); however, bakeries, fudge factories, wine-tasting rooms, and tourist shops are on Copenhagen St., 1 block west. Continue south from Solvang on Highway 246. Hills get steeper and traffic volume increases.

24.5 Turn right (south) on Highway 154. Shoulders remain good for a few miles and then gradually disappear.

30.5 Lake Cachuma County Park, the recommended overnight stop. The campground has excellent facilities, including a hiker-biker site, hot showers, fishing, boat rentals, horseback riding, complete grocery store, swimming and wading pools, a game room, miniature golf, and roller-skating.

36.5 Start of 4-mile climb to San Marcos Pass.

40.5 San Marcos Pass, elevation 2,225 feet. From the summit, it is a rapid 7-mile descent on a narrow, twisting road with heavy traffic.

47.5 Cyclists take the Foothill Rd. exit (State 192). At the base of the exit, turn left on Foothill Rd. and follow it for 2 miles along the outskirts of Santa Barbara.

50.0 At Alamar Ave., turn right and descend to State St.

50.2 Turn left on State St. and ride to the beach to rejoin the Pacific Coast Bicycle Route.

Gaviota State Park to Carpinteria State Beach (44.4 Miles)

The mix of freeways, backroads, farmlands, and cities serves to remind you that you are now well into that very unique area called southern California. Riding conditions are good, the freeway has a wide shoulder, city streets have wide bike lanes, and only one short, steep hill breaks the harmony of gently rolling terrain.

Santa Barbara is the center of interest along this portion of the coast. The day's ride is short, leaving plenty of time to savor the city's strong Spanish flavor in an optional city tour. With just a short side trip off the main route you may visit the Santa Barbara Mission, founded in 1786 and called the "Queen of Missions" because of its stately grace; the county courthouse, which was modeled after a Spanish-Moorish palace with

Mission Santa Barbara, known as the Queen of Missions because of its spectacular grace and beauty, was founded in 1786.

hand-painted ceilings, giant murals, and a sweeping view from the clock tower; El Presidio, a fort built by the Spanish in 1782; and El Cuartel, the second-oldest standing adobe building in Calfornia. The tour ends at Stearns Wharf, where the sight of sunbathers, Rollerbladers, and windsurfers make for a strictly modern view.

Cyclists passing through Santa Barbara in mid-August have a chance to catch the Fiesta Days celebration, which features a parade, street dancing, and every kind of Mexican food imaginable.

Carpinteria State Park, at the end of the day's ride, claims to have the world's safest swimming beach, long and sandy with no undertow. This park was built on an old Chumash native American campsite. On the beach are several tar pits, where natural tar seeps out onto the sand—so watch where you sit and step.

Warning: Santa Barbara has a dizzying array of bike routes. The Santa

Barbara city route, signed as the Coast Route, is not the official Pacific Coast Bicycle Route. If you follow the green signs denoting the Santa Barbara city route, you will eventually head south in the correct direction; however, you will miss some of the city highlights.

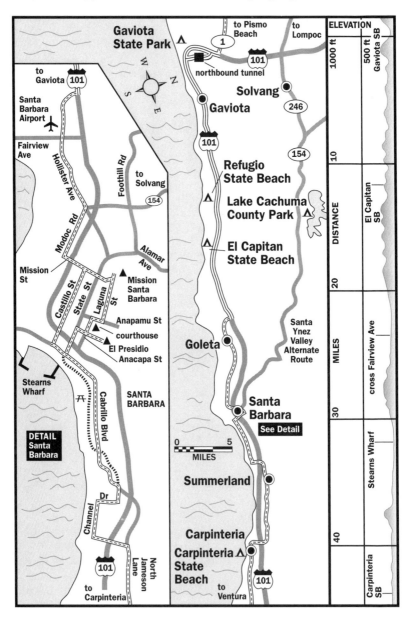

Mileage Log

0.0 The day's ride starts at Gaviota State Park hiker-biker site.

0.5 (mp 46.3) Head south on US 101. The shoulder is broad along the freeway, averaging 4 to 8 feet except at bridges, where it completely disappears. Timing is very important when you cross these narrow bridges in the company of thundering eighteen-wheel trucks; use a lot of caution.

1.8 (mp 44.5) Vista Del Mer; first of two beach accesses.

5.1 (mp 41.00) Vista Point; a chance to get off your bike and stroll over an old highway bridge.

10.0 (mp 36.1) Turnoff to Refugio State Beach; scenic hiker-biker camp, hot showers, and a small store. *Alternate Route:* A 2-mile bike path connects Refugio State Beach with El Capitan State Beach to the south, providing a scenic escape from the noise and dirt of the freeway. Ride down the campground access road from the freeway, then go left on the bike path, which skims along the edge of a bluff overlooking the ocean, with views up and down the coast. The bike path is subject to slides; check with park personnel before starting out.

11.8 (mp 34.30) El Capitan State Beach; large hiker-biker campsite located at the north end of the park in sight and sound of the freeway, hot showers, nature trail, small visitor center, camp store, sandy beach with lifeguards in the summer, and a 2-mile bike path to Refugio State Beach.

18.9 (mp 27.16) Hollister Ave. exit; all bicycles must turn off US 101 at this point.

19.2 At the top of the freeway exit ramp, turn right on Hollister Ave. Numerous grocery stores, bike shops, restaurants, and motels will be passed in the next 20 miles. Traffic is often heavy; however, most roads have a wide lane for bikes.

21.3 Cross Storke Rd., access to UCSB (University of California at Santa Barbara).

23.8 Cross Fairview Ave. at a busy intersection in the center of the town of Goleta. Two large bicycle shops are located within 4 blocks (west). Continue south on Hollister Ave.

27.1 Bear right on Modoc Rd. just before Hollister Ave. passes under a railroad bridge. Modoc Rd. changes to Catania Way after the first mile, which then becomes Parks Rd.

30.2 Turn left on Mission St. at the end of Parks Rd. Cycle under an overpass.

30.4 One block after riding under the freeway, turn right on Castillo St. and follow it for the next 2 miles. (Santa Barbara Tour starts here).

31.9 Castillo St. passes under US 101. (*Warning:* Do not attempt this after a rainstorm.)

32.4 Go left on Cabrillo Blvd. Plaza Del Mar is passed on the right; restrooms. A city bike path is located between the road and the beach for those who wish to brave the perpetual rush-hour traffic of joggers, Rollerbladers, and walkers.

32.8 Pass State St. on the left. Santa Ynez Valley Alternate Route rejoins the Coast Route here.

34.2 Pass the entrance to Santa Barbara's city zoo on the left.

35.0 Opposite the Andree Clark Bird Refuge (just before the road passes under US 101), turn right on Channel Dr.

35.2 Channel Dr. becomes a bike path as it heads to the beach. The bike path soon turns back into a road. Channel Dr. heads inland, becoming Olive Mill Rd. when it crosses US 101.

36.0 Take the first right after crossing the freeway on N. Jameson Lane. The road is shoulderless and moderately busy.

36.4 Pacific Coast Bicycle Route signs indicate that you should return to the freeway at San Ysidro Rd. Unless you have developed an

Southern California is the birthplace of the Olympic sport of beach volleyball.

addiction to freeway riding, or simply are allergic to hills, continue on N. Jameson Lane.

37.6 Go right and ride up Ortega Hill Rd. From the top of this short, steep hill, descend to the small community of Summerland; restaurants and a small grocery store. Paralleling the freeway, Ortega Hill Rd. becomes Lillie Ave., then Via Real.

42.9 Via Real ends. Turn right on Santa Ynez Ave. and cross to the west side of US 101.

43.1 Take a sharp left on Carpinteria Ave. and follow the bike lane through town.

43.8 At the community pool, turn right on Palm Ave. and follow it to the campground. (No signs point to the campground, so watch for the street sign.)

44.4 Carpinteria State Beach; hiker-biker site, hot showers, beach access, a small store, and a visitor center featuring the history of the Chumash people. Several large grocery stores and numerous restaurants are located nearby. Excellent bus service to Santa Barbara. From Carpinteria south, hiker-biker sites have become hangouts for transients. If a regular site is available, you may find it a better bargain than the cheap sites. When you leave camp, carry all your valuables with you, and lock your bike.

Santa Barbara Tour

At the intersection of Mission and Castillo Streets, continue straight on Mission St. After 0.8 mile, Mission St. ends. Turn left and go 0.2 mile up Laguna St. to the Santa Barbara Mission. The mission and museum may be toured for a fee, or you may stay outdoors and enjoy the graceful architecture for free.

From the mission, ride down Laguna St. for 1.1 miles to Anapamu St. Go right 0.2 mile, to Anacapa St., then turn left. The county courthouse, on the left, is the next stop. Walk through the halls and then climb to the top of the clock tower for a view of the whole city. Three blocks farther down Anacapa St., turn left on E. Canon Perdido St. for half a block to El Presidio de Santa Barbara. Go to the visitor center and pay the entrance fee, which allows you to tour the Presidio, as well as the Casa de la Guerra (the oldest adobe home in California) and El Cuartel (the site of the original fortress founded by Spain in 1782). The Historical Society Museum is located 1 block south. After exploring the museum, take the first right and go west 2 blocks to State St. Follow State St. to the beach, and go left on Cabrillo Blvd. to rejoin the bike route. The tour may be continued from the end of State St. by heading out on Stearns Wharf or by cycling right, around the boat harbor and out on the breakwater, a scenic place to watch boats and eat lunch.

Carpinteria State Beach to Leo Carrillo State Beach (47.8 Miles)

Southern California ambiance and plenty of it is found on this fairly easy ride that ends at the outskirts of Los Angeles. With a generous mix of Spanish architecture, palm trees, famous surfing beaches, a national park, and a historic mission, the countryside between Carpinteria State Beach and Leo Carrillo State Beach is fascinating. Scenery varies with nearly every turn of the pedal.

Of course, people play a large role in creating ambiance. Many Californians spend a great deal of time outdoors swimming, sunbathing, sailing, walking, and, of course, bicycling. Take this opportunity to check out some of the extremes in cycling attire. (Some of these fashions will work their way to the rest of the country in the next few years.)

The amazing duality of this area is evident wherever you look; from the beautiful sand-covered beaches with views of offshore oil rigs, to the wilderness peninsula located at the sprawling edge of the megalopolis that is Los Angeles.

Terrain is nearly level, except near Leo Carrillo State Beach, and miles go quickly. One short section of the ride is on the freeway, where broad shoulders give you some protection from the traffic. The most hazardous section is the shoulderless thoroughfares in the Oxnard-Port Hueneme area.

Two side trips are recommended. The first is to visit the restored San Buenaventura Mission and Ventura County Historical Museum in the historic district of Ventura. The historical museum has indoor and outdoor exhibits depicting local history, from the life and culture of native Americans who lived in the area to twentieth-century oil exploration. The mission also has a museum (admission is charged).

Farther south, a second side trip leads to the Channel Islands National Park and Wildlife Refuge Visitor Center. Displays feature the natural history on and around the islands. Charter boats take visitors out for half- or whole-day trips to observe the islands. Reservations for these trips should be made up to two weeks in advance. For the cyclists who do not have a day to devote to the islands, the 30-minute movie at the visitor center is best avoided, as it simply wets the viewers' appetite to visit these isolated islands.

Mileage Log

0.0 Leaving Carpinteria State Beach, follow Palm Ave. back to Carpinteria Ave.

0.2 Turn right on Carpinteria Ave. and head south, paralleling US 101.

2.2 At the end of Carpinteria Ave., turn left, then take an immediate right to descend the on ramp to US 101 (mp 00.43). For the next

4.8 miles you will be riding around the edge of a broad bay on a wide shoulder of the busy freeway. At the north end of this bay is Rincon Point, an area that attracts surfers from around the world.

2.9 (mp 00.00 and mp 43.80) Leave Santa Barbara County; enter Ventura County.

7.0 (mp 39.30) Exit the freeway at the small community of Sea Cliff;

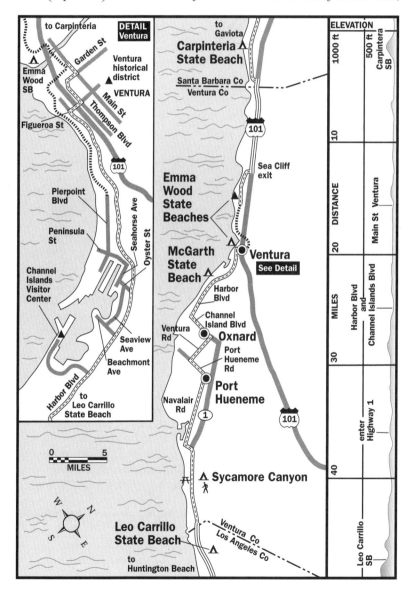

county parks, state beaches, homes, but no stores.

7.2 At the base of US 101 exit ramp, turn right on Old Highway and pass the entrance to Hobson County Park; camping. The road heads south, passing the community of Faria Beach.

9.8 Faria County Park; camping, water, a small store, but no hiker-biker site.

13.3 Ride up the freeway entrance ramp. To the right is the access to the Emma Wood State Beach RV camping area.

13.7 At the top of the ramp, turn right on a narrow bike path, which parallels the coast.

14.6 Ventura city limits.

15.1 Bicycle path enters the south section of Emma Wood State Beach; picnic area, water, hiker-biker site, group campsites, cold outdoor showers, and beach access. Stay on the bicycle path as it passes under US 101 and winds around a commercial campground.

15.6 Cross the Ventura River, then turn left (east) off the bike path to Main St. ***Alternate Route:*** The bike path turns west, offering a scenic route around downtown Ventura. The route heads out to the beach and then skirts the Ventura County Fairgrounds. The bike path passes Surfers Point and then heads through Promenade Park before entering San Buenaventura State Beach, where it returns to the city streets and continues south on Pierpoint Blvd. for 1 mile. Go left on Peninsula St., then right on Seahorse Ave. Turn left on Oyster St., right on Seaview Ave., and left on Beachmont Ave. to return to the bike route at Harbor Blvd.

15.7 Pass Ortega Adobe Historic Site on the left (east) side of Main St. This type of house once lined the streets of town.

15.8 Turn right on S. Garden St. ***Side Trip*** to the historic district of Ventura: Continue straight on Main St. 0.3 mile to visit San Buenaventura Mission. This was the ninth mission built by the great mission builder Father Sierro in 1782. The original mission burned down and then was rebuilt in 1809. One block north of the mission is the Ventura County Museum of History and Art, which is full of fascinating information about the original inhabitants of Ventura and what happened to them when the Spanish arrived. Adjacent to the museum is the Ortega Adobe Historic Site, which features a small home of the type that used to line the streets of Ventura.

15.9 Go left on W. Santa Clara St., following the green city bike route signs.

16.1 Turn right on Figueroa St. and cross under US 101.

16.3 Take a left on Harbor Blvd. immediately after crossing the rail-road tracks.

16.7 Beach Park, a small picnic area with tables but no water.

17.8 Cross San Pedro St. (the turnoff to Buenaventura State Beach;

day-use area with restrooms, water, picnic tables, and beach access).

18.2 Harbor Blvd. passes through a congested commercial area with grocery stores. Continuing south, head through a residential district, then around Ventura Harbor.

20.2 *Side Trip* to Channel Islands National Park and Wildlife Refuge Visitor Center: Turn right into the harbor area and ride west for 1.3 miles to the visitor center at the end of the spit; restrooms, beach access, and running water.

20.7 The road crosses a corner of McGarth State Beach.

21.2 Enter Oxnard.

21.4 McGarth State Beach Campground; hiker-biker area, hot showers, beach access, lake, bird watching, sand dunes, and nature trail. Beyond the park entrance, Harbor Blvd. passes the Mandalay Steam Plant electric generating station and then heads by an exclusive residential area.

24.6 Oxnard State Beach; a picnic area with restrooms, tables, water, and beach access.

25.0 Harbor Blvd. divides; go left, heading east over Channel Islands Harbor into Oxnard, where Harbor Blvd. becomes Channel Islands Blvd. This is the start of a very congested area. Much of the road is narrow without a shoulder. Shops and grocery stores, located on the left (north) side of the road, are the last before Leo Carrillo State Beach.

27.1 At the eastern end of a large golf course, turn right on Ventura Rd. and ride the bike path for the next 1.5 miles. Watch out for the

Channel Islands

Channel Islands National Park encompasses five of a string of eight islands. The park covers 249,345 acres, half of which are underwater. There are 145 species that are unique to the islands, making them a delicate and fascinating place to explore. The closest island to land is Anacapa, located an hour and half from shore by boat. This island has a visitor center, lighthouse, campground, and picnic area, making it a great day trip. Santa Barbara Island has a visitor center and is ideal for hiking and camping. The larger islands, San Miguel, Santa Rosa, and Santa Cruz, require half-day to all-day boat trips to reach their shores and are best for longer visits. All islands offer bird watching and marine-mammal observation opportunities. All water and food supplies must be carried with you to the islands. Contact the national park for up-to-date information on camping and charter boat reservations several months before your visit.

A tour boat cruises near Anacapa Island, in Channel Islands National Park. Overnight or day trips can be arranged.

narrowly spaced posts at the intersections.

28.8 Go left on Port Hueneme Rd. (pronounced "wye-nee-mee") and enter the town of Port Hueneme. This is a navy area, and many side roads are gated. The road is very busy as it leaves the city, heading into farm country; however, the shoulder is good.

33.7 Turn right on Navalair Rd. just before Highway 1, passing naval installations and the airport.

34.3 Intersection. Continue straight, past a display of rockets and jets, or stop and inspect them; picnic tables are located in the shade of the fighter planes.

36.7 Turn onto Highway 1, heading back toward the coast (mp 10.30).

39.2 (mp 7.80) Leave the military reservation and begin public access area. Before long the road enters Point Mugu State Park, which is spread out along the coast. Use caution; the wide shoulder is used as a parking lot for those who do not wish to pay for parking at the state beaches. This nifty system may alleviate parking congestion in the lots, but it forces cyclists onto the highway.

41.2 (mp 6.10) La Jolla Canyon on the left; trailhead and group camp area.

41.3 (mp 6.00) Thornhill Beach Campground, located on a sandy area between the highway and the beach. The campground has cold outdoor showers and chemical toilets, but no hiker-biker area.

42.6 (mp 4.47) Sycamore Cove and Canyon has picnicking at the cove on the west side of the highway and camping in the canyon on the east side; hiker-biker site, running water, and several trails into the canyon. This campground is preferable to Leo Carrillo. If you can manage the longer ride through Los Angeles tomorrow, spend the night here.

47.0 (mp 00.00 and mp 62.87) Leave Ventura County and enter Los Angeles County.

47.8 (mp 62.10) Leo Carrillo State Beach, the last public campground north of Los Angeles; hiker-biker site, hot showers, beach access, and a very small camp store (open summer only). No stores or restaurants nearby. This campground is at the end of the bus line from Los Angeles, providing easy access to and from the city. (If you have the energy, continue on another 12.5 miles to Malibu Beach RV Park. Call ahead. See next section for details.)

Leo Carrillo State Beach to Colonial Inn Hostel (72 Miles)

If you are touring on a tight budget, arrange for your night's lodging or campsite before you start your ride; otherwise you maybe disappointed when you arrive at your chosen destination! The next state park with a hiker-biker site is at Doheny State Beach, 94.4 miles to the south. Newport Dunes Aquatic Park, 78.2 miles south of Malibu, may accept a tent as long as it is free standing; however, it is a very upscale park with numerous restrictions and a declining tolerance for anything but RVs. Tents must be set up without stakes. You must pay for two nights on weekends in July and August. Holiday weekends require that you pay for three nights. Reservations are a necessity during the summer; call ahead: (800) 288-0770. Prices range from high to exorbitant.

As an alternative to camping, there are numerous hotels a few miles inland from the beaches that are moderately affordable. Surf the web for possibilities and make your reservations ahead of time. In 2004, there were two hostels along the route: one at Venice Beach and the other at Huntington Beach. The recommended destination for the day's ride is the Colonial Inn Hostel in Huntington Beach. This hostel is near the beaches, a hangout for surfers, within riding distance of Disneyland, and on bus routes to Hollywood. It is essential to call ahead as early as possible (a month or two ahead would be a good idea); for reservations, call (714) 536-3315. You can also make your reservations on the web for a fee.

Riding through the Los Angeles area is more than just physically demanding; it is mentally exhausting. This long ride will require the use of every riding skill you have. It will require that you are constantly alert and concentrating not only on the traffic around you, but on the directions as well, to avoid missing crucial turns and intersections. Riders

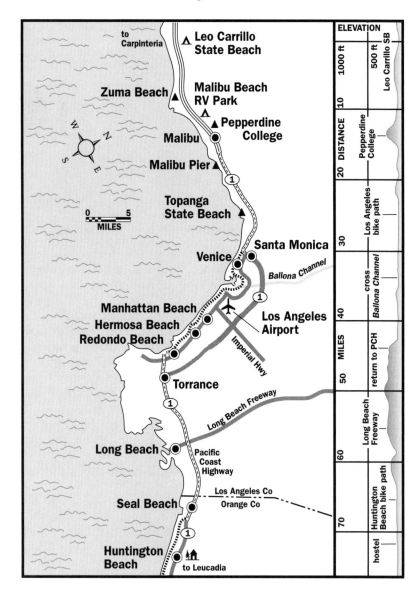

Surfers paddle out to catch a wave near the Huntington Beach pier, the birthplace of surfing on the United States mainland.

who have big-city commuting practice will have a definite advantage.

Heading south from Leo Carrillo State Beach, Highway 1 has a moderate shoulder and low traffic volume (except on weekends) for the first 7 miles. Near Malibu, the amount of traffic increases and the shoulder virtually disappears. While cycling through Malibu, keep in mind that this is one of the few places in the country where hilltop property annually becomes beach-front property. The effects of sliding are visible everywhere.

South of Malibu, Highway 1 (now called the Pacific Coast Highway, or PCH) enters the gigantic urban sprawl that is loosely called Los Angeles by nonresidents. Cyclists must leave the PCH and make their way along a series of hectic bike paths and crowded city streets.

Travel through any large city is demanding. Riding through the nine cities that make up the Los Angeles coast area stresses the word "demanding" to a whole new dimension. Do not expect to make good time, no matter how strong a rider you are. City streets are shoulderless and busy, and progress is constantly interrupted by stoplights. Wildcat growth combined with rolling hills cause the streets to constantly change directions or simply dead-end. The easy-to-follow bike path that weaves along the beaches for part of the way is often jammed with people, causing travel to be slow and frustrating.

South of Redondo Beach, the route leaves the sandy beaches and returns to the Pacific Coast Highway for a 20-mile stretch on the rough, often shoulderless, and frequently busy roadways. The smell of car exhaust and the stench of oil refineries dominate until the route returns to the refreshing ocean air at Seal Beach.

On a rare smog-free day, the Los Angeles area is beautiful. From the bike path, views extend up and down the coast, and east to the San Bernardino Mountains. Start the day at first light to reach the bike path before the midday haze sets in and the crowds arrive. Take your time, enjoy the beaches, and then head back to the city streets by noon to ensure you reach the coast before rush hour.

If you are taking a well-deserved rest day in Huntington Beach, plan a trip to Balboa Island, located a couple of miles south of the hostel. The island specialty is frozen bananas dipped in chocolate, with the topping of your choice—a real taste treat. The island can be reached by a short trip from the hostel or by following an alternate route that takes you to The Wedge (a famous bodysurfing area) before crossing to the island on a ferry.

Mileage Log

0.0 (mp 62.10) Head south from Leo Carrillo State Beach on the Pacific Coast Highway.

1.1 (mp 61.00) Nicholas County Beach; chemical toilet.

2.5 (mp 59.70) El Pescador State Beach, the first of three beach accesses.

5.0 (mp 57.10) Malibu. General urban clutter increases as you ride by expensive houses teetering over sandy beaches.

5.4 (mp 56.70) Zuma Beach County Park, one of many popular Los Angeles County swimming beaches.

12.5 (mp 50.30) Malibu Beach RV Park is located on the left. The park has tent spaces; call ahead for reservations: (213) 456-6052.

14.4 (mp 48.40) Pepperdine University on the left and a community park on the right; restrooms. Official shoulder ends.

15.9 (mp 46.90) Beach access.

16.2 (mp 46.60) Malibu Lagoon State Beach and Museum.

16.4 (mp 46.40) Pass Malibu Pier. This is a favorite hangout for sunbathers and surfers, who flock to the rocky point west of the pier nearly every day of the year.

22.2 (mp 40.60) Topanga State Beach; restrooms.

23.5 (mp 39.30) Will Rogers State Beach (Sunset Blvd. section).

25.2 (mp 37.60) Start Los Angeles Bike Path at the second section of Will Rogers State Beach; restrooms and food available in several locations along the route.

28.4 Ride past a pier and a Ferris wheel.

30.7 Venice Beach, a place where the people of Los Angeles come to look and be looked at. The large pavilion for Rollerbladers, dancers, and weightlifters, as well as masses of people, distinguishes this beach from the others. Check out Muscle Beach, the open-air gym where body builders come to tan their biceps.

31.4 At the end of the Venice Beach area is a pier. Leave the beach path here. Turn left and head northeast on Washington St., following the green bike route signs.

31.9 Ride past a pond. Then, at Milred Ave., go right on the well-signed Marina Del Rey Bike Path.

32.2 Cross Bali Way and follow the bike path through the alleyways and parking lots of the Marina Del Rey boat basin.

32.7 Bike path ends. Turn right on Fiji Way and follow it to its end.

33.4 A traffic circle marks the end of Fiji Way. Ride about three-fourths of the circle, then take a sharp right on a bike path. Go straight up the path for 200 feet, then turn right and ride along a strip of land between Ballona Channel and the entrance to the boat basin.

34.1 Cross Ballona Channel on a wide bridge, then take an immediate right back onto the beach-front bike path for 8 miles of moderately easy riding. If the traffic lights at Hermosa Beach indicate that you must walk, leave the path and go inland 1 block to Beach St. for 0.3 mile. If heading to Los Angeles International Airport (LAX), leave the bike path after crossing Ballona Channel and continue straight onto Pacific Ave. At Vista Del Mar, put in your earplugs, then turn right and ride 1.6 miles along the end of the runway. At Imperial, go left and follow it 0.5 mile before turning left again on Pershing for 2 miles. At Winchester Pkwy., go right and ride 2.5 miles to Sepulveda Blvd. Follow the signs to the airport entrance.

42.8 Beach path ends at Redondo Beach. Go left, then take the first right on Harbor Dr., following the city bike route.

43.5 At Redondo Beach municipal pier, the bike path winds through a parking garage. On the far side you will exit onto the pier. After looking around, go left and leave the bike path in favor of the pier access road. Pass the tour bus loading area and ride up a steep hill.

44.0 Turn right on Catalina Ave.

44.1 Go right on Esplanade and follow the coast.

45.3 Ignore the Pacific Coast Bicycle Route at Ave. H and continue on to make your left turn at Ave. I.

45.5 Turn right on Pacific Coast Highway and enter the city of Torrance. Following the PCH for the next 27 miles is not easy on the nerves. Traffic is very heavy, shoulders irregular, pavement full of potholes and broken glass, and the air truly foul. Don't delay; get busy and get it over with. The beaches ahead are wonderful. If you have lingered until rush hour, linger some more and complete this section as an after-dinner treat.

49.6 Enter Lomalita.

51.7 Pass a regional park on the right; restrooms. Soon after, you will enter Wilmington.

56.5 Ride past an entrance to the Long Beach Freeway. This is a dangerous interchange, with drivers vying for position to get on or off the freeway. Ride with brain engaged and use your hand signals aggressively here.

59.0 Drop down a short hill, then head around a traffic circle. Stay to the right in the well-marked PCH lane. About halfway around, the PCH veers to the right, heading toward Newport. The riding relaxes a bit here, and the streets become wider. However, the traffic is often heavy.

62.6 Leave Los Angeles County and enter Orange County and the town of Seal Beach.

63.6 A bike lane begins at the outskirts of Seal Beach.

65.1 Enter Sunset Beach.

66.5 Enter Huntington Beach. To reach the bike path, turn off the PCH and go right Warner St. Ride halfway around the traffic circle to find the beachside bike path on your right. Restrooms and water are found at the start of the path. (Or you may stay on the PCH, which has a wide shoulder for the next 7.5 miles.)

71.5 Turn off the beach path and go left on 8th St. Ride 4 blocks to Pecan St.

72.0 The Colonial Inn Hostel is located on the corner at 421 8th St. It has twenty-eight beds, showers, a full kitchen, and bicycle storage.

Colonial Inn Hostel to San Elijo State Beach (65.4 miles)

During the warm and smoggy summer months, the coast south of Newport Beach is a popular escape from the heat and stagnant air of the interior. Throughout the warmest season, the four major state park campgrounds and numerous state beaches along this 65.4-mile section are full to overflowing. The coastal towns have attempted to accommodate the vast influx of tourists by lining the streets with restaurants, motels, fast foods, and surf shops.

Fishing dories wait for high tide on busy Newport Beach.

Roads traveled in this section vary from busy thoroughfares to quiet residential streets. Shoulders are nonexistent in towns and are frequently used for beach parking in the country. The best feature of this area is the gently rolling terrain—perfect for riding.

The route follows the busy Coast Highway (Pacific seems to have been dropped from the name at Newport Beach) until it merges with Interstate 5 at Dana Point. The route then heads through a maze of city streets at San Clemente. Then there is a problem. Formerly, beyond San Clemente, the route headed through open country on the nearly deserted roads of Camp Pendleton—deserted unless the Marines are practicing maneuvers. Since the September 11 tragedy, the somewhat trusting nature of the Marine Corp has changed, and nonmilitary personnel are no longer welcome to wander through the camp. Equally frustrating for the touring cyclist is the fact that Caltrans has yet to make a plan for cyclists in this area, leaving the freeway as the only alternative around the military reservation.

Beyond Camp Pendleton, the route winds its way through Oceanside,

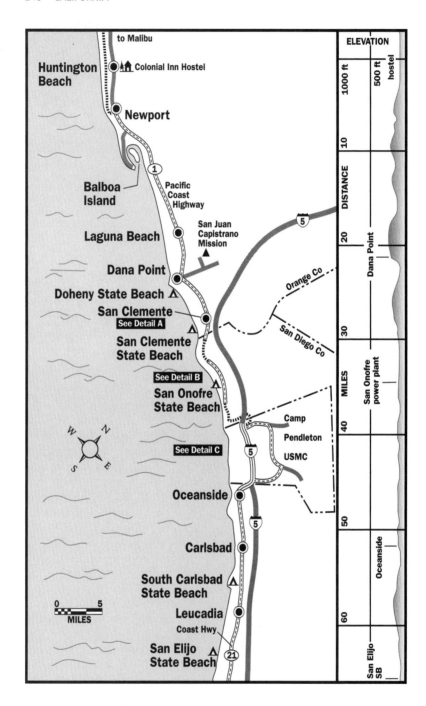

ELEVATION

to Malibu

Huntington Beach ● ☖ Colonial Inn Hostel

Newport ●

1000 ft   500 ft   hostel

Balboa Island

Pacific Coast Highway

1

10

DISTANCE

Laguna Beach ●

San Juan Capistrano Mission ▲

20

5

Dana Point ◉

Dana Point

Doheny State Beach △

San Clemente ●

Orange Co

See Detail A   △

San Diego Co

San Clemente State Beach

30

See Detail B   ▲

San Onofre State Beach

San Onofre power plant

40

Camp Pendleton USMC

See Detail C   5

N W E S

Oceanside ●

5

50

Carlsbad ●

Oceanside

South Carlsbad State Beach △

0   5   MILES

Leucadia ●

60

Coast Hwy

San Elijo State Beach △   21

San Elijo SB

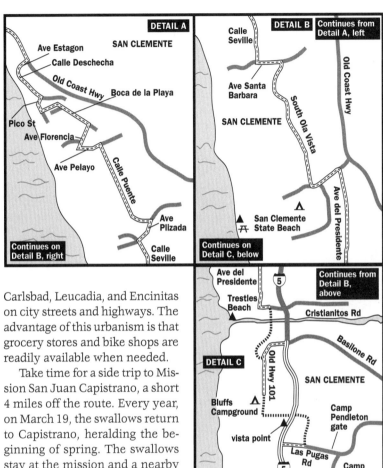

DETAIL A

Ave Estagon

SAN CLEMENTE

Calle Deschecha

Old Coast Hwy   Boca de la Playa

Pico St

Ave Florencia

Ave Pelayo

Calle Puente

Ave Pilzada

Continues on
Detail B, right

Calle
Seville

DETAIL B   Continues from
Detail A, left

Calle
Seville

Ave Santa
Barbara

SAN CLEMENTE

South Ola Vista

Old Coast Hwy

Ave del Presidente

San Clemente
State Beach

Continues on
Detail C, below

Ave del
Presidente

Trestles
Beach

DETAIL C

Old Hwy 101

Bluffs
Campground

vista point

roadside
rest
area

Harbor Dr

OCEANSIDE

Coast Hwy

Continues from
Detail B,
above

Cristianitos Rd

Basilone Rd

SAN CLEMENTE

Camp
Pendleton
gate

Las Pugas
Rd

Camp
Pendleton
USMC

CAMP
PENDLETON
BYPASS

Carlsbad, Leucadia, and Encinitas on city streets and highways. The advantage of this urbanism is that grocery stores and bike shops are readily available when needed.

Take time for a side trip to Mission San Juan Capistrano, a short 4 miles off the route. Every year, on March 19, the swallows return to Capistrano, heralding the beginning of spring. The swallows stay at the mission and a nearby shopping center through the second week of October. Even if you are not on hand when the swallows return, the mission is worth a visit. It was founded in 1776 and destroyed by an earthquake in 1812. A new mission was built behind the ruins of the old church, creating an elegant setting for the gardens.

The day's ride ends at San Elijo State Beach, the last public campground north of the Mexican border. A large grocery store is located across the road from the campground.

Mileage Log

0.0 From Colonial Inn Hostel, ride west on 8th St. to rejoin the bike path.

0.5 Go left on the bike path and continue south down the coast.

0.7 Huntington Beach Pier, the best vantage point along the coast to watch surfers. Surfing was first introduced to California here, and the tradition is still going strong. Continue south on the bike path or the shoulder of the Pacific Coast Highway.

1.7 Huntington State Beach entrance; restrooms, water, and beach access.

3.4 Newport Beach city limits. The Huntington Beach bike path ends; return to the PCH, which is blessed with a wide shoulder in this area.

4.6 Cross Balboa Blvd. This is the start of the Balboa Island Alternate Route (for details, see end of this mileage log). Continuing south, the shoulder disappears as you ride through Newport Beach. The highway descends before crossing a wide bridge across Newport Bay.

7.3 The Balboa Island Alternate Route returns to the PCH here.

9.1 Marguerite Ave. is passed on the right. South Corona Del Mar Beach Park is located 0.3 mile west; restrooms, water, and views north to Newport Harbor, The Wedge, and Balboa Island.

9.9 Start a brief spell through open country.

10.1 Pass a bike path on the right, which descends into Crystal Cove State Beach and returns to the highway 2 miles to the south. This bike path is scenic and passes several restrooms. If you choose the path you will have opportunities to return to the highway at the three auto entrance points.

13.2 Laguna Beach; grocery stores. In 1.1 miles the route will leave the highway and follow side streets in an attempt to avoid some of the congestion.

══════════ California's Mission Chain ══════════

In 1769, King Charles III of Spain sent Father Junipero Serra to Alta, California, to create a chain of missions along the coast. The missions were to be established approximately one day's walk apart along the entire length of the 650-mile El Camino Real. The original missions were all ordered to be similar in appearance. Each mission church was to be equal in height to the tallest tree in the area so the mission could be seen from a great distance. The missions were expected to grow enough wheat, corn, and grapes, as well as sheep and cattle, to feed an entire mission community and have enough provisions left over to serve to visitors and to trade for needed supplies.

13.3 At Cliff Dr., take a right turn off the Coast Highway and head into a residential area. Cliff Dr. bends left, then twists and turns along the top of a bluff overlooking the coast.

14.8 Pass Diver's Cove Park; restrooms, water, benches, picnic tables, and views, as well as access to the beach's ecological reserve area.

15.4 Return to the highway, busy and shoulderless, for the next 0.4 mile.

15.8 At the crest of a steep hill take a left turn on Legion St. (When traffic is heavy you may find the pedestrian signal on the south side of the intersection to be helpful.)

15.9 Go right (south) on Catalina St.

16.3 Catalina St. ends temporarily; turn right on Thalia St., then take the first left back on Catalina St.

16.7 Catalina St. becomes Calliope St. Take the first left on Glenneyre St.

17.0 At Diamond St., turn right and return to S. Coast Highway (Coast Highway has now officially changed names). The highway soon broadens to include a shoulder, which serves as a parking lot. Generally, the riding is less than perfect in this area.

18.7 Aliso Beach County Park entrance; restrooms, water, and a pier.

20.9 S. Coast Highway leaves the urban sprawl for another short stint through open country. A large supermarket is located on the left side of the highway.

21.7 Salt Beach County Park; picturesque day-use area with restrooms, water, pavilion, fountain, and beach access.

22.8 Dana Point; a long, narrow town spread along the highway with grocery stores and restaurants.

23.0 The road divides; stay right on Del Padra Ave. and follow the city bike route signs.

23.4 Go right on Golden Lantern and descend. (Not far ahead, Highway 1 joins Interstate 5 and ends.)

23.7 At the base of the hill, make a left turn on Dana Point Harbor Rd.

24.0 Go right on Park Lantern Rd. and ride into Doheny State Beach. There are hiker-biker sites, showers, and beach access. If you plan to stay at the park, check in at the entrance station. If continuing on, pass the booth and follow the park road as it parallels the S. Coast Highway. When the road forks, stay left on the Old Coast Highway. Cross a short bridge, then ride through the day-use parking area. ***Side Trip*** to Mission San Juan Capistrano: Continue on Dana Point Harbor Dr. for 0.3 mile. Cross S. Coast Highway and continue straight inland on Del Obispo St. After 3.2 miles, go left on Camino Capistrano for a final 0.2 mile to the mission.

25.5 At the end of the day-use parking area, continue south along the edge of the sandy beach on a bicycle path.

25.7 Bicycle path ends at the entrance to Capistrano State Beach. Go left to the Old Coast Highway and continue south on a wide bicycle lane. (Northbound bicycle lane varies from good to nonexistent, depending on recent slide activity.)

27.3 San Clemente; a city whose narrow main roads are avoided by a well-marked bike route starting at the city limits. Take the first right after the city sign on Ave. Estagon and ride to the entrance of the Metro Link (commuter train) parking area.

27.4 Following the city bike route signs, turn left on Calle Deschecha.

27.5 Take a right on Pico St. and follow it through a residential area.

27.6 Go left on Boca de la Playa.

27.7 Turn left again on Calle las Bolas and soon after take a right on Ave. Florencia.

28.1 Go left on Ave. Pelayo.

28.2 Turn right at Calle Puente, which takes you past a city park with restrooms.

28.7 Bear right on Ave. Palizada.

28.8 At Calle Sevill, steer left.

29.1 Go straight on Ave. Santa Barbara.

29.2 Swing right on S. Ola Vista and relax for a bit.

Jumping into the surf is a great way to celebrate a day in southern California.

30.6 Ola Vista ends. Go left and ride uphill. To the right are San Clemente State Beach and Califia Beach Park. San Clemente State Beach has picnicking, camping, a hiker-biker site, showers, impressive views of the ocean, and a nearby store. Califia Beach Park offers picnicking, restrooms, and access to an impressive beach at the base of sandstone cliffs.

30.7 Take a right on Ave. del Presidente and ride south on a wide bicycle lane, sandwiched between I-5 and San Clemente State Beach.

31.7 Leave Orange County and enter San Diego County.

31.9 Avenue del Presidente ends. San Onofre Campground is located to the left, on Cristianitos Rd.; campsites, water, beach access, but no hiker-biker site. Cross Cristianitos Rd. and continue straight on a bike path starting just before the freeway entrance. The bike path parallels I-5 on the Old Coast Highway (Highway 101) passing an access to Trestles Beach, one of the most crowded surfing areas on the southern coast.

33.0 Bike path ends. Go left around the gate at the bike path exit and continue south on a wide bike lane at the edge of the San Onofre State Beach access road (old Highway 101).

34.5 Pass the San Onofre nuclear plant. Expect considerable traffic when the work shifts change.

35.7 Ride past the entrance booth for Bluffs Campground, part of San Onofre State Beach. The bike path heads straight through the 3-mile-long campground, which is located between the freeway and the ocean. Hiker-biker camp, cold outdoor showers, a small store (rarely open), beach access, and no electricity.

38.8 At the southern end of Bluffs Campground, the bike path heads into the Camp Pendleton restricted area. Make sure you can cover the next section to Oceanside before dark. Camp Pendleton closes at dark, and due to the accumulation of garbage on the edge of the freeway alternative, you should certainly plan to be back on city streets before the sun goes down. Gate 25, at the entrance into Camp Pendleton, requires negotiating the narrowly spaced bars on the left side of the gate. Beyond the barrier, the road belongs to bicycles, tanks, and Hummers.

40.5 The bike route turns inland, passing through a tunnel under I-5. Use caution here; the tunnel is not only subject to occasional flash floods, it also is used by military vehicles on maneuvers.

40.7 The road divides; stay right. Watch out for broken pavement and potholes in the old pavement of the abandoned Highway 101, except for a 0.5-mile section that has been resurfaced and is used on occasion as a practice landing strip. When the landing strip is in use, the path is closed. In that situation, you must either wait or ride back through the tunnel under the freeway, then go left on a side road that leads to a small parking area and an access to I-5. The freeway unfortunately is closed to bicycles in this area.

42.1 The road you have been following ends at Las Pulgas Rd. (not marked at the intersection). Go left to the camp entrance checkpoint.

42.3 Camp entrance checkpoint. If you can go forward, great. To enter Camp Pendleton you must wear a helmet, stay on the well-marked route or risk arrest, and carry identification. Continuing, bear right when the road splits. *If Camp Pendleton is closed:* Ride back on Las Pulgas Rd., passing the bike path to reach I-5. Pass under the freeway and then go left, up the freeway on ramp heading south. In exactly 2 miles there is an off ramp to a rest area. Exit the freeway, ride through the rest area, and return to I-5. After 5.5 more freeway miles, exit at Harbor Drive. At the end of the off ramp go straight, crossing Harbor Dr. to reach the North Coast Highway S 21. Now advance to Mileage Log point 51.4.

42.8 Intersection and first stop sign; go right. (Routefinding through the camp is easy; at every major intersection, go right.)

49.6 Cycle around a small pond to arrive at a major intersection. Turn right on Vandegrift Blvd.

51.0 Exit Camp Pendleton and follow Harbor Dr. south.

51.4 After passing under I-5, take the first left on Coast Highway and enter Oceanside. If you had to ride the freeway around the camp, rejoin the route here.

52.3 Turn right (west) on Surfrider Way. (If you are looking for restaurants or groceries, stay on the Coast Highway, busy but rideable if you are hungry enough.)

52.5 Cross railroad tracks, then take a left on Pacific St. *Alternate Route* for southbound riders only: Continue down Surfrider Way 1 more block to palm-lined beaches. Go left on The Strand and follow it to its end. Go left for 1 block, then turn right on Pacific St.

53.6 At Cassidy St., go left under a bridge and head inland.

53.8 Following the city bike route signs, go right on Broadway.

54.1 Broadway ends; take a left on Easton for 1 block.

54.2 Turn right and head south on Coast Highway (also known as State Highway 21).

54.4 Coast Highway dips across Buena Vista Lagoon, a bird sanctuary, and then enters the town of Carlsbad.

55.5 Carlsbad State Beach; no facilities.

58.2 The road divides. Stay right, following the coastline.

59.6 South Carlsbad State Beach Campground; small store, Laundromat, showers, hiker-biker site, and beach access.

61.2 Leucadia; a congested town with small shops and grocery stores.

62.7 Encinitas; a congested town with small shops and grocery stores.

63.4 Pass access to Moonlight State Beach; beaches, restrooms, and water.

64.4 Swamis City Park; roadside park with restrooms and water.

65.4 San Elijo State Beach; hiker-biker site, small store, hot showers, and access to beaches and tide pools. Groceries may be purchased at a store on the far side of the railroad tracks.

Balboa Island Alternate Route

Turn right (southwest) on Balboa Blvd. for a shoulderless 3.5 miles down the long sandspit that protects Newport Bay and Balboa Island. Most of the spit is covered with stores and private homes. The west side has a pier, fish market, and state park, which ends at The Wedge, a famous and very dangerous body surfing area. On the east side are Newport Bay Harbor and Balboa Island. To return to the main route, ride 2.7 miles down the spit and catch the Balboa Island ferry. You will return to the PCH via a bridge on the east side of the island.

San Elijo State Beach to the Mexican Border (45.3 Miles)

The final leg of the California ride, and of the Pacific Coast Bicycle Route, consists of 45.3 challenging miles. The challenge is not the terrain— there are only two hills of notable size; the challenge comes from riding yet another entire day through cities.

The first 6 miles, from San Elijo State Beach to Torrey Pines State Reserve, are the easiest; the towns are small and somewhat spread apart. Beyond the state reserve, it's uphill to La Jolla Mesa and the start of the San Diego urban sprawl. The remainder of the ride is spent weaving through the maze of La Jolla, San Diego, National City, Chula Vista, and finally San Ysidro, on, unexpectedly, exceptionally well-marked bike routes.

San Diego is a friendly city with fascinating places to explore. Make your first stop the Torrey Pines Reserve, one of the last places on earth where these trees grow. A little farther south is the Scripps Institute Stephen Birch Aquarium-Museum. This aquarium is a little less theatrical and not as pricey as the one in Monterey but overall is an excellent way to spend 2 or more hours. Open daily from 9:00 A.M. to 5:00 P.M. except on Christmas and Thanksgiving.

Continuing south, performing sea animals tickle the fancy of the young and old alike at Sea World. Open daily. Cabrillo National Monument lies a short bike ride off the main route and is a highly recommended side trip. It is a historic area with two lighthouses, tide pools, and an almost overwhelming view of San Diego. The monument is open from 9:00 A.M.

to 5:00 P.M. No one is allowed in the monument after closing.

The San Diego area beaches are excellent; surfing is passable, bodysurfing is popular, sunbathing is outstanding, and people watching is as good as it gets. Try Mission Beach if you are staying in the central San Diego area, and Imperial Beach if you are in the south. Rental surfboards, boogie boards, and skateboards are available near the beaches.

If spending a few days in San Diego, visit Balboa Park, home of a fascinating collection of museums, a velodrome, and the famous San Diego Zoo. San Diego Wildlife Park, located 30 miles north of downtown, is an extension of the zoo and well worth the hassle of getting there. The wildlife park may be reached by bicycle, if you don't mind the desert heat, or by bus. Check for information at your hotel or camp-

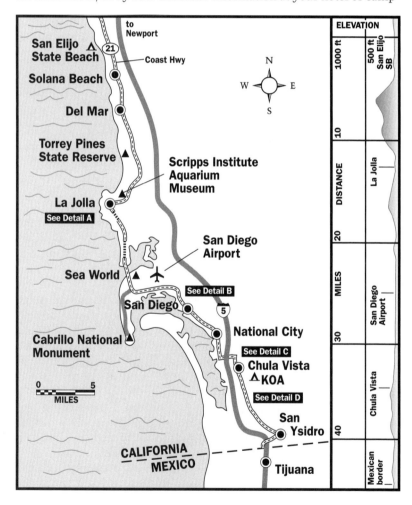

ground office. The Coronado Peninsula makes an excellent, easy day ride. To get to the peninsula, take a passenger ferry from downtown San Diego, or follow the signed bike route from Imperial Beach.

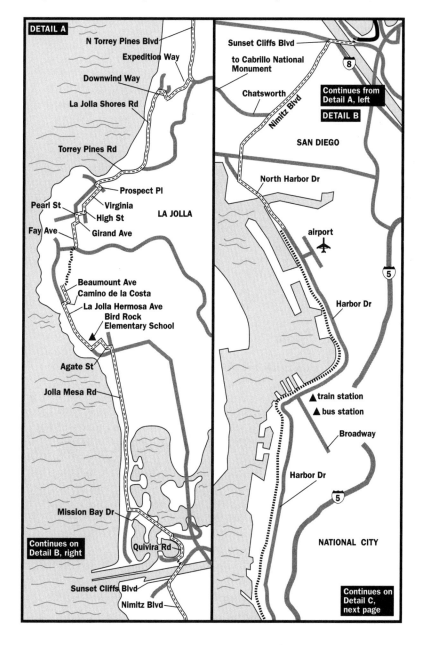

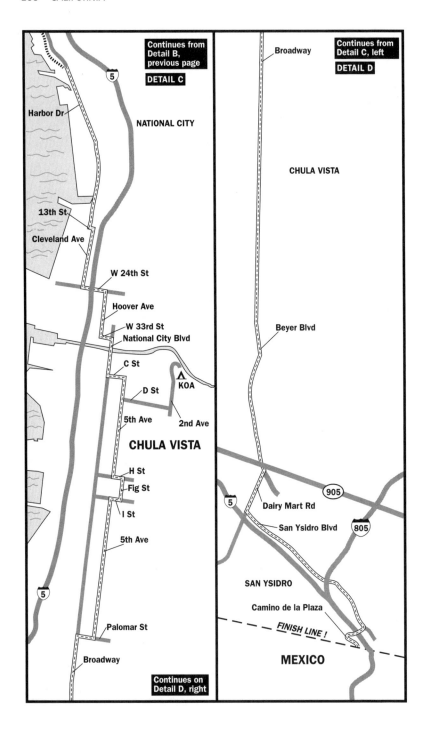

DETAIL C

Continues from Detail B, previous page

5

Harbor Dr

NATIONAL CITY

13th St

Cleveland Ave

W 24th St

Hoover Ave

W 33rd St
National City Blvd

C St

KOA

D St

5th Ave

2nd Ave

CHULA VISTA

H St

Fig St

I St

5th Ave

5

Palomar St

Broadway

Continues on Detail D, right

DETAIL D

Continues from Detail C, left

Broadway

CHULA VISTA

Beyer Blvd

905

5

Dairy Mart Rd

San Ysidro Blvd

805

SAN YSIDRO

Camino de la Plaza

FINISH LINE !

MEXICO

Reaching the California–Mexico border is a thrill. It is also a good place to turn around and head back north. If planning to visit Mexico for a day, it is best to leave your bike in a secure place and take the Red Commuter Train to the border. Unless you are comfortable with riding in downtown Manhattan, the streets and the traffic south of the border are not for gringos on bikes.

The closest campground to the border is the San Diego Metro KOA, in Chula Vista, 7 miles south of the train and bus stations and 9 miles south of the airport. To be on the safe side, secure your spot ahead of time. Call (619) 427-3601 for information and (800) 562-9877 for reservations. San Diego also has two hostels, one in downtown and one at Point Loma, and only the Chamber of Commerce knows how many hotels. No matter what your accommodation choice, secure your reservations at least two weeks ahead of time. For reservations at Point Loma, call (800) 909-4776 hostel code 44. The phone number for reservations at the downtown hostel is (800) 909-4776 hostel code 43.

As noted earlier, San Diego is a bicycle-friendly city, and it is only fitting that the Pacific Coast Bicycle Route should, on the final leg, pass right by the entrance to the airport and within 2 blocks of the Amtrak and Greyhound bus stations.

Mileage Log

0.0 From San Elijo State Beach, continue south on County Highway S21, enjoying the wide bicycle lane.

0.5 Cardiff by the Sea; a sunning and swimming beach with chemical toilets and no running water.

2.1 Pass the Solana Beach County Park turnoff on the right; picnic tables, restrooms, running water, and ocean views.

3.5 Del Mar; town with a Danish theme. Beyond Del Mar the highway rambles along the coast; watch for cars pulling in and out of the unofficial parking area on the shoulder.

5.9 Pass Torrey Pines State Beach on the right.

6.8 The highway begins a long climb to La Jolla Mesa. *Side Trip* to Torrey Pines State Reserve: At the end of the state beach, go left up a steep, mile-long hill to scenic views and the rarest pine trees native to the United States. Trails, restrooms, water, and a visitor center.

8.8 County Highway S21 becomes Torrey Pines Blvd.

9.6 At the stoplight; go right, following N. Torrey Pines Blvd., and ride around the western edge of University of California at San Diego.

11.1 Following signs to the Stephen Birch Aquarium, go right on Expedition Way and begin a steady and often steep descent off La Jolla Mesa.

11.6 Scripps Institute's Stephen Birch Aquarium is located to the left.

The Old Point Loma Lighthouse is just one of the points of interest at Cabrillo National Monument.

You can't miss it. If not stopping for a visit, stay to the right and continue the descent on Downwind Way to Shellback Way for 1 short block.

11.8 Go left on La Jolla Shores Dr.

13.0 Bear right, following Torrey Pines Rd., and enter La Jolla. The route through the town is marked by green bike-route signs.

13.8 Near the crest of a hill, go left on Prospect Pl. for 1 block.

13.9 Turn right on Virginia.

14.3 Go left on High St.

14.4 At Pearl St. go right.

14.5 Take a left on Girand Ave. and follow it up the hill, where it makes a sharp right hook.

14.8 Turn left on Fay Ave.

15.1 Fay Ave. ends at the T intersection with Nautilus St. Cross to the sidewalk on the opposite side, then descend 100 feet to find a bicycle path on the left. This path is 0.7 mile long and easy to follow.

(Northbound riders will have one intersection at 0.4 mile; keep right.)

15.8 At the end of the bike path, go left for half a block, then turn right on Beaumont Ave.

16.2 Turn right on Camino de la Costa for 1 block.

16.3 Turn left on La Jolla Hermosa Ave., still following the city bike route signs.

16.9 Pass Bird Rock Elementary School, then turn left and ride up a narrow alley.

17.1 Pass the school playfield and turn right into another unnamed alley.

17.2 Take a left on Agate St., the second normal-looking street off the alley.

17.3 Turn right at Jolla Mesa Rd. and follow it as it merges with La Jolla Blvd., which, in turn, becomes Mission Blvd.

17.7 *Alternate Route* along the beach: The main route stays on Mission Blvd.; however, if you want a view of San Diego beach life and don't mind cycling through crowds, turn right on Law St. for 0.1 mile, then head left on a bicycle path overlooking the coast. Follow the bike path south for 2.2 miles, then leave it just before passing a large pavilion and amusement center. Go left on Ventura Plaza, which becomes Mission Bay Dr. after crossing Mission Blvd.

19.9 Turn left onto Mission Bay Dr. just before passing an amusement park. Mission Bay Dr. passes a large park (restrooms and running water), then heads across Mission Bay Channel on a wide bridge.

20.8 After crossing the bridge, exit to the right on Quivira Rd., then go left (south), paralleling Mission Bay Dr. *Side Trip* to San Diego Sea World: Turn left after crossing Mission Bay Channel Bridge on Dana Landing Rd. (opposite the Quivira Rd. exit), and follow it to the right for 0.5 mile. Cross a major four-lane road then follow Perez Cove Way to the entrance of Sea World in 0.2 mile. Plan to spend at least 3 hours; large admission charged.

21.3 Following the bike route signs, go left on a bike path that takes you to Sunset Cliffs Blvd. and ride over the San Diego River.

21.8 At the south end of the bridge, merge left in preparation for a left turn on Nimitz Blvd. This is a tricky intersection in heavy traffic, and from this point on traffic is always heavy. You are nearing the heart of San Diego's downtown and business district, so there will be a lot of stoplights and numerous bumpy railroad tracks.

23.0 *Side Trip* to Cabrillo National Monument: Go right on Chatsworth Blvd. and head up and over a hill for 0.8 mile to Catalina Blvd. Turn left for 0.7 mile, then jog right, following the bike route signs to the road paralleling Catalina Blvd. After 0.6 mile the road ends, and the bike route continues on the sidewalk along Catalina Blvd. Shortly after, the road enters the military reservation. Be sure you have enough time to be out of the reservation at 5:00 P.M. In 2.5 more miles (4.7 miles from Nimitz Blvd.), enter the national monument.

24.1 Nimitz Blvd. ends in the heart of the naval training center. Turn left on North Harbor Dr. and ride over a large bridge either on the road or on the wide sidewalk that doubles as a bicycle path. The road now heads around the West Basin of San Diego Bay.

24.5 Spanish Marine Bayside Park. A nice place to relax; restrooms, water, and picnic tables. Leave the road here and ride the meandering bicycle path for the next 6 miles.

25.8 San Diego International Airport exit.

26.6 *Side Trip* to Balboa Park and San Diego Zoo: Turn left on Laurel St. for a very steep 1.7 miles to the entrance of Balboa Park. Continue straight into the park on El Prado to reach the information center, museums, and zoo.

27.8 Intersection of Harbor Dr. and Broadway. The Amtrak station is located 2 blocks left up Broadway at the Santa Fee Train Depot. The Red Commuter Train to the Mexican border station is located just beyond, and the Greyhound bus station is a couple of blocks farther, at the corner of Broadway and First Ave. The passenger ferry to the Coronado Peninsula departs just to the right of this intersection. If not looking for immediate transport to somewhere else, continue straight ahead on Harbor Dr.

28.7 Pass the massive San Diego Convention Center.

32.1 Enter National City.

32.9 Turn right on 13th St. and follow it for 1 short block, then go left on Cleveland Ave.

33.6 Go left on W. 24th St. and ride under I-5.

33.9 Make a right turn on Hoover Ave.

34.6 Hoover Ave. ends; go left on W. 33rd St.

34.8 Go right (south) on National City Blvd. and cross the Sweetwater River.

35.2 At the south end of the bridge take an immediate left on C St., leaving National City and entering Chula Vista.

35.4 Turn right on 5th Ave., entering a residential area. Intersections have shallow culverts across them to drain rain water; ride carefully.

35.6 If planning to spend the night at the San Diego Metropolitan KOA, go left on D St. for 0.7 mile to 2nd Ave. Go left again for 0.7 mile to the campground.

36.9 Further progress down 5th Ave. is blocked by a shopping center. Go left on H St. for 1 block.

37.0 Turn right on Fig Ave. and follow it to I St.

37.1 Take a right on I St., then go left, back onto 5th Ave.

38.9 Turn right (west) on Palomar St. and descend to the second major intersection.

39.2 Go left on Broadway, which soon becomes Beyer Blvd.

42.0 Directly after passing under the Highway 905 freeway, go right on Dairy Mart Rd.

42.6 Turn left (east) on San Ysidro Blvd., just before crossing I-5. Before long the road enters San Ysidro. Streets are jammed with traffic, and the main enterprise here seems to be money changing. Everyone speaks Spanish, but very few will admit to understanding English. (English is much more commonly spoken across the boarder in Tijana.)

44.0 Pass under the US 805 freeway and head into the most congested section of town.

44.7 Turn right on Camino de la Plaza. Cross over I-5, then take the first left, following signs for bus and taxi parking.

45.3 AJÚA! LA FRONTERA MEXICANA, 3,198.2 km al sur de Vancouver, British Columbia. (YAH HOO! THE MEXICAN BORDER, 1,987.3 miles south of Vancouver, British Columbia.)

There is a lot to see and do along the Pacific Coast Bicycle Route. Some riders take longer than others; this cyclist took a very long time.

USEFUL PHONE NUMBERS AND WEBSITES

British Columbia
George Massey Tunnel Office (604) 277-2115
Jericho Beach Hostel in Vancouver (604) 224-3208 or (888) 203-4303
Victoria Hostel (604) 385-4511

Washington
Doe Bay Village Resort Hostel (360) 376-2291
Ocean Shores passenger ferry (360) 289-3389
San Juan County Park Reservations (360) 378-1842;
    www.co.san-juan.wa.us.
Washington State Park Reservations (888) 226-7688

Oregon
Oregon State Park Reservations (800) 452-5687
Oregon State Parks *www.oregonstateparks.org*
Yurt Information (800) 551-6949

California
Año Nuevo Tours (800) 444-4445
California State Park Reservations (800) 444-7275
California State Park Reservations TDD (800) 274-7275
Colonial Inn Hostel (714) 536-3315
Eureka KOA (707) 822-4243
Hearst Castle Tours (800) 444-4445
Malibu Beach RV Park (213) 456-6052
Marin Headlands hiker-biker site (415) 331-1540
Marin Hostel (800) 909-4776 hostel code 73
Montara Lighthouse Hostel (800) 909-4776 hostel code 153
Newport Dunes Aquatic Park (800) 288-0770
Piedras Blancas Light Station Information (888) 804-8608
Piedras Blancas Light Station Reservations (888) 927-6881
Point Loma Hostel (800) 909-4776 hostel code 44
Point Reyes Hostel (415) 663-8811
Redwoods Hostel (707) 464-6101
San Diego Downtown Hostel (800) 909-4776 hostel code 43
San Diego Metro KOA Information (619) 427-3601
San Diego Metro KOA Reservations (800) 562-9877

Youth Hostels
American Youth Hostels *www.111traveldirectory.com*
Hosteling International *www.hihostels.com/opendiscounts.sma*

RECOMMENDED READING

Below is a list of books and VHS tapes that are full of information about bicycle touring, physical fitness, and the all-important subject of bicycle maintenance.

How to Bicycle Tour

Lovett, Richard R. *The Essential Touring Cyclist*, 2d edition. Camden: Ragged Mountain Press/McGraw Hill, 2001.
     This book was written by a real pro and is enjoyable reading, too. The book includes preparation, touring techniques, how to load your gear, bike fitting, cooking, camping, and clothing.

VHS: *The Fundamentals of Bicycle Touring*. Seattle: Elliott Bay Film Company, 1994.
     If you are a visual learner and prefer to get your information in a compact, 60-minute burst, then this video is for you. The presentation was put together in conjunction with REI, Inc., and is extremely full of facts.

Bicycle Maintenance

Langley, Jim. *Bicycling Magazine's Complete Guide to Bicycle Maintenance and Repair for Road and Mountain Bikes*. Emmaus: Rodale Press, 1999.
     When the title says complete, it means exactly that. This is a wonderful resource to have at home.

Van der Plas, Rob. *Simple Bicycle Repair*. San Francisco: Cycle Publishing/Van der Plas Publications, 2003.
     If you are looking for a book to carry along with you on the tour, this is it. This compact little book has complete instructions for all repairs that can be done with a small, bike-bag-size toolkit.

VHS: *The Fundamentals of Bicycle Maintenance*. Seattle: Elliot Bay Film Company, 1993.
     A video is an ideal tool for learning bicycle maintenance at home. The only thing better than a video is a class, where you can talk to your instructor when something doesn't work the way it is supposed to.

INDEX

A

Aberdeen 81, 97, 100
Alder Dune Campground 134
American Camp National Historic
  Park 65
Amtrak 154, 201, 262
Anacortes 61, 67, 70
Andrew Molera State Park 215
Año Nuevo State Reserve 201, 204, 205
Arcadia State Park 119
Arcata 163
Astoria 114, 116
Avenue of the Giants 165

B

Balboa Island 244, 250
Bandon 140, 143
Bastendorf County RV Park 139
Battery Point Lighthouse 154, 157
Bay Center 103, 104
Bay City 81
Beachside State Park 132
Bean Hollow State Beach 203, 204
Benbow Lake State Recreation Area
  172
Beverly Beach State Park 124, 128
Big Basin Redwoods State Park 204
bike boxes 114
Boardman State Park 147
Bob Straub State Park 126
Bodega Dunes State Beach 183, 187
Bogachiel State Park 92
Boiler Bay Wayside State Park 127
Brockton Point Lighthouse 30, 32, 33
Brookings 148
Bruceport County RV Park 104
Buellton 230
Bullards Beach State Park 140, 143
Burlington Campground 165, 171
Bush Pioneer County Park 104
Butchart Gardens 50

C

Cabrillo National Monument 255, 261
Cambria 222
Camp Pendleton 247, 253–254
Cannon Beach 118
Cape Arago 135, 139
Cape Blanco State Park 142, 144
Cape Disappointment State Park 106,
  108
Cape Kiwanda State Park 124, 125
Cape Lookout State Park 123
Cape Meares State Park 123
Cape Perpetua 130, 133
Capistrano State Beach 252
Cardiff by the Sea 259
Carl G. Washburne Memorial State
  Park 134
Carlsbad 248, 254
Carmel 215
Carpenteria State Park 231, 235
Carter Lake Campground 136
Cayucos 222
Channel Islands National Park 236,
  239, 240
Charleston 139, 142
Chula Vista 259
Coho ferry 50, 54, 82, 84
Colonial Inn Hostel 241, 246
Combined Route 101–108
Comox 38, 40
Coos Bay 139
Copalis Beach 98, 99
Coupeville 67, 72
Courtenay 41
Cranberry Lake Campground 70
Crescent City 154, 157
Crofton 48

D

Dana Point 251
Darlingtonia Botanical Wayside 131, 134
Davenport 205
Deception Pass State Park 69, 70
Denman Island 38, 41, 42, 43
Depoe Bay 127
Devils Elbow State Park 130, 134
Devils Lake State Park Campground
  126
Devils Punchbowl State Park 128
Doe Bay Village Resort Hostel 64
Doheny State Beach 241
Dosewallips State Park 76
Driftwood State Park 132

E

Earls Cove 34, 37
East Carter Lake Campground 136
Ecola State Park 109, 118

Eel Creek Campground 138
El Capitan State Beach 233
El Granada 200
El Pescador State Beach 244
elk 181
Elk Prairie Campground 159
Emma Woods State Beach 236
Encinitas 249, 255
English Camp National Historic Park 65
Eureka 164, 166
Eureka KOA 164
F
Fairfax 196
Fairholm Campground 83, 87
Falls View Campground 75
Ferndale 164, 167
Fidalgo Island 67
Florence 134
Fogerty Beach State Park 127
Forks 90
Fort Bragg 177, 179
Fort Casey 69, 72
Fort Clatsop 115, 117
Fort Point 198
Fort Ross State Historic Park 181, 184, 186
Fort Stevens State Park 115, 117, 118
Fort Worden State Park 69, 72
Friday Harbor 64
Fulford Harbor 49
G
Gabriola Island 48
Ganges 49
Garberville 172
Garden Bay 36
Gardiner 137
Gaviota State Park 226, 229
Gazos State Beach 204
Glenada 134
Gleneden Beach Wayside State Park 127
Gold Beach 145
Golden Gate Bridge 198, 200
Golden Gate National Recreation Area 188, 191, 198, 200
Goleta 233
Gorda 219
Governor I. L. Patterson State Park 132
Grayland 103
Grestle Cove Campground 185
Gualala Point Regional Park 183

H
Half Moon Bay State Beach 200
Harris Beach State Park 145, 148
Hearst Castle 217, 220
Heart O' the Hills Campground 87
Hidden Springs Campground 171
hiker-biker sites 19
Hoh River Valley 57, 89, 90, 92
Hoodsport 76
Hoquiam 97, 100
Hornby Island 38, 41, 42, 43
hostels 20
Hug Point State Park 119
Humboldt Lagoons State Park 163
Humboldt Redwoods State Park 168
Humbug Mountain State Park 140, 144
Humptulips 98, 99, 100
Huntington Beach 241, 246
Hurricane Ridge 82, 85, 87
I
Ilwaco 106, 108
J
Jenner 186
Jericho Beach Park hostel 28, 30
Jessie M. Honeyman Memorial State Park 131, 134
Jughandle State Reserve 177, 179
Julie Pfeiffer Burns State Park 213, 216
July Creek Campground 95
K
Kalaloch 88, 89, 92
Keystone ferry 67, 69, 72
Kirk Creek Campground 217
L
La Jolla Mesa 255, 259
Lady Bird Johnson Grove 161
Ladysmith 48
Lagunitas 196
Lake Cachuma County Park 226
Lake Crescent 82, 86, 87
Lake Sylvia State Park 77, 81
Langdale 33
Lantzville 46
Lasqueti Island 42
Leffingwell Landing State Beach 222
Leggett 175
Leo Carrillo State Beach 214
Leucadia 249, 255
Lighthouse Field State Beach 206
Lilliwaup 76
Lime Kiln Lighthouse 65

Limekiln State Park 217
Lincoln City 126
Lincoln County Park 85
Little River, BC 38, 40
Little River, CA 180
Little River State Beach 161, 163
Lochside Regional Trail 50, 51
Loleta 164, 166
Lompoc 225, 229
Lopez Island 61, 62
Los Angeles International Airport 152, 245
Lost Creek State Park 132
Lucia 217
Lund 38, 40, 42

M
MacKerricher Beach State Park 174, 177
Madiera Park 36
Malibu Beach RV Park 154, 241, 244
Manchester State Beach 181
Manchester State Park 60
maps 18
Marin Headlands 188, 191, 192, 198
Marine Garden Club Grove 165, 169
McCay Canyon 217
McCleary 79
McDonald Provincial Park 49, 50
McGarth State Beach 239
Mendocino 178, 179
Mill Creek Campground 157
Mission San Juan Capistrano 249, 251
Misson San Luis Obispo 222, 223
Montara 199
Monterey 206, 210, 211
Montesano 81
Mora Campground 90
Moran State Park 63, 66
Morro Bay 220, 221, 222, 223
Moss Landing 210
Mouat Provincial Park 49
Mount Maxwell Provincial Park 49

N
Nanaimo 44, 46
National City 262
Natural Bridges State Beach 203, 205
Neahkahnie Mountain Trail 119
Nehalam Bay State Park 119
Neilton 99
Neptune State Park 133
Neskowin 126
New Brighton State Beach 206

Newcastle Island 44, 47
Newport 128, 131
Newport Beach 250
North Bend 135, 139

O
Oak Harbor 71
Oakland Airport 201
Ocean City State Park 100
Ocean Shores 96, 100
Oceano Campground 225
Oceanside 248, 254
Oceanside State Park Beach 123
Old Fort Townsend State Park 70, 72
Olympic National Park 74, 77, 82, 85, 86, 87, 88, 89, 90, 92, 93, 95, 96
Ona Beach State Park 132
Orcas Island 61, 63, 64, 66
Oregon Dunes National Recreation Area 131, 135, 137, 138, 139
Oswald West State Park 114, 119

P
Pacific City 126
Pacific Rim National Park 38, 42, 43
Parksville 42
Patricks Point State Park 161, 163
Pescadero State Beach 204
Pfeiffer-Big Sur State Park 213, 216
Pigeon Point Light Station and Hostel 204
Pismo Beach 221, 225
Pistol River State Park 147
Plaskett Creek Campground 218
Point Arena Lighthouse 14, 183
Point Atkinson Lighthouse 23, 32
Point Lobos State Reserve 213
Point Loma Hostel 259
Point Mugu State Park 240
Point Reyes National Seashore 187, 189, 190
Point Reyes Youth Hostel 187, 190
Pomponio State Beach 204
Porpoise Bay Provincial Park 36
Port Angeles 82, 84
Port Hueneme 240
Port Orford 144
Port Townsend 67, 69, 72
Portland 113
Portland International Airport 113
Potlatch State Park 73, 74, 77
Powell River 38, 40
Prairie Creek Redwoods State Park 156, 159

Q
Queets Valley 95
Quinault Rain Forest 96, 99
R
Rathtrevor Beach Provincial Park 42
Raymond 101, 103
Red Commuter Train 259
Redcrest 169
Redondo Beach 244, 245
Redwoods Hostel 158
Redwood National Park 154, 157, 161
Reedsport 138
Reef Campground 186
Refugio State Beach 229, 233
Rialto Beach 90
Richardson Grove State Park 169, 172
Rio Dell 168
River Park Campground 229, 230
Roads End Wayside State Park 126
Roberts Creek Provincial Park 34
Roche Harbor 63, 65
Rock Creek Campground 133
Rockway Beach 121
Rocky Creek Wayside State Park 127
Rosewell Provincial Park 41
Ruckle Provincial Park 49
Russian Gulch State Park 178, 179
S
Salt Point State Park 181, 184
Salt Spring Island 44, 48, 49
Saltery Bay 34, 36, 37
Samuel P. Taylor State Park 187
San Anselmo 196
San Buenaventura Mission 236, 238
San Clemente 247, 252
San Diego 255, 256
San Diego International Airport 154, 262
San Diego Metro KOA 259, 262
San Elijo State Beach 249, 255
San Francisco 191, 192
San Francisco International Airport 201
San Gregorio State Beach 204
San Juan County Park 63, 65
San Juan Island 61, 62, 64, 65
San Juan Islands 57, 61, 63
San Juan Islands ferry 50, 58, 61
San Juan Island National Historic Park 53, 65
San Onofre State Beach 253
San Simeon State Beach 220

San Ysidro 263
Santa Barbara 226, 230, 235
Santa Cruz 205
Scotia 164, 168
Sea Cliffs State Beach 109
Sea Gulch 130
Sea Lion Caves 134
Sea World 255, 261
Sea-Tac International Airport 59
Seal Beach 244, 246
Seal Rock Campground 76
Seal Rock State Park 132
Seaside 114, 118
Seattle 59, 61, 79
Seattle-Tacoma International Airport 59
Sechelt Peninsula 34
Shaw Island 61, 62
Shelton 79
Shore Acres Botanical Gardens 135, 139
Sidney 50, 51, 52
Siletz Bay Park 127
Siltcoos Dunes 135
Skookumchuck Narrows 34, 36
Skunk Railroad 177, 179
Solduc Hot Springs 89
Solvang 226, 230
Sonoma Coast State Beaches 186
South Beach Campground 95
South Beach State Park 132
South Bend 102, 104
Spinreel Campground 139
Standish-Hickey State Recreation Area 170, 173
Stanley Park 26, 28, 31
state park reservations 19
Stewarts Point 184
Stillwater Cove State Park 185
Strawberry Hill 130, 133
Sunset Bay Campground 135, 139
Sunset State Beach 209
Sunshine Coast 24, 34
Sutton Lake Campground 134
Swartz Bay 49
Sycamore Cove 241
T
Tahkenitch Campground 137
Texada Island 38, 40, 42
Thetis Island 48
Thornhill Beach Campground 240
Three Capes Scenic Route 120, 122, 124

Tillamook 120, 122
Tillicum Beach Campground 132
Tolovana Park 119
Tomales State Park 187, 190
Torrey Pines State Reserve 255, 259
Trinidad 161, 163
Tsawwassen 50
tunnels 112, 114, 119, 131, 134
Twin Harbors State Park 77, 81, 100
Tyee Campground 135
U
Ucluelet 38, 43
Umpqua Dunes trailhead 138
Umpqua Lighthouse 135, 138
V
Valley Ford 189
Van Damme State Park 178, 180
Vancouver 26
Vancouver International Airport 29
Venice Beach 245
Ventura 236, 238
Vesuvius Bay 49

Vets Memorial Park 206
Victoria 50, 54
W
Walker Point 75
Washington Park 70
websites 264
Westport 77, 79, 81, 96, 100
Westport Union Landing State Beach 176
Wheeler 121
Whidbey Island 67
Wilder Ranch State Park 205
Will Rogers State Beach 244
William M. Tugman State Park 138
Winchester Bay 135, 138
Woodside Campground 185
Y
Yaquina Lighthouse Wildlife Refuge 128, 131
yurts 19
Z
Zmudowski State Beach 210

About the Authors

Vicky Spring and Tom Kirkendall are both enthusiastic professional landscape photographers. The couple travels the hills in summer with medium- and large-format cameras on their backs looking for exotic and exquisite mountain scenery. When the snow falls they step into cross-country skis and keep adding to their expansive collection of photos. Both Tom and Vicky studied at the Brooks Institute of Photography in Santa Barbara, California. Along the way they decided to share their extensive knowledge of scenic mountain trails with others to entice more people to help to protect these sacred places from exploitation.

They currently live in Western Washington where their two favorite hiking buddies, eleven-year-old Logan and ten-year-old Ruth, attend school.

At the Mexican border crossing, authors Tom Kirkendall and Vicky Spring celebrate the end of one adventure and the start of another.